Essays on the history of Trinity College Library, Dublin

Essays on the history of

Trinity College Library

Dublin

Vincent Kinane *&* Anne Walsh

Editors

FOUR COURTS PRESS

Set in 10.5 on 12.5 point Ehrhardt for
FOUR COURTS PRESS LTD
Fumbally Lane, Dublin 8, Ireland
E-mail: info@four-courts-press.ie
and in North America
FOUR COURTS PRESS
c/o ISBS, 5804 N.E. Hassalo Street, Portland, OR 97213.

A catalogue record for this title
is available from the British Library.

ISBN 1-85182-467-7

Printed in Great Britain
by MPG Books, Bodmin, Cornwall

Contents

List of Illustrations

Editors' Introduction

It will come as a surprise to the researcher interested in Trinity College Library that no full-scale history of it has ever been published. The library is, after all, 400 years old, the foremost and largest in Ireland, and is in the front rank of European research libraries. In comparison several monographs have been written on the histories of the Bodleian Library, Oxford, and Cambridge University Library.

A little reflection will point to a major reason for this neglect: not enough background research on the history of the library has been carried out over the years. There is no critical mass of research to provide an individual scholar with the background with which to tackle a full-scale academic history of the library. An exhaustive bibliography of Trinity College Library, both scholarly and popular works, would run to less than 200 works. Compare that with the 400-plus scholarly works listed for the Bodleian in Cordeaux and Merry's *Bibliography of printed works relating to the University of Oxford* (1968).

Research was not helped by the fact that up until 30 years ago most of the college muniments were not easily accessible to the scholar and had not been professionally listed. This situation was remedied when these papers were transferred to the library in 1969; over the next few years they were sorted and listed by Margaret Griffith. This cataloguing has spawned some scholarly researches, although not as much as would have been hoped. A high point was the publication in 1986 of *Treasures of the library, Trinity College Dublin*, edited by Peter K. Fox. Profusely illustrated, it was aimed at the popular market, and continues to sell steadily in the library shop. Nonetheless all its essays were written to scholarly standards and fully footnoted, and the volume adds greatly to our knowledge of the library's collections.

The catalyst for the present volume was the independent submission in 1996 of two essays on the history of the library to the editor of *Long Room: Ireland's Journal for the History of the Book*. This stirred the idea of the possibility of dedicating an issue of the journal to essays on the library. The idea grew and grew, until a volume was being suggested which would explore the core issues in the history of the library. It was agreed among colleagues that the emphasis should be on the mechanics of how the library operated, and not an exploration of the collections which was the orientation of the 1986 volume. A list of core topics was identified: the buildings, staffing, administration, stock acquisition, legal deposit, the catalogues, readers, binding and conservation. Covering such a broad range of unexplored territory would be an unenviable task for an individual scholar. A list of possible contributors was drafted, with the hope of encouraging as many library staff as possible to undertake the research – after all the basics of collection building, cataloguing, book storage, readers services have not changed radically over the centuries even if the mechanics of doing so has. A meeting of potential contributors took place in the library on 6 August 1996 to discuss the project and to clarify ideas. It was unanimously agreed to go ahead with the undertaking.

The meeting was attended by Peter K. Fox, who had recently resigned his post as Trinity Librarian to take up the same post at Cambridge University Library. For a decade and more Peter had been considering writing a comprehensive history of the library, and in the odd spare hour which he had in his busy schedule would be found in the Manuscripts Room poring over the muniments, noting references to the library. Alas his schedule proved too busy and he had to admit that the writing of the history would have to wait for his retirement. Generously he agreed to make his long list of references available to those undertaking the essays, thus saving them exhaustive trawls through the muniments, and happily preserving the archives from excessive use. In February 1997 the Four Courts Press agreed to publish the volume.

A few contributors fell by the wayside, and others had to adjust their chosen topics for a variety of reasons. So there are still glaring gaps in the history of the library that need to be researched: for example, the acquisition of stock in the seventeenth and eighteenth centuries; the history of the catalogues; provenances in the books; there is even a very lively tale to be told about the theft of books over the centuries. However, this volume takes a significant step towards providing the foundations which will enable a full scholarly history of the library to be undertaken.

Finally, we gratefully acknowledge grants from the Trinity College Dublin Association and Trust, and from the Friends of the Library, which have allowed us to include a special 16-page section of illustrations of bindings in Anthony Cains' essay.

The Librarians of Trinity College

PETER FOX

The office of librarian or library keeper is one of the oldest in the college.[1] The earliest recorded holder was Ambrose Ussher, brother of the great archbishop, who was appointed in 1601, less than ten years after Trinity's foundation. Ussher held the post whilst still a BA but was replaced as library keeper when he took his MA in 1605. The post continued to be held by men of BA status for the next twenty years or so, until, in 1627, 'yᵉ custody of yᵉ Library' was 'devolved to one of yᵉ senior fellowes in perpetuum'.[2]

This 'perpetuity' was in fact short-lived, as the major revision of the statutes carried out in 1637 under Archbishop William Laud, chancellor of the University, laid down that the librarian (*Bibliothecarius*) was to be chosen from among the junior fellows or scholars (*e junioribus Sociis vel discipulis Baccalaureis*) or, if none was willing, from among the Masters (*e magistris*).[3] His duties and hours of attendance in the library were set out, as was the right of the bursar to deduct from the librarian's salary the value of any book lost from the library during his tenure of office. The election of all the college officers, including the librarian, was to take place annually, on 20 November.

For the next hundred years or so, until the 1730s, the post of librarian was normally occupied by the most recently elected junior fellow. The annual election, therefore, usually led to a change of incumbent. Between 1718 and

---

1 Most of the information for this chapter was taken from the Board Register (MUN/V/5/1-), the Bursar's Accounts (MUN/P/7/1-), and the Library Minute Books (MUN/LIB/2/1-). Biographical information came principally from *Alumni Dublinenses*, edited by G.D. Burtchaell and T.U. Sadleir, Dublin 1935, and *Trinity College Dublin record volume 1991*, compiled by D.A. Webb, edited by J.R. Bartlett, Dublin 1992.

2 J.G. Smyly, 'The Old Library: extracts from the Particular Book', *Hermathena* vol. 49 (1935) pp. 166-83.

3 See *Chartae et statuta Collegii Sacrosanctae et Individuae Trinitatis Reginae Elizabethae juxta Dublin*, Dublin 1844; Robert Bolton, *A translation of the charter and statutes of Trinity College Dublin ...*, Dublin 1749.

1720, for reasons which are unclear, the post was filled in succession by three men who were not fellows.

In 1734, two years after the opening of the new building (now the 'Old Library'), the statutes relating to the library were altered by Letters Patent of George II. The librarian henceforth was to be chosen from among the fellows or those Masters of Arts who were not fellows, not on an annual basis but whenever a vacancy arose. In fact, however, for much of the rest of the century, the post did rotate every November. There is no evidence of any of the holders having had much influence on the development of the library, nor, indeed, on anything else; McDowell and Webb dismiss those of the first half of the eighteenth century with the comment 'it must be confessed that few of the Fellows of the time showed evidence of even a blighted promise or of intellectual creativity'.[4]

As far as the library was concerned, the exception to this was Edward Hudson, librarian from 1729 to 1730 and again from 1731 to 1740, a crucial period following the opening of the 'new' library. Hudson organized the move of books and their arrangement in the Long Room and prepared a catalogue of them. His successor, William Clement travelled to Clogher to select books for the library from the collection of Bishop John Stearne. It was, however, the Assistant Librarian, Henry Mercier, also a fellow, who, between 1744 and 1749, had the task of arranging and cataloguing the donation of over 13,000 volumes from Claudius Gilbert's library which had been received in 1743. (As far as I have been able to establish his intention to leave his library to Trinity was made in 1735, but the books were not received until after his death in 1743.)

After Clement's resignation in 1743 until the appointment of J.G. Smyly in 1914 the post of librarian remained almost exclusively in the hands of one of the senior fellows, despite the fact that it and the senior proctorship were the only offices not restricted by the statutes to the senior fellows. From the appointment of 'Jacky' Barrett in 1791, it became more commonly the custom for the librarians to hold office for longer periods, thus having greater opportunities to instigate change. The office holder generally seemed to be selected on the basis of having an aptitude for the post rather than simply being a pressed man as often in the past. In Barrett's case, though undoubtedly an eccentric and no administrator, he nonetheless arrranged and catalogued the enormous Fagel collection, which arrived in 1802, and began the process of putting in order the college muniments, as well as making the important discovery of an early text of St Matthew's Gospel among the manuscripts.

4   R.B. McDowell and D.A. Webb, *Trinity College Dublin 1592-1952: an academic history*, Cambridge 1982, p. 38.

Later in the nineteenth century, J.H. Todd began the work of reorganizing the library whilst he was still the assistant to C.W. Wall and continued it after his appointment as librarian in 1852. More than any of his predecessors since the Copyright Act of 1801, he took the library's legal deposit privilege seriously and began actively to acquire material. He also initiated the compilation of the Printed Catalogue, which is still in use today. His successor, J.K. Ingram, was elected president of the Library Association of the United Kingdom on the occasion of its annual conference in Dublin in 1884.

In 1887 Ingram was succeeded by T.K. Abbott, who remained in office until his death in 1913. A classicist like his predecessor and two successors, he produced catalogues of coins, manuscripts and incunables, and turned the Long Room into a display gallery for plaster casts of classical antiquities and coins as well as printed books and manuscripts, including the Book of Kells. He also had firm views on his predecessors and on the qualities that made a good librarian and, in a memo to the board, bemoaned the fact that the 'Library suffers from the perfunctory manner of earlier librarians'.[5]

J.G. Smyly, who took over from Abbott and became the longest serving librarian in the history of the college, was also one of its least effective, spending his time preparing editions of texts, neglecting the administration of the library and resisting most of the changes suggested by his assistant, Joseph Hanna. It was during his tenure of office that the college nearly lost its legal deposit privilege, mainly as a result of the disorganized state of the library. On his death, H.W. Parke, Professor of Ancient History, took over and began a major reform, turning the library into the modern organization it now is. Parke was the last of the fellow-librarians. Since then the running of the library has been considered a full-time task to be entrusted to professional librarians. All of Parke's successors to date have been appointed to the post in Trinity after having served in libraries elsewhere.

5   Library Minute Book, 17 Oct.1889, MUN/LIB/2/5, fol. 37.

LIST

1601   **Ambrose Ussher** 1601–June 1605
        b.1582?, BA 1601, MA 1605, Fellow 1611. Brother of James Ussher,
        d.1629.
        Prepared library catalogue of 1604.
        DNB.[6]

1605   **John Egerton** July 1605–September 1608
        Scholar 1603, BA 1605, MA 1609, Fellow 1611, Dean of Kildare
        1621, d.1625.

1608   **Edward Warren** October 1608–December 1609
        Scholar 1603, BA 1608, MA 1611, Fellow 1612-17, Dean of Emly
        1620, Dean of Ossory 1626, d. between 1654 & 1661.

1610   **Randall Holland** January 1610–September 1614
        Scholar 1606, BA 1610, MA 1613, d.1672.

1614   **William Smith** September 1614–May 1616
        Scholar 1610, BA 1613, Fellow 1615, MA 1616, Vicar of Kilcock
        1613, Vicar of Kilpatrick 1617.

1616   **Charles Clinton** May 1616–June 1617
        Scholar 1613, BA 1615, Vicar of Sollachodmore 1617, Vicar of
        Kilkamamnane 1629.

1617   **Joshua Hoyle** June 1617–May 1618
        Born Halifax, Yorkshire, BA 1610, Fellow 1617, MA 1618, Professor
        of Divinity 1623-41, Master of University College Oxford &
        Professor of Divinity, University of Oxford, 1648-54, d.1654.
        DNB.

1618   **John Garrald** May 1618–at least December 1624
        BA 1613, MA 1616, Fellow 1620, Philosophy Lecturer, Dean of
        Cork 1628-41, d.1641.

1630   **Thaddeus Lysaght** by April 1630–March 1631
        Scholar 1618, BA 1623, Fellow 1626, simultaneously Senior Fellow,
        Bursar, Registrar, Library Keeper 1630.

1631   **Charles Cullen** March 1631–September 1633
        BA 1631, Fellow 1631, MA 1635, Logick Lecturer, Senior Fellow
        1637, Dean of Ossory 1661.

1633   **Arthur Ware** October 1633–1634
        BA 1631, Fellow 1631-6, MA 1635, Mathematics Lecturer, Greek
        Lecturer, Senior Fellow 1636, Archdeacon of Meath 1643.

1634   **Charles Cullen** [*above*] 1634–Summer 1636

6   *DNB* indicates that an entry for that librarian will be found in the *Dictionary of National
    Biography.*

1636   **Thomas Seele** Summer 1636–June 1637
        b.1611, Scholar 1626, MA 1633, Fellow 1634-7, Senior Fellow 1638,
        Provost 1661-75, Dean of St Patrick's Cathedral 1666-75, d.1675.

1637   **James Bushopp** June 1637–November 1641
        Fellow 1637, Minister at Rathfarnham 1654.

1641   **Richard Welsh [Walsh]** November 1641–at least 1644
        No career details available.

After the rebellion of 1641, the provost and many of the fellows fled to
England. By 1651 the college's student numbers and resources were severely
depleted and, until about 1667, vacancies were left in the body of fellows and
scholars because of lack of funds.

1661   **John Jones** before November 1661–November 1664
        BA 1660, Fellow 1662-6, MA 1664, Chancellor of Cashel 1666,
        d.1678.

1664   **George Walker** November 1664–November 1669
        b.1641 Wellington, Shropshire, Scholar 1660, Fellow 1663-9, Senior
        Fellow 1669-70, d.1670.

1669   **James Kyan** November 1669–November 1670
        b.1648 Dublin, Fellow 1669-71, Senior Fellow 1671-6, d.1682.

1670   **George Mercer** November 1670–November 1672
        b.1645 Darby, Lancashire, Scholar 1664, Fellow 1670-72, Senior
        Fellow 1672, Vice-Provost 1686-7, removed for being married 1687.
        1674: became Library Keeper of Sir Jerome Alexander's library,
        bequeathed to the college in 1670.

1672   **Giles Pooley** November 1672–November 1675
        b. c.1651 Ipswich, BA 1670, Fellow 1672, MA 1673.

1675   **Richard Acton** November 1675–November 1676
        b.c.1646 Overpeever, Cheshire, MA 1672, Fellow 1672-7, Senior
        Fellow 1677, Vice-Provost 1687-9, d.1689.
        Prepared catalogue of Spanish books.

1676   **Edward Walkington** November 1676–November 1677
        b.c.1652 Lochgur, County Limerick, BA 1673, Fellow 1676-82, MA
        1676, Bishop of Down and Connor 1695-9, d.1699.

1677   **John Barton** November 1677–November 1680
        b.c.1653 Poulton, Lancashire, BA 1674, Fellow 1677-85, MA 1677,
        Senior Fellow 1685-96, Regius Professor of Laws 1693, Vice-Provost
        1695-6, Dean of Ardagh 1703-9, d.1718.

1680   **Thomas Smith [Smyth]** November 1680–November 1682
        BA 1674, Fellow 1677-85, Vice-Chancellor of the University 1714-
        21, Bishop of Limerick 1695-1725, d.1725.

1682   **Thomas Patrickson** November 1682–November 1683
         b.1657 County Westmeath, BA 1678, Fellow 1682, d.1689.
1683   **Richard Reader** November 1683–November 1684
         b.1659 Dublin, BA 1680, Fellow 1683-90, Senior Fellow 1690-97,
         Vice-Provost 1696-7, Dean of Kilmore 1700, d.1700.
1684   **Edward Smith** November 1684–November 1685
         b.1662 Lisburn, BA 1681, Fellow 1684-90, Senior Fellow 1690-96,
         Dean of St Patrick's Cathedral, Dublin, 1696, Vice-Chancellor of
         the University 1697-8, Bishop of Down 1699-1720, d.1720.
         DNB.
1685   **John Hall** November 1685–?
         b.1659 County Kerry, BA 1681, Fellow 1685-92, Senior Fellow
         1692-1713, Vice-Provost 1697-1713, Rector of Ardstraw 1713,
         d.1735.
1687   **Jeremiah Allen** November 1687–March 1689
         b.1665 County Down, MA 1687, Fellow 1687-9, d.1689.

Early in 1689 the manuscripts were moved to England, to be followed shortly
afterwards by all but four of the fellows. Between September 1689 and July
1690 the college was occupied by troops of James II's army. The library was
committed to the care of Teigue McCarthy, chaplain to the king, who preserved it and its contents during the occupation. On 20 November 1690 and
1691 the normal elections for officers were held, but the record does not indicate whether this included a librarian.

1692   **William Carr** November 1692–November 1693
         Fellow 1692-6, Senior Fellow 1696-8, d.1698.
1693   **Claudius Gilbert** November 1693–November 1696
         b.1670 Belfast, BA 1691, Fellow 1693-8, Senior Fellow 1698-1735,
         Vice-Provost 1717-35, Professor of Divinity 1722-43, d.1743.
         Bequeathed his library of 13,000 volumes and £500 'for the pur-
         chase of busts of men eminent for learning to adorn the library'.
         Bust.[7] *DNB.*
1696   **Thomas Coningsby** November 1696–November 1697
         b.1672 Neensollars, Shropshire, BA 1695, Fellow 1696-1710, Senior
         Fellow 1710-11, d.1711.
1697   **William Grattan** November 1697–November 1699
         b.1672 County Dublin, BA 1693, Fellow 1697-1701, Rector of
         Derryvullan 1701, Rector of Cappagh 1703, d.1719.

7   For details of busts and portraits of the librarians in Trinity College, see A. Crookshank
    and D.A. Webb, *Paintings and sculptures in Trinity College Dublin*, Dublin 1990.

1699   **John Dennis** November 1699–June 1700
        b.1675 Waterford, BA 1696, Fellow 1697-1700, Headmaster of
        Portora Royal School 1700, Rector of Cleenish 1721, d.1745.

1700   **Matthew French** June 1700–June 1701
        b.1679 Kinsale, BA 1698, Fellow 1699-1710, MA 1701, Senior
        Fellow 1710-14, d.1714.

1701   **Thomas Squire** June 1701–November 1703
        BA 1698, Fellow 1701-9 (removed for being married), Rector of
        Drumragh 1712, Rector of Coleraine, d.1739.

1703   **Robert Howard** November 1703–November 1705
        b.1683 Dublin, BA 1701, Fellow 1703-14, Senior Fellow 1714-22,
        Dean of Ardagh 1722, Bishop of Killala 1727-30, Bishop of Elphin
        1730-40, d.1740.
        DNB.

1705   **John Walmsley** November 1705–November 1706
        BA 1700, Fellow 1703-13, Senior Fellow 1713-23, Rector of
        Clonfeacle 1723, d.1737.

1706   **Robert Howard [*above*]** November 1706–November 1707

1707   **Richard Helsham** November 1707–November 1709
        b.1683? Leggatsrath, County Kilkenny, BA 1702, Fellow 1704-14,
        Senior Fellow 1714-30, Professor of Natural and Experimental
        Philosophy 1724-38, Professor of Physic 1733-8, President, Royal
        College of Physicians 1716 & 1725, d.1738.
        Prepared library catalogue; petition to Irish House of Commons for
        grant of £5,000 for new library 1709.
        DNB.

1709   **George Berkeley** November 1709–November 1710
        b.1685 Kilkenny, BA 1704, Fellow 1707-17, Senior Fellow 1717-24,
        Dean of Derry 1724-34, Bishop of Cloyne 1734-53, d.1753.
        Portraits. *DNB.*

1710   **Charles Grattan** November 1710–November 1711
        b.1688 Dublin, BA 1706, Fellow 1710-13, Master, Royal School,
        Enniskillen, d.1746.

1711   **Thomas Bindon** November 1711–November 1712
        b.1685 Enish, BA 1707, Fellow 1709-17, Rector of Aghalurcher
        1717, Dean of Limerick 1722-40, d.1740.

1712   **John Kearney** November 1712–November 1713
        b.1687 Cashel, BA 1709, Fellow 1712-19, Rector of Derryvullan
        1719, d.1771.

1713   **John Hamilton** November 1713–November 1714
        Scholar 1706, BA 1707, Fellow 1713-22, Dean of Dromore 1724-9,
        d.1729.

1714   **Robert Clayton** November 1714–November 1715
        b.1695 Dublin, BA 1714, Fellow 1714-24, Senior Fellow 1724-8,
        Bishop of Killala 1730-5, Bishop of Cork 1735-45, Bishop of Clogher
        1745-58, d.1758.
        Bust. *DNB.*

1715   **John Kearney** [*above*] November 1715–November 1716

1716   **William Thompson** November 1716–November 1717
        b.1688 County Antrim, MA 1712, Fellow 1713-23, Senior Fellow
        1723-30, Rector of Aghalurcher 1730, d.1754.

1717   **James Stopford** November 1717–November 1718
        b.1697 London, BA 1715, Fellow 1717-27, Vicar of Finglas 1727,
        Bishop of Cloyne 1753-9, d.1759.
        DNB.

1718   **[Thomas?] Skelton** November 1718–February 1719
        b.1691 County Antrim, BA 1713, MA 1717.

1719   **William Lewis** February 1719–December 1719
        b.1692 Waterford, BA 1716, MA 1719, Archdeacon of Kilfenora.

1720   **Joseph Keddy [Caddy]** January 1720–November 1720
        b.c.1694 Ravenglass, Cumberland, BA 1716, MA 1719.
        Prepared new catalogue of library (perhaps the version which was
        printed about this date).

1720   **Charles Stuart** November 1720–November 1722
        BA 1717, Fellow 1720-30, Senior Fellow 1730-8, Rector of Clon-
        feacle, 1738, d.1746.

1722   **James King** November 1722–November 1723
        b.1695 Enniscorthy, MA 1719, Fellow 1720-8, Senior Fellow 1728-
        35, Rector of Raymochy and Clondehorkey 1735, d.1745.

1723   **Lambert Hughes** November 1723–November 1724
        b.1698 Wexford, BA 1719, Fellow 1722-31, Senior Fellow 1731-9,
        expelled (reason unknown) 1739, d.1771.

1724   **Robert Berkeley** November 1724–November 1726
        b.1698 County Tipperary, MA 1724, Fellow 1724-33, Rector of
        Ardtrea 1733, d.1787.

1726   **Richard Dobbs** November 1726–November 1727
        b.1694, BA 1723, Fellow 1724-31, Rector of Desertcrete 1731,
        d.1775.

1727   **John Pellisier** November 1727–November 1728
        b.1703 County Laois, MA 1726, Fellow 1727-38, Senior Fellow
        1738-53, Vice-Provost 1747-53, Professor of Divinity 1747-53, Rector
        of Ardstraw 1753, d.1781.

1728   **Henry Hamilton** November 1728–November 1729
        b.1707 Callen, BA 1726, Fellow 1728, d.1735.

1729   **Edward Hudson**   November 1729–November 1730
b.1703 Ardee, County Louth, BA 1726, Fellow 1728-39, Rector of
Drumragh 1739, d.1757.

1730   **Edward Molloy**   November 1730–November 1731
b.1706 Cork, MA 1730, Fellow 1730-7, Rector of Dunleer 1737, d.1737.

1731   **Edward Hudson** [*above*]   November 1731–July 1740
New Library building opened 1732, Hudson organized move of
books with help of the Revd. Mr Connolly. New catalogue prepared
under Hudson's direction.

1740   **William Clement**   July 1740–March 1743
b.1707 Carrickmacross, MA 1731, Fellow 1733-43, Senior Fellow
1743, Professor of Botany 1733-63, Professor of Natural and
Experimental Philosophy 1745-59, Vice-Provost 1753-82, Regius
Professor of Physic 1761-81, d.1782.
Travelled to Clogher to choose books from Bishop Stearne's library
for the college library 1742.
Portraits & bust.

1743   **John Forster**   March 1743–November 1743
b.1707 Enniskillen, MA 1733, Fellow 1734-43, Senior Fellow 1743-
50, Regius Professor of Laws 1743-7, Rector of Tullyaughnish 1750,
d.1788.

1743   **John Lawson**   November 1743–November 1744
b.1709 Magherafelt, MA 1734, Fellow 1735-43, Senior Fellow 1743-
59, Professor of Oratory and History 1750-59, Professor of Divinity
1753-9, d.1759.
Bust.

1744   **Brabazon Disney**   November 1744–November 1747
b.1711 County Louth, MA 1734, Fellow 1736-46, Senior Fellow
1746-61, Regius Professor of Laws 1747-9, Professor of Divinity
1759-90, d.1790.

1747   **John Lawson** [*above*]   November 1747–November 1750

1750   **John Whittingham**   November 1750–November 1751
b.1712 Wicklow, MA 1735, Fellow 1736-46, Senior Fellow 1746-53,
Regius Professor of Laws 1749-50, Rector of Conwall 1753, d.1778.

1751   **James Knight**   November 1751–November 1752
b.1709 Clownish, County Monaghan, MA 1738, Fellow 1738-50,
Senior Fellow 1750-8, Rector of Drumnagh 1758, d.1767.

1752   **John Whittingham** [*above*]   November 1752–March 1753

1753   **John Lawson** [*above*]   March 1753–January 1759

1759   **John Stokes**   January 1759–November 1760
b.1721 Dublin, MA 1743, Fellow 1746-59, Senior Fellow 1759-
75, Professor of Mathematics 1762-4, Regius Professor of Greek

1764-75, Rector of Raymochy and Clondehorkey 1775, d.1781. Portrait.

1760   **Joseph Grace** November 1760–March 1761
b.1720 County Louth, MA 1742, Fellow 1744-58, Senior Fellow 1758-61, d.1761.

1761   **Thomas Leland** April 1761–August 1761
b.1722 Dublin, MA 1745, Fellow 1746-61, Senior Fellow 1761-81, Professor of Oratory and History 1761-2, Professor of Oratory 1762-81, Rector of Ardstraw 1781, d.1785.
DNB.

1761   **William Martin** August 1761–November 1761
b.1723 Dublin, MA 1746, Fellow 1746-61, Senior Fellow 1761-4, Professor of Hebrew 1762-4, Rector of Killeshandra 1764, d.1787.

1761   **William Andrews** November 1761–November 1762
b.1724 Kilkenny, MA 1747, Fellow 1747-61, Senior Fellow 1761-77, Professor of Modern History 1762-9, Rector of Clonfeacle 1777, d.1783.

1762   **Theaker Wilder** November 1762–November 1765
b.1717 County Longford, MA 1741, Fellow 1744-58, Senior Fellow 1758-69, Regius Professor of Greek 1761-4, Rector of Tullyaughnish 1769, d.1777.
In March 1764 Wilder was given leave of absence for three years, renewed for a further three years in March 1767. In June 1767 he protested that the appointments of Wilson (1765) and Andrews (1766) were against the statutes, which specified an election not each year but when the post was vacant; he was still in post and would not resign unless found guilty of breaches specified in the statutes. The objection was ignored, but a note to its effect was inserted into the board register 'at the request of Dr Wilder'.

1765   **Thomas Wilson** November 1765–November 1766
b.1727 County Donegal, MA 1753, Fellow 1753-67, Senior Fellow 1767-86, Professor of Natural and Experimental Philosophy 1759-86, Rector of Ardstraw 1786, d.1799.

1766   **William Andrews** [*above*] November 1766–November 1768
1768   **Thomas Leland** [*above*] November 1768–November 1769
1769   **Richard Murray** November 1769–November 1771
b.1726 County Down, MA 1750, Fellow 1750-64, Senior Fellow 1764, Professor of Mathematics 1764-95, Vice-Provost 1782-95, Provost 1795-99, d.1799.
Portrait.

1771   **Thomas Leland** [*above*] November 1771–November 1774
1774   **Thomas Wilson** [*above*] November 1774–November 1776
1776   **Thomas Leland** [*above*] November 1776–May 1781

1781   **Henry Ussher** June 1781–November 1781
        b.1741 County Wicklow, MA 1764, Fellow 1764-81, Senior Fellow
        1781-90, Professor of Astronomy 1783-90, d.1790.
        DNB.

1781   **John Forsayeth** November 1781–March 1782
        b.1736 County Cork, MA 1761, Fellow 1762-77, Senior Fellow
        1777-82, Professor of Hebrew 1764-82, Regius Professor of Laws
        1782-3, Rector of Raymochy and Clondehorkey 1782, d.1785.
        Portrait.

1782   **Gerald Fitzgerald** March 1782–November 1782
        b.1740, BA 1763, Fellow 1765-82, Senior Fellow 1782-1806, Regius
        Professor of Laws 1783-5, Professor of Hebrew 1790-1806, Vice-
        Provost 1795-1806, Rector of Ardstraw 1806, d.1819.

1782   **Thomas Wilson** [*above*] November 1782–November 1785

1785   **Henry Dabzac** November 1785–May 1790
        b.1737 Minorca, BA 1757, Fellow 1760-75, Senior Fellow 1775-90,
        Regius Professor of Greek 1775-8, Professor of Modern History
        1778-90, Regius Professor of Laws 1779-82, d.1790.
        Portrait.

1790   **George Hall** May 1790–May 1791
        b.1753 Northumberland, Fellow 1777, Senior Fellow 1790, Regius
        Professor of Greek 1790-92, 1795-6, Professor of Modern History
        1791-9, Professor of Mathematics 1799-1800, Provost 1806-11,
        Bishop of Dromore 1811, d.1811.
        Portrait. *DNB.*

1791   **Arthur Browne** May 1791–November 1791
        b.1756 Newport, Rhode Island, Fellow 1777-91, Senior Fellow 1791-
        1805, Regius Professor of Laws 1785-1806, Regius Professor of Greek
        1792-5, 1797-9, 1801-5, MP for the University 1783-1800, d.1805.
        Portrait. *DNB.*

1791   **John Barrett** November 1791–November 1808
        b.1754 County Laois, MA 1778, Fellow 1778-91, Senior Fellow
        1791-1821, Regius Professor of Greek 1796-7, Professor of Hebrew
        1806-21, Vice-Provost 1806-21, d.1821.
        Edited early palimpsest version of St Matthew (Codex Z) in the
        library; TCD became a legal deposit library following passing of
        Copyright Act 1801; Barrett arranged and catalogued Fagel library
        1802; took delivery of Quin bequest 1805.
        Portrait. *DNB.*

1808   **Joseph Stopford** November 1808–August 1809
        b.1766 Cork, MA 1790, Fellow 1790-1807, Senior Fellow 1807-9,
        Rector of Conwall 1809, d.1833.

1809   **Thomas Prior**   August 1809–November 1809
         b.1767 Tipperary, BA 1789, Fellow 1792-1809, Senior Fellow 1809-
         43, Regius Professor of Greek 1813-21, 1822-3, 1824-5, 1829-33,
         Vice-Provost 1832-3, 1840-3, d.1843.

1809   **John Barrett** [*above*]   November 1809–November 1813

1813   **Thomas Prior** [*above*]   November 1813–November 1814

1814   **John Barrett** [*above*]   November 1814–November 1821

1821   **Franc Sadleir**   November 1821–December 1837
         b.1774 Borrisokane, County Tipperary, MA 1805, Fellow 1805-22,
         Senior Fellow 1822, Professor of Hebrew 1822-4, Professor of
         Mathematics 1825-35, Regius Professor of Greek 1833-8, Provost
         1837-51, d.1851.
         Portrait. *DNB*.

1837   **Charles William Wall**   December 1837–February 1852
         b.1780 County Limerick, MA 1805, Fellow 1805-24, Senior Fellow
         1824-62, Professor of Hebrew 1824-49, Vice-Provost 1847-62, d.1862.
         Portrait.

1852   **James Henthorn Todd**   February 1852–June 1869
         b.1805 Dublin, BA 1825, Fellow 1831-50, Senior Fellow 1850-69,
         Professor of Hebrew 1849-69, President of the Royal Irish Academy
         1856-61, d.1869.
         Reformed many aspects of library procedures, arranged and classi-
         fied the manuscripts; began publication of the Printed Catalogue.
         DNB.

1869   **John Adam Malet**   November 1869–April 1879
         b.1810 Cork, MA 1838, Fellow 1838-67, Senior Fellow 1867-79, d.1879.
         Appointment challenged in 1874 on grounds that he was an undis-
         charged bankrupt; the Visitors held that this was not a statutory dis-
         qualification for the post.
         Author of *A catalogue of Roman silver coins in the library of Trinity
         College Dublin* (1839). 1879 travelled to London to defend legal deposit.
         Bust.

1879   **John Kells Ingram**   June 1879–December 1886
         b.1823 Temple Carne, County Donegal, BA 1843, Fellow 1846-84,
         Senior Fellow 1884-99, Professor of Oratory 1852-66, Professor of
         English Literature 1855-66, Regius Professor of Greek 1866-79,
         Vice-Provost 1898-9, President of the Royal Irish Academy 1892-6,
         President of Library Association 1884, d.1907.
         Published several editions of manuscripts from the library.
         Portrait. *DNB*.

1887   **Thomas Kingsmill Abbott**   January 1887–December 1913
         b.1829 Dublin, BA 1851, Fellow 1854-97, Senior Fellow 1897-1913,

Professor of Moral Philosophy 1867-72, Professor of Biblical Greek
1875-88, Professor of Hebrew 1879-1900, d.1913.
Catalogued manuscripts, incunables, etc.; began display of coins,
plaster casts etc. in Long Room.
DNB.

1914   **Josiah Gilbart Smyly**   January 1914–December 1948
b.1867, Fellow 1897-1927, Senior Fellow 1927-48, Professor of Latin
1904-15, Regius Professor of Greek 1915-27, Vice-Provost 1943-6,
d.1948.
Neglected library; 1941: attack on TCD's legal deposit status on
account of poor state of library.

1949   **Herbert William Parke**   June 1949–July 1965
b.1903 Moneymore, County Londonderry, Fellow 1929-52, Senior
Fellow 1952-73, Professor of Ancient History and Classical Archaeology 1934-73, Vice-Provost 1952-73, Curator of the Library 1965-
73, d.1986.
Began process of reorganization of library into a modern university
library. Wrote *The library of Trinity College Dublin: an historical
description* (1961).

1965   **Francis John Embleton Hurst**   July 1965–March 1967
b.1921 Leeds, Assistant Librarian, Manchester City Libraries 1950-
8, Deputy Librarian TCD 1958-65, University Librarian, New
University of Ulster, 1967-84, Research Librarian, University of
Ulster 1984-5, d.1989.

1967   **Edward Frederick Denis Roberts**   June 1967–September 1970
b.1927 Belfast, Secretary of the Library, National Library of
Scotland 1966-7, Librarian, National Library of Scotland 1970-90,
CBE 1989, d.1990.
New (Berkeley) Library opened 1967; carried out restructuring of
library staff.

1970   **Peter Brown**   October 1970–January 1984
b.1925 Wanstead, Essex, Deputy Keeper, British Museum Library
1959-65, Keeper of Catalogues, Bodleian Library Oxford, 1966-70,
Fellow of Nuffield College Oxford 1966-70, d.1984.
Edited *British Museum catalogue of printed books*, author of *Computer
activities at the Bodleian Library* (1971), *The use of computers in university libraries* (1974). Established computer-based cataloguing
system at TCD; Santry Book Repository opened 1974; Lecky
Library opened 1978.

1984   **Peter Kendrew Fox**   July 1984–September 1994
b.1949 Beverley, Yorkshire, various posts Cambridge University
Library 1973-9, Deputy Librarian TCD 1979-84, University Lib-

rarian, University of Cambridge 1994-, Fellow of Selwyn College Cambridge 1994-.

Map Library opened 1987; Hamilton Science Library opened 1992; Colonnades exhibition gallery opened 1992. Wrote *Trinity College Library, Dublin* (1982). Edited *Treasures of the library, Trinity College Dublin* (1986) and facsimile edition of Book of Kells (1990).

1994   **William George Simpson**   November 1994

b.1945, Liverpool, University Librarian, University of Surrey 1985-90, University Librarian, University of London 1990-4.

Custodes librorum: Service, Staff and Salaries, 1601-1855

LYDIA FERGUSON

The first library keeper was appointed in 1601, in which year he had sole charge of less than 400 books. By 1855 there were 15 members of staff, taking care of over 100,000 books. This essay charts the progress of the library over its first two and a half centuries from the point of view of the staff, their salaries and duties. A cut-off date of 1855 suggested itself for various reasons: at the end of that year the librarian James Henthorn Todd persuaded the board to appoint full-time assistant librarians instead of junior fellows being elected into the post, and the Lending Library became a department of the library rather than being in the care of the junior dean. It was also a couple of years since the Dublin University Commission had presented its report and there had been time for its recommendations to be noted, if not yet put into effect. Most of the evidence here regarding staffing has been taken from the board minutes and the library minutes, while the bursars' account books have given more detailed information regarding payments and salaries. The latter are summarized in the two tables appended to this essay. The information in the minute books is unfortunately often tantalisingly brief; it would be interesting to discover why a particular member of staff was dismissed or a particular payment made, but there is generally insufficient material to justify even informed speculation.

CREATION AND DEVELOPMENT OF
THE LIBRARY KEEPER'S POST

According to the Particular book of Trinity College, the oldest muniment of the college to have survived, Ambrose Ussher was the first keeper of the library, for which he was paid a salary of £2 5s. per annum. He, like his immediate successors, was at that time a graduate of the college who was working towards his MA. His duties as library keeper do not appear to have been onerous. The library was divided into an inner and an outer room, and only the provost, fellows, and resident bachelors of divinity were allowed into the inner room to take down the books themselves, while the keeper supplied books to those admitted

25

to read in the outer room. Most of the early keepers applied themselves to listing or cataloguing the books, but from references in the *Particular book*, it is.
clear that they were often paid extra for doing this. In March 1611, Randal
Holland was paid six shillings 'for makinge an index of library bookes',[1] a size-
able sum to add to his quarterly salary as keeper of 11s. 3d. The early keepers
remained in their posts for several years, usually until they took their MA.

In 1627, the status of the keeper of the library was changed: 'The
Register's place and the custody of the library is devolved to one of the Senior
ffellowes in perpetuum; his stipend is six pounds per annum.'[2] By this stage
the library was growing in size and it had obviously been realized that the job
of looking after it was of some responsibility and should be reckoned on a par
with the other officers in the college. Like the other officers, the keeper of
the library was now being elected annually. However, the practice of choos-
ing a senior fellow as library keeper was not kept up for long as the next mention of a keeper in the board minute books is in 1637 when a junior fellow
named James Bishop was elected.[3] This change was set out in the college
statutes compiled by Chancellor Archbishop William Laud in 1637. These
statutes elaborated on the keeper's role as follows:

> But forasmuch as of all the College Goods the books are most valu-
> able, our will is, that one of the Junior Fellows or Scholars who are
> Batchelors, or (in case such of the Fellows or Scholars, who are
> Batchelors, as are fit shall refuse) one of the Masters, who is careful,
> who generally keeps at home, is given to study, and a lover of books,
> shall be appointed to this charge; yet so, as that having made a Register
> of the books he shall oversee them, give security to make them good,
> and swear that he will faithfully execute his office.
>
> The Librarian shall attend every day from eight of the clock in the
> forenoon to ten, and again from two of the clock in the afternoon to four.[4]

The library keeper's salary, according to these statutes, was fixed at £3, on a
par with the allowance for junior fellows of £3. By 1677-8, the keeper's salary
had increased to £8, while the payment for being a junior fellow was £10.
These were the standard payments for junior fellows and office-holders by
the late 1670s, although some senior offices such as bursar were worth more.

1 TCD Library, *Particular Book*, MUN/V/1, f.54a. A facsimile of this work was published in
   London in 1904. (Hereafter MS references are to TCD Library.)
2 Board Minute Book, 19 August 1627, MUN/V/5/1. This sum included the fellow's allowance
   of £3.
3 Ibid., 7 June 1637. James Bishop is also known as John Busshopp.
4 Robert Bolton, *A translation of the charter and statutes of Trinity-college, Dublin*, Dublin 1749,
   p. 89.

Senior fellows were paid £30 per annum and the provost received £200. These salaries were to stay the same until 1722 when there was all at once a big increase, the first since 1676. The librarian's salary was then raised to £15, on top of the junior fellows' allowance of £15, while the senior fellows and provost received £48 6s. 8d. and £376 respectively.

The keeper of the library throughout the seventeenth century was still awarded extra payments over and above his salary when he performed tasks beyond his normal duty, either compiling catalogues or doing other unspecified work. On 20 November 1675 it was 'Ordered ... the same day by the Provost and Senior Fellowes that Mr Acton should have ten pounds allow'd him in consideration of the pains he tooke in writeing a catalogue of the Spanish bookes'.[5] Claudius Gilbert was given £6 15s. 6d. in 1694 and £4 5s. in 1696 for 'diligence' and 'service in the Library'.[6] This practice of rewarding extra service, even by such senior members of the college as fellows, continued throughout the eighteenth century, when numerous references appear in the board minutes to 'extraordinary trouble' undertaken in the library, especially, of course, in connection with the move to the new library building in the 1730s. Often, however, the reason given for the payments is very vague, leading one to wonder how easy it was for a case to be made for extra money. Salaries were laid down in the college statutes and so could not readily be changed by the board: *ex gratia* payments were the one way they had of rewarding work carried out beyond the normal call of duty.

The library keeper remained as sole custodian of the library during its first century. In 1674 the college received the books bequeathed by Sir Jerome Alexander. The latter also left an annuity to pay for a librarian and George Mercer, a junior fellow, was duly appointed as Keeper of Sir Jerome Alexander's Library. The books were, however, kept separate from the college library and in due course were incorporated into the Lending Library which was established in 1800. The first mention of payment to the Keeper of Sir Jerome Alexander's Library does not appear in the bursar's accounts until 1723, when the keeper was paid £7 8s. per annum.[7]

EXPANSION AND CONSOLIDATION IN THE
EIGHTEENTH CENTURY

During the eighteenth century the number of staff in the library increased slightly: a porter was assigned to do duty there from the early years of the century, with a second one employed from 1757, while an assistant librarian

5 Board Minute Book, MUN/V/5/2.
6 Ibid., 20 November 1694 and 20 November 1696.
7 Bursar's Account Book, Sept.–Dec. quarter 1723 *et seq.*, MUN/V/57/2.

was appointed from the mid-1740s. By the end of the century the new building was being manned by the librarian and his assistant, both fellows elected
annually, two porters, and a cleaning woman.

The first time that an assistant to the librarian is recorded in the board minutes of the annual election of officers is in 1743 when James Knight, a junior
fellow, was appointed. From that year, the librarian was chosen from among
the senior fellows, thus ensuring that he was senior in standing to his assistant.
The librarian had had occasional assistance before that, nevertheless. In 1705
Richard Helsham, to become librarian himself two years later, was paid £8 'for
his care in assisting the Library-keeper'[8], while in the years 1735-9 various payments were made to a Robert Lester and others for writing the catalogues in
the library. The assistant librarian was paid £30 per annum in 1746, the first
year for which a record of his salary survives. The librarian at that stage was
being paid £60, having been awarded a substantial increase in 1735 from £15.
The increase was set out in the statutes brought in under George II in 1734
and was in recognition of the extra duties and responsibility involved in the
new library building. The librarian at the time of the move, Edward Hudson,
had already been granted several extra payments for additional trouble and
attendance in the library in 1732-5: £30 in November 1732, £60 in November
1733, and finally a lump sum of £112 in March 1735, the latter 'on acct. of
the trouble he has taken and is herafter to take in settling the Library'.[9] The
college seems to have been particularly well-disposed towards Hudson: many
years later, in 1748, he was granted £228 3s. 2¼d. for 'his trouble in settling
the books in the new Library and making a Catalogue of them'.[10] By this stage
he was no longer even a fellow, having resigned in 1739 for a parish appointment, let alone library keeper, and it would be interesting to know what exactly
he accomplished that merited him a payment of nearly four times the annual
salary of the then keeper. Unfortunately no detailed explanation survives.

In the second half of the century, the librarian and assistant librarian managed the day-to-day running of the library between them. Along with other
interested fellows and with the approval of the board, they selected books as
well as compiling lists and catalogues, and helped readers, some of them visiting scholars. At times they called on others, not necessarily members of the
college, for expert assistance. Maurice Gorman was paid £1 2s. 9d. in 1767
'for classing the Irish M.S.S.'[11] and in 1784 'Mr Heydeck was appointed to
making a catalogue of the Hebrew and Rabbinical books at present in the
College Library and not enter'd in the catalogues.'[12]

8 Board Minute Book, 20 November 1705, MUN/V/5/2.
9 Ibid., 25 March 1735.
10 Board Minute Book, 29 June 1748, MUN/V/5/3.
11 Bursar's Account Book, Jan.–March quarter 1767, MUN/V/57/4.
12 Board Minute Book, 19 June 1784, MUN/V/5/5.

The fellows of the college were regularly granted leave of absence by the board for various reasons, particularly ill-health or travel, and if they were holding the office of librarian or assistant librarian at the time, a substitute was appointed on a temporary basis, with the approval of the board, even if it was only for a couple of weeks. This arrangement led to some disputation in 1767 when Theaker Wilder returned to the college after three years' leave of absence, during which time the office of librarian, which he had held on his departure in 1764, had not been kept open for him. He lodged an official protest to the board, claiming that the elections in 1765 and 1766 had been unfair.[13] Although his protest was recorded in the board's minute book, Wilder was not appointed librarian again. Most of the fellows' absences were, of course, of much shorter duration: according to the statutes, they had to receive a royal dispensation in order to be away from the college for more than 63 days in the year. In 1749, while he was assistant librarian, Henry Mercier had received a royal dispensation for leave to travel abroad 'for the recovery of his health and his improvement in learning';[14] he, however, had not tried to hold on to the office of assistant librarian while he was away.

In 1752 the librarian's salary was raised from £60 to £100. Even allowing for the extra work associated with the new library building, this was a very big increase, particularly considering that the salary had already been raised in 1735 and had therefore gone from £15 to £100 in only thirty years. It was, however, to stay at this rate, as did the assistant librarian's salary of £30, until 1817, when an increase of one quarter was sanctioned by the board in recognition of longer opening hours.

The only other person working in the library in the early decades of the eighteenth century was a porter. There was a porter in attendance from at least 1708, when payment to the library porter is listed separately in the bursar's accounts. At that time the porter was paid £2 per annum but this sum was doubled to £4 at the end of 1720, when James Matthews had been in the post for at least ten years. There were plenty of opportunities for the library porter to supplement his income and earn some extra money when the library was transferred to the new building in the 1730s, as extra manpower was needed to move and reshelve the books. Several references occur in the bursar's accounts to payments 'To the Porter for carrying books to the Library'.[15] Although it is not specified whether these payments were to Roger Matthews, the library porter who succeeded James Matthews, or to other college porters whose help was enlisted, Matthews certainly had extra work to do. In 1735 he was given an *ex gratia* payment of £6 'for work extraordinary

---

13 Board Minute Book, 3 June 1767, MUN/V/5/3.
14 Ibid., 19 May 1749.
15 Bursar's Account Book, 1732-1733, MUN/V/57/2.

in the Library'.[16] By 1744, the library porter's salary had increased substantially, to £20, having remained at £4 until at least 1739 (the bursar's accounts from 1739 to 1746 have not survived so that it is not known exactly when the porter's salary went up). According to the headings under which it is listed in the bursar's account book, half of the £20 was paid out of the college funds and half out of the library fund. It is probable that this increase was due to the greater work involved for the porter in the new building, possibly with a wider range of tasks and longer hours of attendance. He still had other duties around the college when not in the library: 'He is also to attend the Park-Gate, & when he is employ'd in neither place, to assist the Head Porter.'[17] By 1757 a second porter was attending the library as well, at a salary of £10.

The porters were well looked after by the college overall, perhaps because they in turn devoted their working lives to Trinity. When Roger Matthews, library porter for 26 years, became ill in 1756, the board ordered £3 8s. 3d. to be paid for him, as well as £3 5s. 11d. for the coffin and funeral which proved necessary shortly afterwards.[18] Another library porter later on in the century, Robert Whyte, was paid extra for work well done: 'The Bursar was this day ordered to pay Robert Whyte the Library Porter the sum of ten pounds as a reward for his long diligent and faithful discharge of his duty; and particularly for his care and attention in detecting lately the taking of books out of the Library'.[19] Later that same year, 1784, Whyte was given a further five guineas 'as a gratuity for his extraordinary attention to his duty'.[20] As with many small, close-knit institutions, those who gave evidence of loyalty and dedication were well taken care of, while those who misbehaved were quickly removed. Only a few years after Whyte was rewarded, another library porter, Corky, was dismissed, 'being judg'd unfit for his situation',[21] while there are regular references in the board minutes to porters around the college being dismissed for drunkenness.

One of the library porter's main tasks in the early days of the century was to clean the library, but this changed once the books were moved into the new building as it was obviously a much larger area to keep clean. Also, the porter was kept busier supervising readers and doing other tasks such as shelving books. Instead, a woman was employed to do the cleaning. She is listed in the accounts from 1746, being paid £3 per annum, but from at least 1737 a team of women had been brought in once a year to wash down the library. This practice of washing the library every year was continued into the nineteenth century in

16   Ibid., June–Sept. quarter 1735.
17   Board Minute Book, 18 June 1744, MUN/V/5/3.
18   Bursar's Account Book, March-June quarter 1756, MUN/V/57/3.
19   Board Minute Book, 14 February 1784, MUN/V/5/5.
20   Ibid., 22 November 1784.
21   Ibid., 8 February 1788.

spite of a regular cleaning woman, or maid, being employed. The library porters could still be called on to help out with cleaning, though, as in 1815, 'The Board ordered ... the Library to be swept once a month by the Library Porters.'[22]

1800-55: MORE BOOKS, MORE READERS, MORE STAFF

Although the number of staff in the college library had increased slightly in the eighteenth century, it was not until the nineteenth century that any real expansion in numbers took place. A Lending Library had existed in the eighteenth century, but at the beginning of the nineteenth century it seems it was reconstituted, giving undergraduates the use of a library in the college, since admission to the main library at this date was restricted primarily to graduates and fellows. The Lending Library consisted of Sir Jerome Alexander's books, supplemented by others bequeathed by Claudius Gilbert and Provost Richard Murray. The assistant librarian in charge was equivalent to the assistant librarian of the college library, being chosen annually from among the junior fellows (and in practice usually the junior dean) and paid a salary of £30. His salary, however, unlike the main assistant librarian's, did not increase over the years since it came from the interest on £500 left by Claudius Gilbert for that purpose. It was still £30 in 1852. He only attended for four hours weekly (two hours out of term) and his duties included lending out books to readers and writing a report of the condition of the library and the books missing each year.[23] The terms under which books could be borrowed were, in fact, very restrictive until 1838 (a deposit for the books had to be paid by readers to the librarian), when Todd reformed them, so that the library was probably not heavily used before then. The regulations of the Lending Library as laid down in 1800 were to be strictly enforced, and the librarian penalized if not:

> The Lending Library shall be visited by the Provost and Senior Fellows; or by such persons as they shall appoint, in the first week of November in each year: and if it shall appear on inspecting the Books, that the Librarian has omitted to punish Persons committing offences against the Regulations of the Library, he shall pay to the Fund for purchasing Books for said Library, double the Amount of the Punishments so omitted; and if he shall appear to have been negligent of the Trust committed to his care, he shall forfeit to the Fund of said Library, such sum as the Provost and Senior Fellows shall direct.[24]

22 Library Minute Book, 16 October 1815, MUN/LIB/2/1.
23 Ibid., 8 November 1800.
24 Ibid.

There is in fact no record of this punishment having been meted out to any of the junior fellows in charge of the Lending Library. From 1835 the librarian was assisted by one of the library clerks who took over the job of handing out books to readers. The first holder of this post, a Mr Dobbs, was paid £20 in the beginning, as a junior clerk, but this had increased to £80 by 1841. In that year Dobbs was also paid £10 for compiling a catalogue of the Lending Library, a task that was obviously considered beyond his normal duty.[25] At the end of 1855, the Lending Library became a department of the main library, under the librarian, instead of being in the care of the junior dean. It was still staffed by a junior clerk.

The workload for the staff in the main library increased significantly in the early years of the century with the extension of the Copyright Act to Ireland whereby Trinity became a legal deposit library. Around the same time, the Fagel Collection was acquired by the college. Although it came with a classified catalogue of sorts, the printed sale catalogue, the books still had to be arranged on the shelves and catalogued as part of the library's collections. John 'Jacky' Barrett was paid £100 in October 1807 'for his extra trouble in arranging and making a catalogue of the Fagel Library'[26] and a further £200 was paid to Richard Graves in March 1809 for arranging it. Various students were also enlisted to help with the work of putting the books on the shelves, for which work they were well paid.[27]

As the number of books in the library increased, so did the number of porters. Once the Fagel Library was put in place it required supervision. A retired porter called Cross was paid a 'gratuity' of £10 for three months at the end of 1807 for helping in the Fagel Library, and after that period another porter, O'Neil, was designated the 'Fagel porter' and employed at a salary of £50 (recorded in the board minutes as £40 with commons and chambers) to look after that part of the library. He continued as such until he was dismissed in 1816 ('for insolence to the Librarian').[28] It was customary after that time for one of the library porters to be designated as being specifically in charge of the Fagel Library. The two porters in 1817 were paid £24 per annum, considerably less than O'Neil was paid but perhaps he had other duties as well. This had increased to £41 10s. 8d. by 1837, by which stage the number of porters had grown as well: from 1822 there were three library porters, and from 1837 four of them, rising to a maximum of six in 1842 and falling back to four again by 1852. In the bursar's accounts from around 1810 there is a distinction made between book porters and library porters, but it is not clear exactly how their duties were divided up. Obviously there was much more work for the porters

25 Board Minute Book, 13 November 1841, MUN/V/5/8.
26 Board Minute Book, 24 October 1807, MUN/V/5/5.
27 Bursar's Account Book, Jan.-Sept. quarters 1808, MUN/V/57/8.
28 Board Minute Book, 14 September 1816, MUN/V/5/6.

to do in the nineteenth century, with the huge expansion in the size of the collection: there were more readers to supervise and more books to fetch and return to the shelves. Porters had been fetching books for readers since at least 1817 when new library regulations were introduced, partly in response to theft. The new regulations included longer opening hours, the seating of readers in full view of the library staff and no longer in the recesses of the bays, and the introduction of a system of dockets for requesting books, which were then delivered by the porters (the fellows were exempt from these rules, although encouraged to abide by them). These regulations cannot have been strictly adhered to because in 1842 the provost and senior fellows issued a decree, sanctioned by the Visitors in the following year, stating that readers were no longer allowed to take down books from the shelves themselves: the books were to be given out by the porters and replaced by them afterwards.[29] This reiteration of the regulations was probably considered necessary after one Robert Harman was arrested for stealing books from the library in 1840. Two of the porters were able to give evidence that Harman had been in the library on specific days:

> The days on which the prisoner was in the Library can be proved by the porters Maurice & Hayward, and by the book which is kept, and in which the name of every person who enters the Library is put down every day. It is the duty of Maurice to make these entries – Hayward's duty is to walk about the Library to see that no person is abusing or injuring the books, or in any way violating the statutes and regulations of the Library – and to report all such persons to the Librarian.[30]

The porter Maurice was in fact demoted two years later for being 'wholly inefficient'.[31] He and another porter were henceforth to spend their time 'dusting the books and keeping them in their places; in carrying up such books as may be required by the Library Clerks, and in the necessary messages of the Library.'[32] One of the porters was given the position of reading-room attendant, but Todd, the assistant librarian in the 1840s, was constantly trying to get this changed. In 1844 he petitioned the board,

> If any arrangement could be made by which attendants of a better class could be provided, it would materially promote the convenience of readers. I therefore strongly recommend the appointment in future of men of some literary attainments to this office instead of the Porters, who often unintentionally give offence, and are unable to afford read-

29 Board Minute Book, 17 November 1842, MUN/V/5/8.
30 Library Minute Book, 11 April 1840, MUN/LIB/2/3.
31 Ibid., 18 October 1842. Maurice is also referred to as 'Morris'.
32 Ibid., 22 October 1842.

ers any assistance in looking for books, from having no education of
their own.[33]

Todd did not in fact succeed in getting attendants of a different class while
he was librarian and his poor view of the abilities of the porters cannot have
been wholly warranted. In 1850, the library porter Beardsworth was paid £30
'in consideration of the important extra services rendered by him in preparing the slips for the new Catalogue of the Library',[34] a task which a library
clerk might have been more likely to carry out.

The main burden caused by the extra intake of books under legal deposit
was the job of cataloguing them. The board's initial solution to this was to
pay for additional temporary help, but in this case their choice was unfortunate. From 1812 there are references in the board minutes to Edward Barwick,
a resident master in the college, being employed to draw up a 'catalogue
raisonnée of the Library'.[35] Payments to him for this work continued up to
November 1815, at which point it was agreed by the board 'that Mr. Barwick
shall have access to the said Catalogue to inspect & amend the same from
time to time.'[36] Two years later, books from the library turned up at the
London booksellers Longman, Hurst & Rees, who notified Trinity. Barwick
had taken advantage of his 'peculiar facilities for plundering [the library]'[37]
and had done just that. Longman & Co. had been sold the books by a Mr
Henry Osborne of Belfast (presumably Barwick) in July 1814 and May 1815.
Barwick's response when accused of the theft was to deny it categorically:

> I am fully aware that a general prejudice will exist against me, as enjoy-
> ing an opportunity above others, of secreting the above vol. [a book
> printed by Wynkyn de Worde] and I must confess that I always felt a
> sort of reluctance in accepting of a situation in the library, knowing
> that in the case of the loss of books, my enemies might indulge their
> envious or malicious inclinations by charging me with them, especially
> as I was well known to be a collector.[38]

In spite of Barwick's protestations, the board was sufficiently convinced of
his guilt to ban him access to the library.[39] The books stolen numbered some

33 Library Minute Book, 21 October 1844, MUN/LIB/2/4.
34 Board Minute Book, 22 June 1850, MUN/V/5/9.
35 Board Minute Book, 3 October 1812, MUN/V/5/6.
36 Ibid., 25 November 1815.
37 Ibid., 31 October 1817.
38 Library Minute Book, April 1817, Letter from Barwick to the provost, inserted into
    MUN/LIB/2/2.
39 Board Minute Book, 20 September 1817, MUN/V/5/6.

231 items. Fortunately Longman & Co. were prepared to sell them back to Trinity for £130, the sum which they had paid for them.

A more satisfactory strategy for dealing with the demand for processing and cataloguing new books was the employment of graduates as library clerks, a practice that appears to have started in 1816 when mention is first made in the board minutes: 'Sir Downes & Sir Russel were elected into the office of Library Clerks.'[40] It is not known how much they were paid, since they are not listed in the bursar's accounts at this time. These early library clerks tended to stay only for a few years at most, perhaps for the length of time it took them to complete their MA, rather like the early keepers of the library in the seventeenth century. This cannot have been very satisfactory from the library's perspective since they did not have time to build up expertise. It was not until Todd was elected assistant librarian in 1834 that he persuaded the board to appoint clerks on a more permanent basis and from the late 1830s their salaries are entered into the bursar's account book.

During the 1830s, there was more and more pressure on the library staff to try and keep up with the growing influx of books. Several fellows offered their services to help out without pay, starting with Todd in 1831. He was followed by George Smith later that year and Samuel McClean, Charles Wall and John Meade all in 1833.[41] Once Todd was formally appointed as a salaried assistant librarian he was able to press the board for funds and extra staff to work on a printed catalogue of the library, a catalogue which was now badly needed. The process got under way in February 1837 when the board,

> Ordered, that two hundred pounds per Annum be applied out of the Library fund to preparing a copy of the Library Catalogue for the press, under the superintendence of Mr. Todd.[42]

At the end of the year a graduate called Gibbings was appointed to work on the catalogue, at a salary of £50. Two years later, Gibbings' salary was increased to £120 and the board 'Resolved that Mr. Todd be requested to look out for four persons whom he may recommend as Library Clerks, in order to complete the Catalogue in two years.'[43] Todd was obviously anxious to make progress with the catalogue for within two weeks he had put forward three names of potential clerks to the board, with a further one chosen a month later. All were given a salary of £60 per annum. Gibbings meanwhile

40 Ibid., 20 January 1816. Since the early seventeenth century, 'Sir' had been the title used for postgraduate students.
41 Board Minute Book, 23 & 26 November 1831, 16 February 1833, 13 July 1833 & 9 November 1833, MUN/V/5/7.
42 Ibid., 11 February 1837.
43 Ibid., 2 November 1839.

continued as chief library clerk working on the catalogue, but he managed in 1840 to negotiate to work shorter hours. He may have hoped that his salary would remain at the same level, as this board minute suggests:

> Dr Wall read a letter from Mr Gibbings respecting his attendance in the Library. Ordered that Mr Gibbings be informed that the board will consent to give him £100 per annum for four hours attendance in the Library daily, and that if the catalogue be completed in three years, the difference between his present salary, and the reduced salary, viz. £60, shall be given to him.[44]

Thus was Gibbings given a carrot to try and speed up the work on the catalogue, but it was to no avail as he resigned his position in any case ten months later.

Throughout the 1840s and 1850s the number of library clerks was between three and five, most of them working predominantly on the catalogue and earning between £50 and £150 per annum. The salaries and duties of the clerks in 1848, for example, were as follows: Dr Thomas Fisher was paid £150 as head library clerk for working on preparing the catalogue for printing, organizing stationery for the other clerks and the porters, and supervising the latter. Mr Thorpe was paid £80 as second library clerk and was responsible for cataloguing all new books and looking after other books such as novels, which were not catalogued. Mr Hitchcock and Mr Hunt were paid £60 each, the former claiming new publications under the Copyright Act and dealing with new material prior to it being catalogued, as well as taking care of day-to-day work such as checking accounts, counting books, keeping minutes and cataloguing, while Hunt was in charge of the Lending Library, as well as assisting Fisher with preparing the catalogue for the printers.[45] This number of library clerks was still not sufficient for getting the catalogue ready for printing. One of the recommendations of the Dublin University Commission of 1853 was in fact that 'a large number of persons should be employed so as to have the whole work [of a catalogue] speedily completed'.[46] But this had not been put into effect by 1855 at least as there were then still only four library clerks.

The status of the assistant librarian also changed significantly in the middle of the nineteenth century. Having been assistant for many years, Todd had to resign this post in March 1850 when he was elected a senior fellow. In February 1852 he was chosen to be librarian and, with the board's agreement, proceeded to give £60 out of his librarian's salary of £115 7s. 10d. to pay for

---

44 Board Minute Book, 5 December 1840, MUN/V/5/8.
45 Library Minute Book, 29 September 1848, MUN/LIB/2/4.
46 Dublin University Commission, *Report of Her Majesty's commissioners*, Dublin 1853, p. 77.

a second assistant librarian from among the junior fellows. He did this on condition that he also held the post of bursar or senior lecturer, evidently considering that his income would be sufficient if he were being paid for holding either of these offices. Within three years he had persuaded the board that the assistant librarians should not be elected from among the fellows, presumably because they had little experience of library work and did not provide continuity. They also had other jobs in the college as well and so could not dedicate themselves wholeheartedly to the library. In 1855 Dr Fisher, formerly the chief library clerk, and Rudolf Thomas Siegfried, another library clerk up to then, are listed in the bursar's accounts as the assistant librarian and junior assistant librarian, alongside three library clerks and a junior library clerk.[47] All of the staff in the library except the librarian were now full-time library staff rather than academics elected annually or graduates employed temporarily.

It was not until the second half of the twentieth century that the librarian was no longer chosen from among the academic staff, though there is evidence that there was in fact some feeling in the college at this time that the librarian should at least work full-time in the library and not have other duties. One of the suggestions put forward by a committee of the board to the Commissioners of the 1851 inquiry was as follows:

> It would also, we think, be a great benefit to the Library if such a salary could be given to the Head Librarian as would detach him from other offices, and enable him to devote his whole time to the duties of the Librarianship.[48]

This was not to happen for many years yet, but the library in 1855 had certainly come a long way since its foundation. Instead of the solitary *custos librorum* of the early seventeenth century, there were now four library porters, four book porters, four clerks, as well as the librarian and two assistants. In place of the 400 books in the care of Ambrose Ussher was a collection of nearly 120,000 works, a collection still not adequately catalogued but one of established renown. Although the printed catalogue had still not been completed, much progress had been made and Todd in particular must take much of the credit for bringing the library up to the standard of other large university and research libraries in the nineteenth century. He was to remain as librarian until his death in 1869, a signal exemplar of the zeal and loyalty demonstrated by many library staff over the years.

47 Bursar's Account Book, October–December quarter 1855, MUN/V/57/12.
48 Dublin University Commission, p. 298.

Table 1. Salaries of the Librarian and Assistant Librarian

	1601	1627	1678	1722	1735	1752	1817	1826*	1855
Librarian	£2 5s. 0d.	£3	£8	£15	£60	£100	£125	£115 7s. 10d.	£115 8s. 0d.
Assistant Librarian	–	–	–	–	–	£30	£42	£38 15s. 6d.	£150** / £100

*All salaries were adjusted slightly in 1826 when the Irish currency was assimilated into the English under the terms of the Currency Act, 1825, which took effect on 5 January 1826. The English pound was worth more than the Irish had been so that salaries had to be reduced. They were not, however, reduced until October, whereas the new rates for chambers in College, for instance, were brought in from January.

**From 1855 the Assistant Librarian was a full-time member of the library staff, receiving a full salary, and no longer a Junior Fellow paid an allowance for holding the office of Assistant Librarian.

Table 2. Salaries of the Library Clerks, Porters and Maid

	1708	1720	1746	1790	1810	1820	1840	1850	1855
Clerks	–	–	–	–	–	–	£120 £60 (x 3)	£150 £80 £60 (x 2)	£80 £60 (x 2) £30
Porters*	£2	£4	£20	£20 £10 (Fagel porter)	£20 £50 (Fagel porter)	£45 (1st book porter) £42 (3 book porters) £24 (2 library porters)	£55 7s. 8d. (1st book porter) £51 13s. 8d. (3 book porters) £41 10s. 8d. (4 library porters)	£55 7s. 8d. (1st book porter) £51 13s. 8d. (3 book porters) £41 10s. 8d. (4 lib. porters) £60 (attendant)	£55 7s. 8d. (1st book porter) £51 13s. 8d. (3 book porters) £41 10s. 8d. (3 lib. porters) £60 (attendant)
Maid	–	–	£3	£6 16s. 6d.	£9 2s. 0d.	£13 13s. 0d.	£16 16s. 0d.	£16 16s. 0d.	£16 16s. 0d.

* From 1839 the porters' and maid's salaries were no longer listed separately in the bursar's account book. The figures for their salaries in 1840–1855 are taken from MUN/V/75/21, porters' salaries 1832–1859. The library porters' salaries for 1850 are slightly different to those given by J.H. Todd in his replies to the Dublin University Commission, where he lists two porters receiving a salary of £51 10s. 8d., another receiving £41 10s. 8d., and the attendant earning £50 (*Report of Her Majesty's commissioners*, p. 179). I have not been able to account for this difference. Todd does not mention the book porters at all.

The Function of the Library in the Early Seventeenth Century

ELIZABETHANNE BORAN

Collegium hinc pulcherrimum e regione prospectat (quo loco olim Omnium Sanctorum monasterium visebatur) Sanctae et Individuae Trinitatis nomini consecratum : quod a felicissimae memoriae Elizabetha regina academicis donatum privilegiis, insignique nuper instructum bibliotheca, spem ostendit non exiguam, ad Hiberniam (quo veluti ad mercaturam bonarum artium confluxerunt aliquando exteri) et religionem et cultiores omnes disciplinas tanquam ad avitum hospitium postliminio reversuras.[1]

This extract from a letter of James Ussher to William Camden, dated 30 October 1606, is one of the few glimpses we have of the function of the library of Trinity College Dublin in the early seventeenth century. Our sources for the early history of the library, while fruitful in areas such as finances and arrangement of the collections, say very little about the role the library was intended to play within the institution. The chief book buyers of the library, Luke Challoner and his son-in-law James Ussher, were unfortunately far more reticent about their aims in developing the library than their counterparts in Oxford, where Thomas Bodley and his librarian Thomas James kept up a frequent correspondence on the subject.[2] Documents such as the Trinity statutes give us much more information about the regular workings of the library than any explanation about its importance within the university.[3] However, an

---

1 C.R. Elrington ed., *The whole works of the most reverend James Ussher, D.D.*, Dublin 1864, vol. XV p. 11. 'A handsome college, consecrated to the name of the Holy and Undivided Trinity, is situated in the place where once the monastery of All Saints might be seen; having been given academic privileges by Queen Elizabeth of most happy memory, and recently distinguished by a well equipped library, it displays the not inconsiderable hope that all the inhabitants will return to Ireland, whence like a merchandise the good arts used to flow abroad, as well as both religion and all the more cultivated disciplines once more as to the ancestral hospitality'.

2 See G.W. Wheeler ed., *Letters of Sir Thomas Bodley to Thomas James*, Oxford 1926.

3 The Temple Statutes may be found scattered among the following manuscripts: TCD

examination of the early seventeenth century debate about the function of libraries can augment our understanding of the motivations of the founders of the college library, while internal evidence from the college itself allows us to analyse how far TCD's library mirrored the perception of the function of libraries then prevalent in Europe. For Challoner and Ussher were very much aware of these new developments. Their frequent trips to England to buy books necessarily occasioned contacts between them and Thomas Bodley, the founder of the Bodleian, and through their connections with him and scholars in Oxford and Cambridge, they would have kept up to date with current developments.[4]

The growth in the size of libraries, occasioned by the printing revolution, had led to the creation of treatises concerned with the care and history of libraries. One of the first works to attempt a history of libraries was Justus Lipsius's *De bibliothecis syntagma* of 1602, a treatise which ran to a number of editions.[5] It was by no means the only work on the subject and throughout the seventeenth century we find such works as Gabriel Naudé's *Advis pour dresser une bibliothèque* of 1627, John Dury's *The reformed librarie keeper* of 1650, and Johannes Lomeier's 1669 treatise *De bibliothecis*. Lipsius's treatise, as the first work to investigate the history of libraries, proved very influential, and his differing definitions of what the term 'library' meant – either a place where books were kept, or a collection of books or a shop where books were sold – were later repeated by Naudé in 1627 and Furetière in 1690, both of whom added yet a further explanation, namely, that a 'bibliotheque' or 'library' could also mean a compilation of books by authors on the same subject.[6] All these varying definitions are represented in the library of Trinity College Dublin where one finds firstly a building designated as the library, secondly a collection of books and finally, within that collection a series of compilatory volumes which include tracts by different authors on a similar subject. In this paper 'library' will be taken to indicate both the building and

Library, MUN/P/1/201; MUN/P/1/105; MUN/P/1/168; MUN/P/1/171 and MUN/P/1/173. (Hereafter MS references are to TCD Library unless otherwise stated.) A Latin version of the Bedell Statutes may be found in the appendix to J.P. Mahaffy, *An epoch in Irish history*, Dublin 1904, pp 327-75. Finally, an English translation of the Laudian Statutes was made by Robert Bolton: *A translation of the charter and statutes of Trinity College Dublin*, Dublin 1749.

4 Nicholas Bernard, *The life and death of the most reverend and learned father of our Church, Dr James Usher, Late Arch-Bishop of Armagh and Primate of all Ireland*, Dublin 1656, pp 42-3.

5 Thomas D. Walker, 'Justus Lipsius and the historiography of libraries', *Libraries and Culture: a Journal of Library History* vol. 26 no. 1 (1991) pp 49-65.

6 Justus Lipsius, *A brief outline of the history of libraries*, 1602, in J.C. Dana and H.W. Kent eds., *Literature of libraries in the seventeenth and eighteenth centuries*, New Jersey 1967 vol. V p. 31. For Naudé and Furetière see Roger Chartier, *The order of books*, Oxford 1994, p. 65.

the collections within it, but the emphasis will be on an examination of the function of the collection rather than an investigation of the structure which holds them.

There were in fact a number of functions that could be ascribed to a library of the early seventeenth century, whether it was a college library or not. Renaissance discussions of the topic were apt to emphasize the aesthetic role of the library. An inscription on Federigo da Montefeltro's library of 1474 emphasized that one of the goals of a library was to present an attractive setting in which the real treasures, that is, books, could be properly displayed.[7] Central to this thought was the idea of the book as a costly object and in Federigo da Montefeltro's library great attention was given to expensive bindings.[8] This view of the book as either a costly object or, indeed, sacral object – as David Cressy has shown in his study of attitudes to the Bible in seventeenth century America – held implications for the housing of books.[9]

Beauty as a function of libraries continued to be extolled into the seventeenth century. Justus Lipsius, in his *De bibliothecis syntagma*, was anxious that the Roman fashion of sumptuous decoration should be continued, particularly the habit of placing busts of learned men within the library.[10] Gabriel Naudé in referring to the seizure of the library of Mazarin, described it as 'the most beautiful and the best furnished of any library now in the world' in spite of his insistence that content and not decoration should be the guiding principles behind the development of a library.[11] Library decoration was not solely for the reason of making libraries beautiful places to work in, but could also play a vital part in signposting to the reader where books were kept, as the example of the Bodleian frieze demonstrates.[12] As such then, decoration could be an essential tool of cataloguing.

More importantly, the care given to enhancing the beauty of both the library building and the books themselves act as pointers to another great function of the Renaissance and Early Modern library – the library as commemorative act.[13] One sees this quite clearly in the decoration of the Montefeltro Library where the owner of the library is portrayed surrounded by scholars – an attempt by Montefeltro to depict himself as a patron of the

7 Lisa Jardine, *Worldly goods: a new history of the Renaissance*, London 1996, p. 185.

8 Ibid., p. 140.

9 David Cressy, 'Books as totems in seventeenth century England and New England', *Journal of Library History* vol. 21 no. 1 (1986) pp 92-106.

10 Lipsius, *History* (as note 6), p. 103.

11 Gabriel Naudé, *News from France or a description of the library of Cardinal Mazarin before it was utterly ruined, sent in a letter from Monsieur G. Naudeus, Keeper of the Publick Library*, London 1652 in Dana and Kent, *Literature of libraries* (as note 6) vol. vi, p. 63.

12 André Masson, *The pictorial catalogue: mural decoration in libraries*, Oxford 1981, p. 5.

13 Ibid., p. 75.

arts and grandee rather than a successful condottiere.[14] Likewise the Bodleian, where one finds the roof of the library decorated with seven seals and three ducal crowns, and the painted arms of Bodley himself.[15] The chief function of the library here is quite clear – it is to add to the honour and prestige of the donor.

This theme is readily apparent in the early seventeenth century formulations on the subject. Lipsius addressed his patron in the following manner:

> Consider, O Most Illustrious Prince, how this love of books brings favour and high renown – such favour and renown as should be granted without limit to great men like yourself.[16]

Naudé elaborates on the theme in his seminal treatise on libraries, his *Advis pour dresser une bibliotheque* of 1627, which he dedicated to Henri de Mesmes, president at the parlement de Paris:

> For not to go far from the nature of this Enterprise, common sense will informe us, that it is a thing altogether laudable, generous, and worthy of a courage which breathes nothing but Immortality, to draw out of oblivion, conserve, and erect (like another Pompey) all these Images, not of the Bodies, but of the Minds of so many gallant men …[17]

Later, in the middle of the seventeenth century, the English writer John Dury, a correspondent of James Ussher's, placed particular emphasis on the role of a library of Wolfenbüttel as monument to the donors, Dukes Julius and August of Brunswick and Lüneberg:

> Bibliotheca Augusta quae hodie Guelpherbiti, antiquissimam Ducum Brunovicensium Sede visitur, sive locum, sive armaria, sive ipsam denique molem, & congeriem Librorum, sub eo nomine intelligas, primum, & unicum, Autorem habet, Serenissimum Illustrissimum Principem, ac Dominum, Dominum AUGUSTUM, Ducem Brunovicensem & Lunaeburgensem, qui, ut à primis adolescentiae annis, artium cultor solertissimus, & ingeniorum censor acutissimus, ità etiam, quod

---

14 Jardine, *Worldly goods* (as note 7), p. 194.
15 William Dunn Macray ed., *Annals of the Bodleian Library Oxford*, Oxford 1890, pp 17-18.
16 Lipsius, *History* (as note 6), p. 91.
17 Gabriel Naudé's *Advis pour dresser une bibliotheque* was translated by John Evelyn, *Instructions concerning erecting of a library: presented to My Lord the President De Mesme by Gabriel Naudeus, And now interpreted by Jo. Evelyn, Esquire*, London 1661, p. 6.

istis adhaeret, praestantissimorum in omni eruditionis genere Librorum amantissimus.[18]

In Dury's view, the dukes of Brunswick and Lüneberg, by establishing a library at Wolfenbüttel, were underlining their princely station. Both Dury, Naudé, and indeed, Lipsius, were anxious to list the names of the many kings who in ancient times had been responsible for the construction of libraries and who had in turn been immortalized by these actions.[19]

Such considerations were also very much at the forefront of Bodley's mind, not only as regards his own immortality as we have seen, but also in connection with the fame of the many benefactors to the Bodleian, without whose aid the library could not have come to fruition. In his statutes for the Bodleian he declared that the librarian's chief 'Function and Charge' was to take care of the Register Book, in which the names of all the benefactors to the Bodleian had been listed, not only those who had given much money and books but also 'others of mean and vulgar Callings' whose generosity 'must be respectively remembered'.[20] Bodley's emphasis on this as the initial task of the librarian is echoed by his decision to adorn the register book with silver gilt and the arms of the donor, and a suitable title.[21]

This obsession with the library as guardian of the donor's immortality was also evidenced by an interest in bookplates. We see an example of this trend in TCD with the negotiations in the 1670s concerning two bequests of books. In a letter dated 23 December 1670 a college official (Thomas Madden), discussing the bequest by the countess of Bath of her husband Henry Bourchier's books to the library, declared that 'She was ready to contribute £200 to the College towards the perpetuating of her Lords memory.'[22] The countess had already expressed this sentiment in an earlier letter: 'whereas formerly I had an intention to present ye College of Dublin with some few bookes to preserve ye memory of Henry late Ea. Of Bath my Deceased Husband who had his cheefe Education in yt university ...'[23] However, the countess on this occa-

---

18 John Dury, *The reformed librarie keeper*, London 1650, p. 49. 'The Augusta Library, which today may be visited at Wolfenbüttel, the ancient seat of the Dukes of Brunswick, whether you understand by it a place, a book cupboard, or finally just a huge heap or accumulation of books, had as author, first and solely, the most serene and illustrious prince and lord, Lord Augustus, Duke of Brunswick and Lüneberg, who, from his earliest adolescent years, was an expert supporter of the arts and the keenest judge of talents, and something pertaining to this, a most excellent lover of the outstanding books of every kind of erudition'.

19 Ibid., pp 50-3. See also Lipsius, *History* (as note 6) and Naudé, *Advis* (as note 17).

20 Sir Thomas Bodley's *First draught of the statutes of the publick library at Oxon*, in Dana and Kent, *Literature of libraries* (as note 6), vol. iii, p. 71.

21 Macray, *Annals* (as note 15), p. 19.

22 Letter dated 23 Dec. 1670 by Thomas Madden, MUN/LIB/10/13b.

23 Letter dated December 1670 by the Countess of Bath, MS 2160/8/1.

sion not only had her husband's memory in mind, but also her own as her decision that each book should bear their crest of arms and the following inscription 'Ex Dono Rachael Comitissae Bathon Dotariae. An Dom. MDCLXXI' demonstrates.[24] Madden recounts this, and, as if this was not enough, says the Countess also wanted bookplates put inside the volumes.[25] Similarly in another bequest to TCD of the same year, Sir Jerome Alexander stipulated that his library was 'to be called the Alexander library' – as an attempt to ensure his eternal fame.[26]

The library of TCD was in a somewhat extraordinary position when it came to acting as an immortal reminder of a benevolent act, for the money which had financed the purchases of the main library in the first two decades of the seventeenth century had been the gift of a rather anonymous body of people – 'the Lord Deputie & captins of her maiesties armie here in these partes'.[27] Unlike the vast majority of college libraries elsewhere which were the result of benefactions of books, the library of TCD was the result of a donation of money which came to the College in 1601.[28] It appears that in 1592 a group of officers and soldiers had promised a sum of over £600 for the college.[29] Due to the Nine Years War this payment was deferred until after the victory at Kinsale in 1601 and it is in 1601 that the first records of a major book-buying expedition occur.[30] The new President of Munster, Sir George Carey, was instrumental in ensuring that the money got to the college.[31] (Carey had come to Ireland along with Lord Deputy Mountjoy, who proved to be equally interested in the advancement of learning as his substantial benefaction to the Bodleian testifies.[32] Mountjoy's decision in 1602 to grant £100 to the Bodleian may have been intended as a continuation of this policy of encouraging learning and piety).

The fact that the reference to Carey is one of the few pieces of evidence we have for the early benefaction suggests that the function of a library as an eternal indication of the honour of the donor was not the most important element of the Dublin library. Indeed, this particular view of the function of libraries was easier to attribute to private libraries such as Mazarin's or the

24 Print of arms of the countess of Bath (for stamp to be placed on her books), c. 1671, MUN/LIB/10/16.
25 Letter dated 18 Apr. 1671 from Thomas Madden to Provost Seele concerning the Bath bequest, MUN/LIB/10/15a.
26 Copy of portion of the will of Sir Jerome Alexander, 1670, MUN/LIB/10/17.
27 MIC 130 MS Add. C 297, fol. 116r.
28 H.L. Murphy, *A history of Trinity College Dublin from its foundations to 1702*, Dublin 1951, p. 45.
29 Ibid.
30 MS 2160a no. 10 and no. 12. These are two accounts dated 1601.
31 As note 27.
32 Macray, *Annals* (as note 15), p. 27.

library of Henri de Mesmes than institutional libraries where a number of founders might be involved. That being said, the early members of Trinity College Dublin obviously paid it some credence judging by their declaration in a petition of 1643 to the Dublin Government that a 'great wrong would be done to the college and to the memories of those benefactors' if the government did not help in the restitution of books which had been taken from the college library.[33]

Proponents of the fame function of a library were apt to link this theme to the size of the collection. Naudé specifically states in his preface that in order to ensure lasting fame Henri de Mesmes should collect as many works as possible, so that his library may be 'without equal'.[34] Size was also intimately connected with the use of the library and the *public utility* of the library was one of the most dominant themes of all the early seventeenth-century formulations on library development. If the library was to be a true social instrument for the common good the collections had, in the eyes of Naudé, to be as complete, as universal, as possible:

> And therefore I shall ever think it extremely necessary, to collect for this purpose all sorts of Books (under such precautions, yet, as I shall establish) seeing a Library which is erected for the publick benefit ought to be universal, but which it never can be, unless it comprehends all the principal Authors that have written upon the great diversity of particular Subjects, and chiefly upon all the Arts and Sciences.[35]

Not all writers on the subject agreed with Naudé that all works should be included. Bodley, in a letter to Thomas James in 1602, advised him that selection of books might be necessary: 'In any wise take no riffe raffe bookes (for suche will but proue a discredit to our Librarie).'[36] John Dury, writing some 48 years later, outlined a possible solution to the problem posed by the need to collect everything in order to be considered a universal library, an act which would necessarily bring into the library, and hence make available, works which might be better left hidden. In his 'Second letter to the reformed librarie–keeper' he suggested that the library should be as comprehensive as possible, yet works which might potentially be dangerous should be kept apart from the main collections and a separate library catalogue should be made for them. Above all, 'discretion must bee used and confusion avoided'.[37]

33 Petition of 1643 from TCD to the Dublin Government, MS 2160/14a.
34 Naudé, *Advis* (as note 17), pp 4-5.
35 Ibid., pp 19-20.
36 Wheeler, *Letters* (as note 2), p. 35.
37 Dury, *Keeper* (as note 18), p. 23.

That this was a problem which the book buyers of the library of TCD also had to face may be seen in the discussion held between Ussher and Challoner about the placing of books by English Roman Catholics in the library. The presence of these books was vital if the library was to function as an intellectual powerhouse of the Reformation, and yet they could well prove dangerous to impressionable minds. Ussher did not choose to ignore these pernicious works but instead suggested to Challoner that 'you may do well to have a care that the English popish books be kept in a place by themselves, and not placed among the rest in the library'.[38] He would have agreed with Naudé's later judgement that it was 'no extravagance or danger at all, to have in a Library (under caution nevertheless of a license and permission from those to whom it appertains) all the Works of the most learned and famous Hereticks ...'[39]

The comprehensive nature of the collection was intimately connected to the use of the university library as a research facility, but utility did not stop there.[40] In order to be truly useful the library had not only to be complete but also public. On this point all commentators were agreed. In 1602 Lipsius had asked the pointed question concerning the use of libraries: 'If they stand empty, or with only an occasional visitor; if students do not frequent them and make use of their books, why were they ever established, and what are they save that "idle luxury in the garb of scholarship" to which Seneca alludes?'[41] Bodley constantly drew attention to this function of the Bodleian. He was anxious that the opening of the library be publicly notified, since it was a 'worke of so great a publike benefit'.[42] His autobiography was entitled *The life of Sir Thomas Bodley, the honourable founder of the publique library in the University of Oxford*. His-oft quoted statement of his motivation for setting up the library likewise emphasized that it was for 'the publique use of Students', a public nature acknowledged by the Company of Stationers in the grant of a copy of every book to the library in 1611.[43] French authorities agreed. In the ninth chapter of his treatise Naudé argued that the true goal of any library should be to become as accessible as possible and that it mattered little if a collection was large if the owner of the library had 'not a design to devote and consecrate them to the publick use, or denies to communicate them to the least, who may reap any benefit thereby'.[44]

38 Elrington, *Ussher Works* (as note 1) vol. xv, p. 74.
39 Naudé, *Advis* (as note 17), p. 33.
40 See an important article on this aspect of the early modern library by Paul Nelles, 'The library as an instrument of discovery: Gabriel Naudé and the uses of history' in Donald R. Kelley ed., *History and the disciplines. The reclassification of knowledge in early modern Europe*, New York 1997, pp 41-60.
41 Lipsius, *History* (as note 6), p. 111.
42 Wheeler, *Letters* (as note 2), pp 33 and 88.
43 Macray, *Annals* (as note 15), p. 44.
44 Naudé, *Advis* (as note 17), p. 87.

This theme was expanded on by John Dury in his seminal treatise of 1650, *The reformed library keeper*, in which he categorically stated that:

> It is true that a fair Librarie, is not onely an ornament and credit to the place where it is; but an useful commoditie by it self to the publick; yet in effect it is no more then a dead Bodie as now it is constituted, in comparison of what it might bee, if it were animated with a publick Spirit to keep and use it, and ordered as it might bee for publick service.[45]

Dury drew an invidious comparison between the public Bodleian library and the library of Heidelberg, which he said was kept 'as an idol, to be respected and worshipped for a raritie by an implicite faith, without anie benefit to those who did esteem of it a far off'.[46] Nicholas Bernard, Ussher's seventeenth-century biographer, tells us that Ussher made use of his own library 'for the publick good'.[47]

It is clear that certain private libraries of the sixteenth and seventeenth centuries were increasingly being made available to a wider group of people. The most obvious examples of this are the royal libraries, whether they were the libraries of François I of France or Zygmut I Stary of Poland, which were used by the court, a tendency repeated again in the seventeenth century in libraries such as Jean Baptiste Colbert's.[48] Yet we must ask ourselves what in fact does 'public' mean in a seventeenth century context, and when we examine the stipulation at the Bodleian it soon becomes clear that Bodley's 'publique Librarie' was not quite so public as one might imagine. In effect it is a question of *extent* of access. Bodley declared in his statutes that the library was for 'the Publick and Perpetual Commodity of Students' but that 'some choice Limitation, in the Admission of Such Persons, as are to study in the Library' was necessary.[49] True access to all the public would, in Bodley's eyes, be counter-productive: 'For that a Graunt of so much Scope would not minister Occasion of daily pestering all the Room, with their gazing; and babling, and trampling up and down, may disturb out of Measure the Endeavours of

45 Dury, *Keeper* (as note 18), p. 17.

46 Ibid., p. 27.

47 Bernard, *Life* (as note 4), p. 7.

48 For François I's library see Naudé, *Advis* (as note 17), p. 9. See also Jan Pirozynski, 'Royal book collecting in Poland during the Renaissance', *Libraries and Culture: a Journal of Library History* vol. 24 no. 1 (1989) pp 21-32 and Stewart Saunders, 'Public administration and the library of Jean-Baptiste Colbert', *Libraries and Culture* vol. 26 no. 2 (1991) pp 283-99. Wolfgang Schmitz has a discussion of the rise of the court libraries in his *Deutsche Bibliotheksgeschichte*, Bern 1984, pp 76-88.

49 Bodley's *Statutes* (as note 20), pp 77 and 93.

those that are studious.'[50] He therefore declared that 'no Man shall enjoy the Freedom there of Study, but only Doctors and Licentiats of the Three Faculties, Bachelors of Divinity, Masters of Arts, Bachelors of Physick, and Law, Batchelors of Arts of two Years standing, and all other Batchelors'.[51] However, with ever a watchful eye on a potential donor, Bodley declared that 'Among these in like manner for special Respect, we do reckon the Sons of the Lords of the Parliament (for of the Lords themselves there may be no question) and as many besides of all Degrees, as of their zealous Affection to all kinds of good Literature, have inriched that store-House with their bountiful Gifts.'[52]

Yet in spite of this the Bodleian could justifiably call itself a public library when compared with the college libraries of Oxford and Cambridge. That the library of TCD followed the example of the Bodleian rather than the more restrictive Oxbridge college model where, for the most part, only masters and fellows had direct access to the books, may be seen in chapter 20 of the Laudian statutes of 1637, the text of which is based on chapter 19 of the 1628 Bedell Code. This chapter issued the following stipulations concerning access to the library of Trinity College:

> Moreover our Will is, that none but the Provost, Fellows, or such as have been Fellows, and Batchelors of Divinity living in the College (although no fellows) shall have Access to the inner Library to make use of the Books: As for any others who have a Mind to make use of the Conveniency and Benefit of the Library, they shall sit in the outer Library and borrow such Books from the Librarian as they are desirous of Reading on Condition that they shall return them before they depart.[53]

This division into outer and inner libraries is paralleled in the arrangement of the books themselves, which fell into two main classifications: Humanities and Theology. Undoubtedly the former were the books in the outer library, and it was these works which formed the backbone of the undergraduate and non-theological postgraduate curriculum. The decision to restrict access to the theological books may well have had something to do, as we have seen, with a fear that access to works by Roman Catholic apologists might have a destabilizing effect on younger members of the college. Undergraduate access

50 Ibid., p. 94.
51 Ibid.
52 Ibid., p. 95.
53 Bolton, *Statutes* (as note 3), p. 89. For restrictions elsewhere see Philip Gaskell, *Trinity College Library [Cambridge]: the first 150 years*, Cambridge 1980, p. 76.

to part of the library may well have been deemed a necessity, and hence the desire to found as large and comprehensive a library as possible, given the undeveloped state of the local book trade, and the fact that Dublin did not present the same opportunities for scholarly book borrowing networks and cheaper editions as Cambridge and Oxford would have done. The presence of one or two names of book borrowers on a 1638 petition, who are not mentioned in either the *Particular Book* or the *Alumni Dublinenses*, is tantalising, but we should be wary of jumping to conclusions and postulating a wider access level for the Dublin library.[54] Our records for the early intake of students in TCD are problematical and the stipulations in the statutes concerning retrieval of books strongly suggest that the users are solely members of the college.[55]

The library of Trinity College Dublin was above all intended to be as useful and as complete as the financial circumstances would allow. The ultimate function of a library to be useful had, of course, been expounded before this – one has only to look at Sebastian Brant's satire on the Book Fool, who, surrounded by books, merely dusts them rather than reads them – but a new emphasis was placed on it, possibly because of the Baconian insistence of utility.[56] Bacon had congratulated Bodley on his initiative and his 'ark to save learning from the deluge', but he made it quite clear that preservation of knowledge, while an important function of any library, was not enough.[57] What is particularly striking is the common use, both in Oxford and Dublin, of the catchphrase 'the Advancement of Learning' which is constantly applied to both Bodley's endeavours and the aims of the founders of the Dublin library.[58] The prerequisite in the drive to advance learning, rather than to simply transmit old learning, was to be as up-to-date as possible and an investigation of the library collections of TCD demonstrates above all the desire of the book buyers to be at the cutting edge of scholarship – even when they did not agree with the new ideas.[59]

The sheer influx of texts in the Renaissance had shown scholars such as Thomas More how dangerous it was to be dependent on only a percentage

54 See G.D. Burchaell and T.U Sadleir *Alumni Dublinenses*, Dublin 1935, J.P. Mahaffy ed., *The Particular Book of Trinity College Dublin*, London 1904, and Alan Ford, 'Who went to Trinity? The early students of Dublin University' in H.R.H. Robinson-Hammerstein ed., *European universities in the age of reformation and counter reformation*, Dublin 1998, pp 53-74.

55 Bolton, Statutes (as note 3), p. 90.

56 Sebastian Brant, *The ship of fools*, edited by E.H. Zehdel, New York 1944, pp 62-3.

57 Ian Philip, *The Bodleian Library in the seventeenth and eighteenth centuries*, Oxford 1983, p. 3.

58 Macray, *Annals* (as note 15), p. 44 and MS 2160/14a, which is a 1643 Petition to the Dublin Government on behalf of the college.

59 See Elizabethanne Boran, 'Libraries and learning: the early history of Trinity College Dublin from 1592 to 1641', TCD PhD thesis 1995 for detailed discussion of the subject.

of the true textual inheritance, as his satire on the Utopian text bank, which
was solely based on the travelling collection of Raphael Hythlodaye, demonstrates.[60] Hythlodaye's description of the books he brought with him on his
travels and the impact his selective collection of books had on intellectual
life in Utopia, indirectly sheds light on the importance of the library for the
members of TCD. The fictional Hythlodaye felt it necessary to bring his
books – albeit only a part of his library – with him on his travels. As David
Hall has shown for seventeenth- and eighteenth-century America, colonists
considered their libraries to be of too great importance to leave behind in
the Old World.[61] In effect, colonists' libraries acted as the touchstone of their
identity. So too in Trinity College Dublin, where the knowledge held within
the library was essential for the propagation of civility and confessionalization of the natives – for that, after all, was the chief function of the new
University of Dublin.[62] In America the role of the seventeenth-century library
as an agent of civility may also be seen in the construction of the so-called
'Indian Library' – not a building, but a collection of key texts translated into
the various native American languages.[63] This undertaking was designed to
spread the culture of the colonists. Likewise in Brazil and elsewhere Jesuit
missionaries placed inordinate emphasis on the development of libraries for
the proper instruction of the native peoples.[64] Indeed, Peter Canisius went
so far as to say 'Better a College without a Church than a College without a
library.'[65]

Expenditure on a private library in the Renaissance was taken by scholars
such as Vespasiano da Bisticci to indicate, as Lisa Jardine has pointed out,
that the donor was 'humane'- a civilized man.[66] In the library of TCD we see
this theme on a public scale. The purchase of a library as extensive as that
of Trinity's was intended to be interpreted as an indication of the *civility* of
the instigators of the scheme. Such an endeavour strengthened the sense of
identity of the members of the college as purveyors of civility in a relatively
hostile environment. That the TCD library was perceived as being essentially
an agent of civility is best demonstrated by the various petitions the mem-

---

60 Jardine, *Worldly goods* (as note 7), pp 210-11.
61 David D. Hall, *Cultures of print: essays in the history of the book*, Amherst 1996, p. 60.
62 See Elizabethanne Boran, 'Perceptions of the role of Trinity College Dublin, from 1592 to
    1641' in Andrea Romano, ed., *Universita in Europa: le istituzioni universitarie dal Medio Evo
    ai nostro giorni strutture, organizzatione, funzionamento*, Messina 1995, pp 257-66.
63 Alden T. Vaughan, *New England frontier: puritans and Indians 1620-1675*, Toronto 1979,
    pp 276-9.
64 Mark. L. Grover, 'The book and the conquest: Jesuit libraries in colonial Brazil', *Libraries
    and Culture* vol. 28 no. 2 (1993) pp 266-83.
65 Schmitz, *Deutsche Bibliotheksgeschichte* (as note 48), p. 73.
66 Jardine, *Worldly goods* (as note 7), p. 191.

bers of college made to the Dublin Government in 1638 and 1643 respectively, asking the authorities to aid in the recovery of stolen books.[67] The college did not resort to this extreme measure solely because of their isolated political situation in Dublin.[68] Rather, they felt that it was natural that they should be helped by the government in this regard as their library was 'a publique monument of piety'. The fact that Lord Deputy Wentworth looked into the matter for them demonstrates that he concurred in this view.

If utility was the basic function of any seventeenth-century library, in an Irish context utility inevitably meant to be an agent of civility, the inculcation of which would lead to obedience in subjects. Coupled with this was the role of the library as an agent of confessionalization – civility and reformation were perceived to be interlinked. The sacral function of a sixteenth- and seventeenth-century library was acknowledged by all and was certainly dominant in the eyes of the founders of the TCD library. Luther had stated that libraries were necessary for 'the welfare and salvation of all Germany' and had advised the councilmen of German cities:

> To provide good libraries or book repositories, especially in the larger
> cities which can well afford it. For if the gospel and all the arts are to
> be preserved, they must be set down and held fast in books ... Indeed,
> all the kingdoms which ever amounted to anything gave careful atten-
> tion to this matter.[69]

The moderate Puritans responsible for the development of the TCD library whole-heartedly concurred with this view and they were not alone in their analysis, as many declarations by Bodley, specifically referring to the Bodleian as being for the 'honour of God', testify.[70] Both Thomas James and James Ussher felt that libraries could play an important role in the fight against papism and the collections of both the Bodleian and the library of TCD were developed with this in mind.[71] Thomas James's use of the *Index* of prohibited books as a guide on what to read was mirrored by his colleagues in Dublin, while the concentration in the theology section of the Dublin library of works by Roman Catholic apologists demonstrates the perception on the

---

67 MUN/LIB/10/7 which is petition of 1638 to the Dublin Government, and MS 2160/14a a petition of 1643.

68 Elizabethanne Boran, 'Town and gown; Trinity College Dublin and the City of Dublin from 1592 to 1641' in *History of Universities* XIII (Amersham 1995) pp 63-85.

69 Martin Luther, 'To the councilmen of all cities in Germany that they establish and maintain Christian school' 1524, edited by Walther I. Brandt, in James Atkinson ed., *Luther's Works*,vol. 44. *The Christian in society*, Philadelphia 1966, p. 373.

70 Mackay, *Annals* (as note 15), p. 412.

71 Philip, *Bodleian* (as note 57), p. 2.

part of Ussher and Challoner that the chief function of the library was to be a polemical instrument in the intellectual war against papism.[72] As Buzas states, such university libraries were viewed as arsenals in the confessional wars of sixteenth- and seventeenth-century Europe.[73]

The 1643 petition on behalf of the library to the Dublin Government is one of the few instances we have where the function of the library is clearly stated: '... a publique monument of piety & helpe for advancement of learning in ye sayd college ...'[74] We have seen the implications of this conception of the public, sacral and educational functions of the library, all functions that were agreed upon both by the members of the college and by outsiders. Utility was the paramount objective and money was channelled into developing a large library of useful books that could be used by scholars, rather than paying for unnecessary decorations. The size of the collections demonstrate that the library of Trinity College Dublin was intended to be an equal to any university library and the relatively generous access stipulations were designed to make sure that the collections would be utilized by all who needed them. And yet, an examination of the collections demonstrates that there were two contrasting perceptions of function alive in the minds of the founders: on the one hand, they wanted a large, public library which would cover all areas of knowledge; on the other, what they actually constructed was an arts–theological library, with sections on law and medicine which, though substantial when compared with college libraries of the time, were far outweighed by their sister subjects. In this the library mirrored the differing perceptions of the function of the University of Dublin.[75]

The role of the library as the central institution on the early college cannot be over-estimated. The outlay of so much capital at a time when the college was going through a serious financial crisis in itself underlines the priorities as perceived by its early members, as does the entrusting of the work of developing the library to its two leading lights. Evidently the library was regarded as the most important element of the institution to develop. As such it served to define the new college-university. Thomas Carlyle once stated that 'the true university is a collection of books' and the truth of this statement is nowhere more apparent than in Trinity College Dublin, where, among the many possible functions of the library, the principal function was ultimately to mirror the aspirations of the members of the early seventeenth-century college-university.[76]

---

72 Ibid. For Trinity College Dublin see Boran thesis (as note 59), pp 196-229.
73 Ladislaus Buzas, *German library history, 800-1945*, translated by William D. Boyd, Jefferson 1986, p. 261.
74 MS 2160/14a.
75 See Boran, *Perceptions* (as note 62).
76 C.H. Holland, 'Trinity College Dublin, and the idea of a university' in C.H. Holland ed., *Trinity College Dublin and the idea of a university*, Dublin 1992, pp 9-10.

The Long Room Survey of Sixteenth- and Seventeenth-Century Books of the First Collections

ANTHONY CAINS

An invitation by the editors to write about the bindings in the Long Room for a volume of essays on the history of the library drew me to a period as yet largely untouched by our historians – retail bindings of the sixteenth century and the first decade of the seventeenth century.[1] For anyone who studies the provenance and decoration of the book and its cover, and also the construction of the book, the sixteenth century is of particular interest: it was a dynamic period of innovation and change in mass book production with which the bookbinder had to keep pace.

In his book on the history of the college, *An epoch in Irish history*, J.P. Mahaffy describes the books of the first collectors (Luke Challoner, James Ussher and Provost Henry Alvey) as being 'bound coarsely in brown calf with black labels, the mere working tools of scholars, teachers, preachers'.[2] His use of the word 'coarse' is valid to a point, but is ill chosen in my opinion in that it may give the reader the impression that the bindings have little worth; that they are crude and poorly made. The case was very different, as will be seen.

Although there had been many changes in bookbinding practice in the fifteenth century in response to the increased use of paper and the massive production of the presses (Stanley Morison observes that as many as 4,000 or more texts or editions were produced in Venice during this century),[3] at the beginning of the sixteenth century the construction of a typical binding still

---

1   William O'Sullivan, 'The eighteenth century rebinding of the manuscripts', *Long Room* no. 1 (Spring 1970) pp 19-28; Maurice Craig, *Irish bookbindings 1600-1800*, London 1954; Joseph McDonnell and Patrick Healy, *Gold-tooled bookbindings commissioned by TCD in the eighteenth century*, Leixlip 1987.

2   John Pentland Mahaffy, *An epoch in Irish history: TCD, its foundation and early fortunes, 1591-1660*, London 1906, p. 143. (The black labels were added much later, probably in the eighteenth century. The books were originally shelved with their fore-edges facing outwards with the shelf-mark written in black ink on the coloured edge (usually yellow) to view. There is also evidence of a paper label or flag surviving on many volumes stuck to the back fly leaf which may have borne the title of the book; the exposed projecting tab having long since decayed).

3   Stanley Morison and K. Day, *The typographic book 1450-1935*, London 1963, p. 30.

retained many of the robust features of the medieval period, from the time before printing, when books were written on tough skins of parchment. The text gatherings and endleaves would have been sewn onto several double thongs of leather or cord to give three or more 'raised bands'. The ends or slips of these supports would then have been laced (or even nailed) into the prepared wooden book boards (usually quarter cut oak or beech), thus securing them firmly to the text block and at the same time providing a flexible and durable hinge. Prior to this the book edges would have been trimmed level and perhaps coloured or gilded, perhaps tooled or gauffered, and the spine lined with parchment; the head and tail bands would have been securely sewn on and their slips laced into the boards, frequently with a decorative overlay of coloured silk threads; and then the whole would have been covered in a vegetable tanned or tawed leather made from goat, calf or sheepskin. For the 'mere working tools of scholars' the retailed books, if bound at all, would have been sewn in the same robust way but then simply covered in a parchment wrapper through which the slips would have been laced to give a firm attachment.

Although the tradition of binding texts in wooden boards continued well into the seventeenth century, and even the eighteenth in some areas,[4] by the end of the first quarter of the sixteenth century wooden boards had been largely replaced in the major centres of book production by pasteboards made from pasted sheets of paper or printers waste, or formed from thick sheets of pulpboard prepared from the off-cuts of book margins. Other economies become evident such as the adoption of a simple primary endbanding method (although I have noted Italian bindings of the late sixteenth century with coloured silk and even bullion secondary sewings), and the substitution of metal clasps by simple leather or silk ribbon ties – no doubt due to the difficulty of pinning the plates to the relatively soft paper board and its lack of rigidity. By the middle of the sixteenth century a modern form of humanist binding had emerged, one suited to the light papers and small formats of the printed book, that was yet still well made, hard-wearing and elegant. Until the third quarter of the century it would seem that these standards were maintained, but by the end of the century one can observe a deterioration in the quality of the common retail bindings, and as this is the period in which our first collections were formed (1601-13), may justify the Mahaffy's epithet 'coarse'. But the first collections also included many second-hand books, and the books brought to Trinity College by the founding fellows, donors and our

4   For example the revival of their use in Oxford noted by Neil Ker in *Fragments of medieval manuscripts used as pastedowns in Oxford bindings with a survey of Oxford bindings c.1515-1620*, Oxford 1954; the contemporary (1658) instruction of Dirk de Bray, *A short instruction in the binding of books*, translated by H.S. Lake, Amsterdam 1977; and also examples in my own collection.

'chief of the College' Dr Luke Challoner, which had imprints mainly from the middle of the sixteenth century, were in contemporary bindings from the major European centres of book production, but more specifically from London, Oxford, Cambridge and Dublin.

Following the editors' invitation I conducted a trial survey of a few hours duration and to my delight found a number of centre-piece and centre ornament panel bindings bearing the fore-edge press-mark of the first collection. I was told by Dr Elizabethanne Boran that she had record of 7,235 bibliographic items (in about 4,900 physical volumes) from her study of the first catalogue of the library (MS 2), made by Ambrose Ussher starting in 1604.[5] At that stage I was unaware of any concordance between this manuscript and the Printed Catalogue (which records the books in the library as they stood in 1872; it is still in use today). The condition of books in the trial sample concerned me, so that with the agreement of Charles Benson, Keeper of Early Printed Books, I initiated a survey of the Long Room collections, the objectives being as follows:

1 To identify the surviving books of the first collections (still bearing internal evidence of their provenance) purchased by Luke Challoner, James Ussher and Provost Henry Alvey for the college during the period 1601-13, and to produce a concordance with current shelfmarks.

2 To describe their bindings and condition, and to integrate those records with the Long Room project survey data. (This project is an on-going programme of text cleaning and leather treatment started in 1979.)

3 To make observations on provenance and other bibliographic data of technical and historical interest, such as the bookseller's price code (usually next to the imprint).

4 To note in particular, items still in original condition retaining complete documentary integrity.

5 To give 'first-aid' treatment to prevent further loss of components, e.g. headbands, and to box them (phase-boxes or book-shoes).

My trial survey items provided the appropriate headings for the field survey sheet which was composed and printed by my colleague Raymond Jordan. Ray and I started the survey work in late August 1997; he continued through the month of September assisted by an intern from Camberwell College in London, Andrew Megaw, completing the major part of the survey together by the end of the month. During this final phase of the survey a book from

5 TCD Library, MS 2 (References hereafter to MSS are to TCD Library). Elizabethanne Boran, 'Libraries and learning: the early history of TCD from 1592 to 1641', TCD PhD thesis 1995.

the library of John Dee was discovered in the collection of Archbishop James Ussher (BB.i.23). Following a further quartering of this collection by Raymond Jordan further books from Dee's library were found. These items will be the subject of a paper now in preparation by Raymond Jordan (see plates 1, 2).

After the survey was completed, a chance conversation with the previous Keeper of Manuscripts, William O'Sullivan, revealed that a concordance did exist, this being the work of Dr J.G. Smyly (MS 5208) written about 1934.[6] The saving of time would have been considerable if we had known – but then the survey would have been too narrowly focussed and as a consequence the many unrecorded books from the library of John Dee and other treasures would not have been discovered.

INTERNAL EVIDENCE

As I have mentioned above the first collection can be identified by the shelf-mark written in iron gall ink on the cut and coloured fore-edge of each item. These shelfmarks consisted of four parts: first the letter H for Humanities or T for Theology followed at the same level by two groups of numbers – the first is the class division, there being 10 for Humanities and 12 for Theology, and the second the shelf number; below this line is placed the individual item's number on that shelf.[7]

These marks are frequently written upside down. The earliest marks are written in a neat and clear hand, the later ones in a much larger, rougher and careless hand. Each item is recorded in the catalogue (MS 2) compiled initially by Ambrose Ussher, the first library keeper, which he began in 1604. Ambrose, the less successful but learned brother of James, held this post from 1601 until 1605. The latest date of any of the books entered is 1611 and this would account for the different hands evident on the fore-edges – Ambrose's hand being perhaps the neatest!

In the absence of these early shelfmarks or MS ex libris we have discovered during the survey another indelible mark of early college ownership. This takes one of two forms of awl- or chisel-stabbed perforations driven into the text from the titlepage to the depth of from just a few gatherings to about 15mm or more in some cases (see pl. 3).[8] For the former a pointed awl was

---

6   Note also items MSS 5206 & 5207. 5207 has Smyly's observation on price codes.

7   Norma MacManaway and Charles Benson, ' "A sceliton with taffety hangings' ": the early college library', in David Scott ed., *Treasures of the mind: a TCD quatercentenary exhibition*, London 1992, pp 143–50.

8   For example two stab perforations, to a depth of 12mm, are to be found in the lower margin of MS 313, Iacobus De Voragine, 'Legenda sanctorum', Italian, late 14th century, membrane. (Described, without noting the stab marks, in M.L. Colker, *Trinity College Library*

used to form two perforations, one each side of the imprint, penetrating into the lower margin of the text; for the latter a single vertical chisel cut or slit was made, set just about in the centre of the titlepage. I have not determined which was used first or whether the different forms have any significance. However it can be suggested that the practice ceased with the ending of Ambrose Ussher's tenure as librarian in 1605. The last volume in a set of five (M.n.14-18, Matthaeus Dresserus, *Isogoges historicae*, Leipzig), with publication dates between 1587 and 1606, is not stabbed. These books were rebound and cut-down in the last century and for the moment we do not have original shelfmarks for them, but they are certainly first collection items. The double-stabbed books are in the (T) theological part of the collection now located in Long Room bays A-H and the (H) humanities from I-S. The chisel-stabbed items start at Q and continue to S, with transitional areas of mixed chisel- and awl-stabbed items between (Q.aa-Q.ff).

There are also groups of unstabbed texts, for example O.cc.1-O.dd. (about 20 volumes), and another at M.cc.2-18. The fact that these were not stabbed may be due to an initial oversight, later acquisition or to their location in the library – the 'inner library' for fellows living in the college and the 'outer library' for others, described in the Particular Book (f.53b) as 'the upper and lower library'. Of the many hundreds of books rebound and cut down in the eighteenth century following the building of the new library, many bear these stab marks as the only form of evidence of their early provenance (other than the booksellers' codes of which we understand little at present).

Occasionally there is a written ex libris of the college in Latin, for example 'Collegii Sanctae et individuae trinitatis juxta Dublin' in B.f.6 (see pl. 4). This is rather lengthy, so it is not surprising that a more rapid and indelible system of marking was adopted in view of what Mary Pollard has termed the 'momentum of acquisition'.[9] A number of the books bear the signatures of notable people, such as the Reverend Richard Latewar, the first and most colourful of our donors, who gave the library a number of books and manuscripts – and 'a faire silver pott'. He was a fellow of St John's College, Oxford, and was brought from his living in Finchley, Middlesex, to be chaplain to Lord Mountjoy's forces in Ireland. He died from a bullet wound during a skirmish near Benburb, County Tyrone, on 17 July 1601.[10] We have a number of books bearing the signature of Luke Challoner and his favourite daughter Phebe (Phoebe), wife of James Ussher. Luke Challoner's signed books are to

Dublin: descriptive catalogue of the Mediaeval and Renaissance Latin manuscripts, Aldershot 1991, pp 634-5. Also noted in J.G. Smyly, 'The Old Library: extracts from the Particular Book', *Hermathena* v. 49 (1934) pp 166-83, at p. 182, where it is reported as missing!)

9   Mary Pollard, *Dublin's trade in books 1550-1800*, Oxford 1989, p. 37.

10 Mahaffy, *Epoch*, p. 141.

be found in the first collections and in the Ussher collection, some with Phebe's name over that of her father – those she inherited but including a number of her personal books, usually in the vernacular, one of which bears the signature of another important figure in the history of education in Dublin in that period, James Fullerton (CC.p.44). This intimate link between Fullerton and Phebe Challoner is an interesting one. Mahaffy notes that in 1588 James Fullerton and his assistant James Hamilton came to Dublin to work in a school and it was to this boys' school that James Ussher was sent when a precocious child. Could it be that Phebe was also taught by Fullerton, the book being the evidence for this, despite the 'boys only' rule?

THE BINDINGS

The first aid work was conducted at intervals during the survey by the interns Andrew Magaw and Ann O'Rahilly, and subsequently by myself and another member of my staff John Gillis. About 100 items were treated in the laboratory, and a portion of these form the basis of this study. The bindings can be grouped into period types by their construction and the covering material used, but more specifically by the general arrangement and design of the decorative elements used by the binder or finisher. Neil R. Ker in reference to bindings in Oxford of this period divided them into roll-stamp and associated ornaments (single hand-held tool), centre-piece (a stamp of a surface area requiring mechanical pressure – a screw press or lever) and centre-piece with ornaments, and bindings with ornaments, with single and multiple impressions as the central motif.[11] Our survey revealed only a small sample of roll-stamp bindings. The most common type we found is well represented by the plain sheepskin binding by the Dublin printer John Franckton (shelfmark B.aa.4). The *Particular Book* has the following entry in respect to this binding:[12]

1608 f. 34a   To Jhon Frankton for byndinge
                             Lorinus uppon ye actes   3s

The plain calf bindings supplied by the London bookseller Gregory Seton (see below) are very similar in construction, and like the Franckton binding decorated with only a border of blind lines. The next main group of bindings of this period are constructed in the same way, but decorated with the blind centre-piece on both the front and back covers. Large formats are occasionally decorated with one or two inner panels of tooled lines with ornaments placed at each corner of the frames.

11 Ker, *Fragments*.
12 J.G. Smyly, 'The Old Library'.

All the books are blind tooled with fillets or pallets. These lines, defining the general arrangement of the decorative tooling, are of several types. A blind two or three line border or a complex arrangement of many lines in groups of four or four plus three, for example. The most common three line fillet is the one I call the french three line, in which the centre line is thicker than the ones each side of it, and is universally the most common to be seen on our sample. In some cases a blind two line fillet, but widely spaced, is given a single gilt line at the centre. The cover may be tooled yet again within this border to form a panel, and on large formats yet another panel or frame within the first.

The decorative ornaments, the centre-pieces and corner tools are placed in relationship to the blind lines. For the centre tool or block, a centring mark or scribe line is frequently evident – not always at the centre! Most of the later centre-piece bindings are in blind, the earlier ones gilded or silvered. The silver leaf is now oxidized to a leaden metallic grey colour and could be interpreted as blind impressions, but on close examination the metallic lustre is clearly evident. Usually the centre ornament is silvered and the corner ornaments gilded, or they are all silver or all gold.

It will be observed that the gold leaf was cut very carefully to avoid waste, and on many examples the tool impression is not fully covered, and clearly no attempt was made to make good the deficiency. The spine panels are usually decorated with a small gilt or silvered motif, and on some the same tool is repeated at the panel formed between the kettle stitches and the caps. The blind line work is usually with a single lined pallet to emphasize the raised bands, and in some cases to panel the spine. Pallets were also used to create hatched lines at the head and tail kettle stitch panels, caps and board edges. On the later centre-piece bindings spines were simply left with the tie marks as decoration.

Each centre-piece block or ornamental tool is unique in the detail of its engraving and its condition or 'state' at the moment of use. A centre-piece chased and engraved from the same design pattern may be nearly identical to another in form and arrangement of the decorative elements, but one will have an azured or hatched ground and the other a dotted or punched ground or differ in some detail, such as the angle of the hatching or its inclination to left or right. Other examples may display exactly the same pattern but one is engraved in the positive and the other in the negative. By these means the tools and their general arrangement, along with construction details, may allow one to confirm the identity of the binder first noted by documentary reference, such as a receipt or the record noted above.

Of the 11 books that survive largely intact from the 145 titles purchased by Luke Challoner from Gregory Seton in 1601,[13] two display a centre-piece

13 William O'Sullivan, 'The library before Kinsale', *Friends of the Library of TCD Annual Bulletin* (1952) pp 10-14.

of the same basic template and design as Ker's type XIV: C.dd.4 (see detailed description below and pl. 5) and K.m.17; this centre-piece design is to be seen on at least ten other bindings. Close examination divides them into four or more different blocks or cuts. Only two bindings bear the actual Ker centre-piece XIV (B.c.16 and L.aa.17), which was used by the Oxford book-binder Roger Barnes, the brother of the bookseller Joseph Barnes, from whom Challoner purchased books in 1608.[14] The C.dd.4 cut is shared with M.bb.16, which is not on the Seton list, and similarly the K.m.17 cut is displayed on H.c.19 and F.c.1. The impression on L.aa.17 is too degraded to allow certain identification except that it is linked by the presence of the same Ker ornament 68.

A particularly fine example of an Oxford binding is W.k.5 (see detailed description below and pl. 6) with a gilt centre-piece (Ker VII), which is a positive identification and proves that the illustration on Ker's plate VII is inverted, so beware! Although not a first collection item it is the only Oxford binding I have found that has the typical full leaf manuscript parchment paste-downs noted by Ker. Related to this centre-piece with its diagonal hatching (random angle) is VIII with horizontal hatching, which I note on four of our bindings (N.d.11 with Ker ornament 59, L.oo.60, S.mm.18, M.ff.11), and another of the same template and design cut in the reverse mentioned above (C.m.40).

Of the three portrait medallion centre-piece bindings found (BB.ii.48 (see detailed description below and pl. 7), L.oo.59, I.m.8), BB.ii.48 displays the engraved portrait of a lady, not unlike those illustrated by the Lyons printer Guillaume Rouillé.[15] This book belonged to Luke Challoner's daughter Phebe, which seems appropriate. As for the Cambridge purchases made at the same time, and for which we have no surviving lists, one may be represented by G.n.37, a blind centre-piece binding. The impression is very degraded but is the same template as the binding illustrated by David Pearson and noted as bound by John Sheres in Cambridge.[16]

Of the total of 38 centre-pieces (nos. I-XXXVIII) and associated ornaments (nos. 1-71) reproduced by Neil Ker, we have nine examples.[17] We have taken rubbings from about 130 centre-piece bindings for our records. They display about 50 distinct designs of which 21 are found on two or more bindings, like the Gregory Seton example noted above. The remainder are single examples. We have recorded a further 50 items decorated with either a centre ornament,

14 Smyly, 'Old Library', p. 173.
15 Morison and Day, *Typographic book*, plate 120.
16 David Pearson, 'English centre-piece bookbindings 1560-1640', *The Library* ser. 6, v. XVI (March 1994) pp 1-17.
17 Ker centre-pieces VII, VIII, XIV, XV, XVI, XIX, XXII, XXX, XXXII.

or centre and corner ornament panel binding, some of which are the same or very similar to the tools published by Ker. There are also a few similar panel bindings on texts from Paris and Lyons bearing religious centre ornaments (IHS etc.) rather than the humanist ornaments of the English bindings (C.oo.55, Paris 1562; C.nn.47, Lyons 1571; C.nn.43, Lyons 1573). These are an interesting reflection of the political and religious upheaval in France during this period, alluded to by the historian S. H. Steinberg.[18]

In this context it is useful to look at another of our survey finds, a London binding, G.n.28 (Geneva 1552 – see detailed description below and pl. 8), and to compare it to a very fine Lyons binding, gold lettered and dated 1550 from another collection (C.III.29 in the Biblioteca Communale di Montefalco; see pl. 9). Both are decorated with a gilt double impression of an identical tool in the centre of both boards (photocopied transparencies of both rubbings overlay each other in perfect register). A similar motif is to be seen on bindings attributed to G.D. Hobson's 'King Edward and Queen Mary Binder',[19] with another similar item illustrated by Denis Gid as tool number 3 from a Lyons workshop of this period.[20] I think that this similarity is more than mere coincidence and indicates a very intimate link between the craft traditions of the two cities. Neil Ker notes the significance of the arrival in Oxford of the Frenchman Dominique Pinart in 1573, and his use of a particular centre-piece (Ker VII).[21] (As noted above this identifies him as the binder of W.k.5).

I will mention two other London bindings that are technically very similar to G.n.28, but which display only a single gilt centre tool: G.n.8 (see detailed description below and pl. 10) and F.nn.39 by the same hand. The centre tool, probably one of a pair (handed, left and right) is related to a family of solid arabesque tools of the period, examples of which I have illustrated in an article on a Rome binding of 1545-7.[22] A very similar pair of tools can be seen on a Paris 'trade' binding of the same period in the Bodleian Library.[23] From the evidence provided by the printed endleaves, G.n.8 is linked to the London printers Richard Jugge and John Cawood.

18 S.H. Steinberg, *Five hundred years of printing* 2nd ed., London 1961, pp 79-93.

19 G.D. Hobson, *Bindings in Cambridge libraries*, Cambridge 1929, plate XXV, p. 24; Mirjam M. Foot, *The Henry Davis gift: a collection of bookbindings*, London 1978-83, vol. I, plate on p. 19 and vol. II no. 36.

20 Denis Gid, 'Un atelier lyonnais vers 1550: l'atelier au compas', in *De libris compactis miscellanea*, Brussels 1994, pp 117-31, tool no. 3.

21 Ker, *Fragments*.

22 A.G. Cains, 'A recently discovered Apollo and Pegasus medallion binding', *Long Room* no. 41 (1996) p. 21.

23 Bodleian Library, *Fine bindings 1500-1700 from Oxford libraries*, Oxford 1968, item 29, p. 22 and plate VI.

Finally we have recorded a small sample of roll stamp panel, and roll stamp with centre ornaments of the early to mid sixteenth century, one of which (E.ee.33, 1517; see pl. 11) relates to Ker's ornaments nos. 1-18 and rolls illustrated in plates I-V of that publication. A similar (non-survey) item (Q.dd.31, Basle 1526; see pl. 12) displays a stamp of identical design to his no. 14, plate XII. They are both calf over oak boards and originally had covered endbands.[24] E.ee.33 is a contemporary London or Cambridge binding that can be attributed on the basis of its fine impression of a gothic roll decorated with mythical beasts and animals in foliage to either J.B. Oldham's 'Unicorn' or 'Monster' binders (roll no.928).[25] Q.dd.31 was bound, probably not later than 1531, in London and has a similar Netherlandish design (Oldham roll no.884).

In his history of English bookbinding Bernard Middleton transcribes a list of tools and equipment detailed in the will of an immigrant bookbinder and stationer working in Cambridge during the second half of the sixteenth century, a Frenchman named John Denys, who died about 1578.[26] This wonderful list, read but perhaps not completely understood by a modern bookbinder, gives a graphic insight into the type of humanist bindings the Denys' 'workhouse' could produce. These coincide in every detail with the earlier of the bindings I illustrate. To discuss the forwarding equipment briefly, it is clear that he could produce wooden boarded bindings. This is indicated by his stock of woodworking tools, with which he also no doubt prepared many items of his own equipment, as we do today, items such as backing, cording and pressing boards. (These items are vividly represented in the illustrations of Dirk de Bray referred to above.) No stock of wooden boards is recorded but there is a stock of paste boards – a dozen and a half at eight pence and a dozen sixpenny boards. (These are terms I would have understood as an apprentice in reference to the gauge of millboards!)

Similar examples to Denys' stock of finishing tools (petit fer) and centre- and corner-piece blocks are well represented in our sample, for example the Challoner items referred to above. He had two 'prints', which I interpret as centre-piece blocks or 'ovals' as given in an Oxford inventory of Roger Barnes noted by Ker;[27] also a gilding cushion with a knife to cut gold leaf; a single line pallet for tooling the spine; a three line pallet for the sides and a fillet (of three lines?), polishing irons and burnishing 'teeth' for book edge gilding and polishing coloured edges. He had a great corner flower and a little corner

24 Bernard Middleton, *A history of English craft bookbinding technique*, New York and London 1963, pp 103-4.
25 J.B. Oldham, *English blind-stamped bindings*, Cambridge 1952.
26 Middleton, *English craft bookbinding*, pp 246-8.
27 Ker, *Fragments*, p. 215 n. 1.

flower (a lily or fleur de lis) and a rose for the back (ie. the spine) and a little pink (*pincke*). In addition to the two 'prints' he owned pairs of large and small corner-pieces for gilding. The type of binding that Denys could produce with this equipment can be represented by one of Luke Challoner's signed books (M.n.20 – see detailed description below and pl. 13) from the first collection to be used as a college library, and probably acquired during his student days in Cambridge. It is a gilt oval centre-piece panel binding with gilt corner and spine ornaments.

We have found only one example of a full gilt centre- and corner-piece binding in the survey group (E.gg.36 bought from Gregory Seton – see detailed description below and pl. 14). On the endpapers of one of our items we have an ink proof of a binder's corner-piece (G.m.25 – see detailed description below and plates. 15a, b) and another rare find is the leatherseller's stamp on the calfskin cover of S.mm.5 (see detailed description below and pl. 16). John Waterer notes that in 1592 one Edward Darcy obtained the monopoly to inspect skins for sale and to stamp approved ones – for which he charged from 1*d.* to 10*d.* a skin according to quality![28]

Of relevance to the present-day condition and appearance of our survey volumes, compared to their original pristine condition, is the Denys inventory's reference to the making of black ink (iron-gall ink) along with four colour pots and three dishes. The black ink was used to stain the calfskin after covering and the colours for the book edges. With few exceptions where the calfskin cover was stained with stable and benign organic red (i.e. cochineal), all the vegetable tanned leather covers in our survey were stained with this black dye (ferrous sulphate, copperas), which over time has caused great chemical damage to the grain layer of the skin and consequent loss of surface detail, such as cording and board marks and has degraded the definition of the blind, gilt and silvered tool impressions. This grain loss might persuade the observer to describe the cover as reverse calf (flesh or suede side out) but this is rarely the case in our sample; some grain fragment is always to be found.[29] This surface disfigurement may also be the reason why Mahaffy described them as 'coarse' on the basis of the tactile quality of the covers alone. Another factor that bears on their present state of preservation is that they have been housed on open shelves and often subject to the intense light

---

28 John Waterer, *Leather in life, art and industry*, London 1946, pp 60-1.

29 A note of warning: taking rubbings of the tooling on such degraded leather is damaging and will cause further loss of grain layer and detail, unless the leather has been treated with a consolidant. I have recommended the use of a 10-20g/l solution of the hydroxy propyl cellulose KLUCEL G in ethanol since 1980. The surface can be further reinforced by a sparing application of hard microcrystalline wax (Renaissance Wax) applied with the warm bare hand and polished. See also Anthony Cains and Katherine Swift, *Preserving our printed heritage: the Long Room project at TCD*, Dublin 1988.

over the centuries. But examination of their contemporaries in our collection, acquired later and with a better history of care, can lead one to imagine just how splendid they must have appeared.

DESCRIPTIONS OF REPRESENTATIVE BINDINGS

Blind centre ornament binding (see plates 1, 2)

Author:	Clemens I, Pope.
Title:	*De rebus gestis, peregrinationibus, atque concionibus sancti Petri epitome.*
Imprint:	Paris, 1555.
Format:	4°, 232 x 168 x 15mm.
Shelfmark, current:	BB.i.23.
Shelfmark, early:	E.4.18.
Provenance:	John Dee 1555 29 Sept.; James Ussher.
Binding:	Brown vegetable tanned calf in fine condition stained with reddish dye after covering, over paste boards. Sewn on five, regularly spaced, veg. tanned (?) (looks like brown stained kidskin) thongs all laced. (Recently repaired with original threads preserved in-situ, rebacked.) Tailband intact, a two thread, two colours indigo and pink(?). End leaves a 4° of white each end, sewn all along (watermark of a dagger in horned bulls head with letter at the mouth). Larger than usual squares and not parallel, edges coloured yellow and appear to have been planed rather than ploughed.
Decoration:	A blind centre-piece or tool the same as Ker Ornament 34 with a complex blind border of single french three-line fillets, with the band slips emphatically tooled in a vee shape with a single line pallet. Spine fragments indicate a blind single line frame in each panel. Single crease along squares.

Blind centre-piece binding (see pl. 5)

Author:	Clemens, Titus Flavius, Alexandrinus.
Title:	*Opera ...*
Imprint:	Heidelberg, 1592.
Format:	2°, 351 x 218 x 35 mm.
Shelfmark, current:	C.dd.4.
Shelfmark, early:	T.2.2.6.

1 A blind centre ornament binding (see p. 64)

Joannes Dee 1555. 29. Sep.

ΚΛΗΜΕΝΤΟΣ ΕΠΙΣΚΟΠΟΥ

Ρώμης, σε ὶ τῶν σε ράξεων, ὁπιδημιῶν τε καὶ κηρυγμάτων τῶ ἁγίου Πέτρου ὑπιτομή, σε ρὸς Ἰάκωβον ὑπίσκοπον Ἱεροσολύμων.

ΤΟΥ ΑΥΤΟΥ ΚΛΗΜΕΝΤΟΣ ΒΙΟΣ.

CLEMENTIS ROMANI EPI-

ſcopi, de rebus geſtis, peregrinationibus, atque
concionibus ſancti Petri epitome, ad Iacobum
Hieroſolymorum epiſcopum.

EIVSDEM CLEMENTIS VITA.

Βασιλεῖ τ᾽ ἀγαθῷ κρατερῷ τ᾽ αἰχμητῇ.

PARISIIS   M. D. LV.

Apud Adr. Turnebum typographum regium.

Ex priuilegio Regis.

2 The titlepage of the volume whose binding is illustrated in plate 1 showing
John Dee's signature (see p. 64)

ce. Ordinò i confini de' popoli secondo il numero de' fi=
gliuoli d'Israel . Contra questi scriue Giouanni Annio ,
nel lib.2. sopra Beroso & rēde giusta ragione, mostran=
doper quel cap. che fossero settanta sole , non nume=
rando Noè, Sem, Cham et Iaphet:percio che tante perso=
ne si nominano da questi , o uero fossero settanta non
piu, ilche è il piu proprio. Però che non s'hanno da nu=
merare senon quelli , che nacquero infin'a Falec , nel
cui tempo fu la diuisione delle lingue . Di qualunque
sorte che sia stato del numero delle lingue nel principio,
certo è c'hora non è del modo ch'allhora fu : percio che
sono piu ò meno lingue di quelle , ch'allhora furono .
Dico che sono piu , per cagione delle mescolanze che
s'hanno fatto intanti anni che dura il mondo , che me=
schiandosi l'une genti con l'altre , si corruppero quelle
prime fauelle , & si fecero altre fauelle terze, come nel
principio della habitatione si fece , uenendo quelli delle
lingue nuoue , nelle terre che prima furono gia habi=
tate da Noè , & sempre dopo è stato il medesimo ,
con tante guerre , come sono state al mondo . o forse
che sono hora manco . Percio che quelli , i quali fu=
rono patroni delle terre , per hauer meglio il Domi =
nio in esse , procurarono d'introdurre la loro lingua
con esse , & far dimenticare quella , ch'esse haueuano
per propria , non altrimente che , come fecero i Ro =
mani in Hispagna , introducendo la lingua latina , &
precipitando quella , che parlauano propria , laqua =
le era la Viscaglina , Nauarra , & altre simili . Ve=
rissimo è questo gia , & molti hanno scritto alcune

3 An indelible mark of early college ownership – awl- or chisel-stabbed perforations
driven into the text (see pp 56ff)

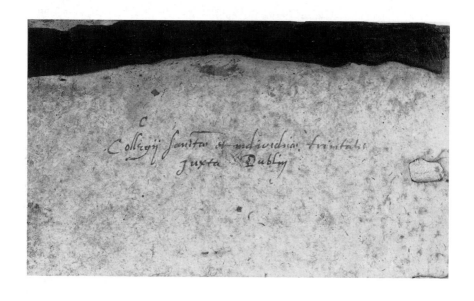

4 Ex libris of the college written in Latin (see p. 57)

5 A blind centre-piece binding (see pp 60 and 64)

6 A gilt centre-piece and corner tool, blind panel binding (see pp 60 and 65)

7 A blind portrait medallion centre-piece binding (see pp 60 and 66)

8 A gilt double centre tool binding (see pp 61 and 66)

9 Another example of the use of the same tool in an identical fashion to the binding
shown in plate 8 (see pp 61 and 67)

10 A binding similar to that shown in plate 8 but which displays only a single gilt
centre tool (see pp 61 and 70)

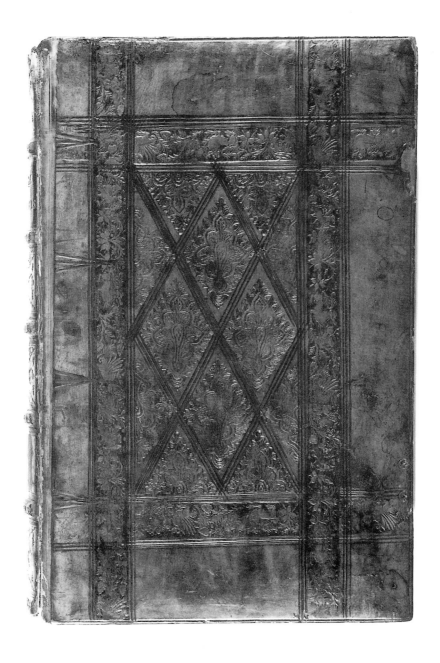

11 An example of a roll stamp panel binding of the early to mid sixteenth century
(see p. 62)

12 Another instance of the type of binding illustrated in plate 11 (see p. 62)

13 A gilt centre-piece and corner tool, blind panel binding described in detail on p. 67

14 A full gilt centre and corner-piece binding described in detail on p. 68

15 a and b A binding (a) and (b) an ink-proof of a binder's corner-piece described
in detail on p. 69

16 Silvered centre and corner tool, blind panel binding described in detail on pp 69ff

Provenance: Bookseller Gregory Seton; no stab marks.

Binding: Tanned calf stained dark brown after covering, over (pulp) paste-board each with a single white lining applied after lacing in. Sewn on six tanned thongs all laced (except one station at front board fifth from head). Endpapers: at front a single folded white with joint of plain parchment, at the back two hooked white leaves reinforced with MS (English) in two lengths (lacks one leaf). Endbands intact but faded, tied down three times to deep set kettle stitches. No spine linings. Ploughed edges stained yellow.

Decoration: Blind centre-piece of the same basic design as Ker XIV but with hatched ground instead of punched and a different arrangement around central oval, height 90 x 64mm wide (same dimensions). Border and spine bands blind tooled with french three line fillet; cord tie marks, no hatching.

Gilt centre-piece and corner tool, blind panel binding (see pl. 6)

Author: Appianus, Alexandrinus.

Title: *Delle guerre civili et esterne de Romani.*

Imprint: Venice, 1555.

Format: 8°, 160 x 107 x 50mm.

Shelfmark, current: W.k.5.

Binding: Fine vegetable tanned calf, stained brown after covering, over coarse fibred pulpboards. Sewn on five single vegetable tanned thongs, all laced in. Note pin holes in the front board slips. Head and tail-bands intact (secured with modern plain thread tackets) of two thread, two colour (indigo and pink) with vegetable tanned cores. Endleaves each composed of folded white with a hooked full leaf of MS parchment (sheepskin) as a pastedown (now detached). Edges shaved rather than ploughed with no evidence of colour surviving. Author's name written at head of fore-edge.

Decoration: Panel blind tooled with french three line fillet, with double border of the same tool. Gilt centre-piece (silver content partially oxidized) same as Ker VII with gilt lily corner tool (not in Ker); a small lily at the centre of each spine panel; panels tooled with a narrow single line pallet, and heavy tie marks (but no hatching).

Binder: Dominique Pinart (after 1573).

Note: Conserved 1987.

Blind portrait medallion centre-piece binding (see pl. 7)

1 Author:	Knewstub, John.
Title:	*A confutation of monstrous and horrible heresies ...*
Imprint:	London, 1579.
2 Author:	[Foxe, John].
Title:	*The Pope confuted ...*
Imprint:	London, 1580.
Format:	4°, 206 x 137 x 38mm.
Shelfmark, current:	BB.ii.48.
Shelfmark, early:	Upside down H.5.5 on fore-edge and other marks.
Provenance:	Luke Challoner, Phebe Challoner, James Ussher.
Binding:	Vegetable tanned calf stained black with copperas over back-cornered paste-boards. Sewn on four single tawed thongs, two sections on (to view); all slips laced in. Endbands lost but remains of three tie downs. Endleaves each constructed of a fold of white paper (gauntlet hand watermark) with a joint of MS parchment, front MS on calfskin with rubrication and blue pigment (fourteenth-fifteenth century English (?)) and the back reinforcing strip from another MS Latin (?). Ploughed edges, pale yellow pigment.
Decoration:	Border of a heavy three line fillet with fine portrait medallion centre-piece in an elaborate baroque frame, the subject a bust of a lady facing slightly to her left in the manner of the Lyons printer, Guillaume Rouille, 1553.

Gilt double centre tool binding (see pl. 8)

Author:	Viretus, Petrus.
Title:	*De origine veteris & novae idololatriae* (and another text).
Imprint:	Geneva, 1552.
Format:	8°, 157 x 100 x 31mm.
Shelfmark, current:	G.n.28.
Shelfmark, early:	T.6.2.21 (also T.6.3.16).
Provenance:	Bookseller's code, double stab, Richard Smithe, merchant.
Binding:	Tanned calfskin stained with black dye after covering, over paste-boards with chamfered joint edge. Sewn on four single tawed thongs, all laced, sewing all along with alternate stations by-passed, missed at the two central thongs. Endbands intact of two colours faded but exposed thread ends indicate indigo and pink. Endleaves each of two bifolia (4°) with parchment reinforcing strips. Remains of two

	narrow pale green ribbon fore-edge ties (4mm). Ploughed edges stained yellow after endbanding.
Decoration:	A gilt centre tool composed of two 'mirrored' impressions of the same tool within a blind french three line border.
Observations:	The spine grain layer damaged but small gilt centre tool and single line pallet work evident. Head and second panels lost.
Binder:	See also *Ethicorum Aristotelis*, Lyons, 1548, same tool used in identical fashion on binding dated 1550, with title lettered on front cover, in Biblioteca Communale di Montefalco, C III 29 (see pl. 9).

Gilt centre-piece and corner tool, blind panel binding (see pl. 13)

Author:	Beuter, Pedro Antonio.
Title:	*Cronica generale d'Hispagna.*
Imprint:	Venice, 1556.
Format:	8°, 162 x 105 x 40mm.
Shelfmark, current:	M.n.20.
Shelfmark, early:	H.8.6.27.
Provenance:	Luke Challoner (two 15mm deep stab perforations).
Binding:	Vegetable tanned calf stained black after covering with copperas, over back-cornered paste boards. Sewn on four double thongs, the thread worked all along, missed station herringbone (to view). The third thong down from the head is tanned and the others tawed, all laced in. Lacks front flyleaves and title-page (an ancient loss) but front lambskin parchment joint in place (two column Latin with rubrication and blue pigment); back blank paper endleaves (bifolium) intact (with remnant of a fore-edge tab label in place) and calfskin parchment joint strip (ruled only) component sewn on separately. Endbands intact, sewn with double linen thread each colour, indigo/natural or faded yellow, indigo thread tied-down four times. No spine linings. Ploughed edges stained green-yellow.
Decoration:	Panel and border blind tooled with french three line pallet or fillet; gilt arabesque centre-piece with gilt panel corner tool, a large lily, and a small lily at the centre of each spine panel; tie marks and possibly a single line pallet – the spine leather is degraded.
Binder:	Same binder as B.f.18.

Full gilt centre and corner-piece binding (see pl. 14)

Author:	Villagagno, Nicolas Durand, chevalier de.
Title:	*Ad articulos calvinianae de sacramento Eucharistiae traditionis ... responsiones.*
Imprint:	Paris, 1560.
Format:	4°, 162 x 154 x 30mm
Shelfmark, current:	E.gg.36
Shelfmark, early:	T.9.5.19.
Provenance:	Initials PW. Purchased for the college by Luke Challoner from the London stationer, Gregory Seton. Two deep stab perforations at tail.
Binding:	Rebacked in the nineteenth century and conserved 1980 in library Conservation Laboratory. Light brown vegetable tanned calf (in fine condition) over paste-boards. Sewn on five equally spaced double tawed thongs, all laced in, each slip recessed in a triangular groove and flush with the inside surface of the paste-board. Original endpapers lost but MS parchment joint lining fragments found under modern machine made endpapers removed during conservation. Sewing supports cut off in nineteenth century. Text block resewn in-situ to preserve the solidity of the original gilt edges. Endbands, modern linen thread.
Decoration:	A gilt centre- and corner-piece binding (the only one found in the first collections) with additional small tools, all hatched (or azured) set around the centre piece, three distinct elements, plus one extra tool of related type added later each side of the centre piece to hide the originally gilded initials PW tooled on both boards. Some gilding of the letter W remains on the front board. Border framed with blind french three line fillet with gilded single gold line within; a round dot tool at each corner and the corner-pieces aligned and abutting the line. The azured flower tool covering the letters is similar in design to Ker Ornaments 50, 59 & 60 and to several of our centre and corner tool panel bindings.
Binder:	Suggest a Paris binder from the quality of the forwarding alone, in particular the neatly recessed slips not found on any other binding in our sample, which are mainly London, Oxford, Cambridge and Dublin bindings.

Vine-in-pot silver centre tool and gilt corner tool, blind panel binding (see plates 15a, b)

Author:	Acosta, Emanuel.
Title:	*Rerum a Societate Iesu in oriente gestarum ad an. 1568, commentarius.*
Imprint:	Cologne, 1574.
Format:	8°, 163 x 107 x 35mm.
Shelfmark, current:	G.m.25.
Shelfmark, early:	T.11.2.23.
Provenance:	Bookseller's code.
Binding:	Tanned calfskin stained with black dye after covering, grain layer very degraded. Paste-boards inside back cornered. Sewn on four single tawed thongs, all laced. Endbands intact – two thread two colour faded, tied down three times on core of rolled vegetable tanned leather. Endleaves of folded and hooked white; the front bears two impressions of the same binders' corner-piece motif on the verso of the flyleaf facing titlepage; front and back pasted down, stub about 15mm wide. Ploughed edges stained yellow. Remains of two fore-edge ties of russet coloured ribbon (5mm) under board paper.
Decoration:	A silvered vine-in-pot centre tool (24 x 20mm) within a french three line blind panel with gilt four petalled corner tool (6 x 6mm), most tool impressions worn or lost to grain erosion. Spine has evidence of tie-mark but otherwise too superficially damaged. A blind single line fillet along squares is noted.
Note:	All the silver tooled impressions have oxidized to a leaden grey colour, but the metallic sheen is evident and should not be confused with blind tooled impressions.

Silvered centre and corner tool, blind panel binding (see pl. 16)

Author:	Corradus, Sebastianus.
Title:	*Egnatius, sive quaestura cujus praecipua capita haec sunt.*
Imprint:	Basle, 1556.
Format:	8°, 185 x 122 x 42mm.
Shelfmark, current:	S.mm.5.
Shelfmark, early:	H.7.6.7.
Provenance:	Bookseller's code, double stab.
Binding:	Vegetable tanned calf, stained with black dye after covering, over back cornered paste boards. The back cover at

Decoration:

the tail edge bears a tanner's or leather-seller's search or view mark (?) of two punched letters possibly MC. Some grain layer remains. Sewn on four single tawed thongs, all laced. Endbands intact of two threads, yellow and natural, of disparate guages, tied down three times. Ploughed edges either not coloured or faded. Remains of two foreedge ties of green ribbon (6mm) set into slots at front. Endleaves of folded hooked white (stub *c*.25mm), front pasted, back free.

A blind french three line panel binding with silver centre tool similar to Ker Ornament 62 (20 x 16mm) and silver corner tool, a lily (11 x 9mm). The centre of each spine panel has a six petalled flower (prob. silver now oxidized), tie marks and kettle stitch panel hatched in blind (head panel lost), edges not tooled but single creaser marks evident along edges and squares.

Gilt centre tool and corner tool panel binding (see pl. 10)

Author: Utenhovius, Joannes.
Title: *Narratio de instituta ac demum dissipata Belgarum ...*
Imprint: Basle, 1560 (colophon).
Format: 8°, 169 x 109 x 26mm.
Shelfmark, current: G.n.8.
Shelfmark, early: T.3.3.29.
Provenance: Bookseller's code 'E' and double stab at date '1560'.
Binding: Tanned calf, stained black after covering over inside backcornered (obtuse 45° angle) paste boards; remains of two pink fabric (5.5mm) fore-edge ties. Sewn on four single tawed kid thongs, all-along, all-around and all laced in (to view, head spine panel lost). Endbands intact, of two thread indigo, tied down three times, and two thread white stained yellow with edge colour. Endpapers, each a bifolium of the same (duplicate) printer's waste – *Book of Common Prayer* (fragment Dii) in English black letter with the following imprint 'Imprinted at London in Poules Church Yarde by Richard Iugge and John Cawood prynters to the Quenes Maiestie. Cum priviligie Regiae Maiestatis.' The front parchment joint has fragment of illuminated MS on the inner stub, the back joint still pasted down displays gesso gilded illumination with evident pallet of red lead, azurite (offset) *verde di gris*, carbon

	black. MS large gothic hand. Ploughed edges coloured green-yellow after endbanding (seen on many books).
Decoration:	A gilt centre and corner tool binding panelled in blind with narrow three line fillet (lines equal guage). The single centre tool is one of the great family of solid arabesque tools of the period and is probably one of a pair. The gilt corner tool is an arabesque lily; the spine panels are tooled with a small gilt six point star with another placed below the kettle stitch at the tail (head panel lost); tie marks and single line pallet.
Binder:	Same binder as F.nn.39 (T.6.6.16).

The Library Buildings up to 1970

BRENDAN GRIMES

The contents of the library are housed in several buildings both on and off the campus. The library buildings on the campus are the Old Library (1732), the Hall of Honour and Reading Room (1937), the Berkeley Library (1967), the Lecky Library (1978), the Hamilton Library (1992), and the Map Library has been housed in the Gymnasium (1860) since 1988. Outside the campus there is the John Stearne Library at the Trinity Centre for Health Sciences at St James's Hospital, Dublin, a small specialist branch library at the School of Occupational Therapy in Dun Laoghaire, and the book repository in Santry, Dublin, where about 70 per cent of the library's 3.7 million books are held. This article gives some account of the Old Library, the 1937 Reading Room, and the Berkeley Library.

In the early 1700s the need for a suitable library building was pressing, and conditions for building looked favourable because of the settled political climate in the country after the upheavals which had lasted for most of the seventeenth century. Some of these troubles had visited the college with its occupation in 1689 by Jacobite troops who caused much damage. Fortunately the contents of the library were spared due to the efforts of Fathers Teigue McCarthy and Micheal Moore; a brass tablet in the 1937 Reading Room commemorates this episode. In the same year, owing to the disturbed state of the country, none of the college tenants was paying rent; and as a result only one meal a day was being served in the college.[1] These problems were now in the past; the college had adequately demonstrated its loyalty to the new Government and the House of Commons of Ireland resolved on 1 June 1709 that

> ... taking into consideration the proceedings of the University of Trinity-College near Dublin, in censuring *Edward Forbes*, by Degradation and Expulsion, for speaking dishonourable of, and aspersing the glorious Memory of his late Majesty King *William* the Third,

1 Constantia Maxwell, *A history of Trinity College Dublin 1591-1892*, Dublin 1946, p. 81.

and also the steady Adherence of the Provost and Fellows of the said College to the late happy Revolution, her present Majesty's Government, and the Succession in the Protestant Line as by Law established, *for the Encouragement of good Literature and sound Revolution Principles*, do address his Excellency the Lord Lieutenant, that he will lay before her Majesty the humble Desire of this House, that 5000 l. be bestowed by her Majesty on the Provost, Fellows, and Scholars of Trinity-College, near *Dublin*, for creating a publick Library in the said College.[2]

In November of the same year the 24-year-old junior fellow George Berkeley was appointed to serve as librarian for the following 12 months. Thomas Burgh, Chief Engineer and Surveyor-General of his Majesty's Fortifications in Ireland was chosen as architect for the new library, and it is possible that Berkeley and Burgh discussed some of the requirements for the new building. The library at Trinity College Cambridge, designed by Sir Christopher Wren, provided an example to be studied, and Archbishop Marsh's Library, Dublin, built in 1703 to the designs of Sir William Robinson (Burgh's predecessor as Surveyor-General), must have provided some inspiration. One of Wren's designs for Trinity College Cambridge was for a circular building, but the scheme adopted was a long rectangular building with the library on the first floor over an open arcade (this sensible arrangement ensured that the books were kept away from rising dampness and the same idea was used in Dublin). Inverted arches, as described by Alberti, were used for the foundations to the arcade in Cambridge.[3] The building work started in 1676 and when the library was finished in 1684 it was the grandest of its kind in Britain. Now the Board of Trinity College Dublin was about to build an even grander library and on the 12 May 1712 the provost and fellows attended the laying of the foundation stone for their new library.[4] During the course of construction an application to Parliament was made on 21 September 1717 for another £5,000, with the declaration of the college's '... resolution to instruct the Youth under their Care in Principles of Zeal and Affection to the Constitution in Church and State, and of Duty and Loyalty to his Majesty King George and his Royal Family ...' This request

2 *Journals of the House of Commons of Ireland*, Dublin 1796, vol. 2, p. 596. Edward Forbes, a graduate about to be conferred with an MA, declined to drink a toast to the memory of King William, and compared him to a highwayman who had recently been hanged (R.B. McDowell and D.A. Webb, *Trinity College Dublin 1592-1952: an academic history*, Cambridge 1982, p. 33).

3 Howard Colvin, 'The building', in David McKitterick ed., *The making of the Wren library, Trinity College Cambridge*, Cambridge 1995, p. 41. No information on the contruction of the foundations to the Old Library, TCD has been found.

4 TCD Library, Board Minute Book, 12 May 1712, MUN/V/5. (Hereafter references to MSS are to TCD Library unless otherwise stated.)

was granted and so was another for £5,000 made on 6 October 1721. As with the previous applications the provost and fellows were at pains to assure the Government of their '... inviolable Attachment to the late happy Revolution...' Furthermore they were prepared (they said) to '... continue utterly to discountenance and exterminate ... all Principles of a contrary Tendency...'.[5] When the library was being conceived it must have been difficult to imagine the shelves full. In the early eighteenth century the library probably had less than 15,000 volumes but the new building was designed to hold about 45,000 volumes in the stalls of the main room. (In comparison the new library at Cambridge was designed to hold at least 30,000 volumes.)[6] Not all the building was intended for library accommodation; some of the space in the end pavilions was to be for lecture rooms.

The building of the eastern range of Library Square (the Rubrics) was completed within a few years of 1700 and the other ranges were begun in the 1720s. The new library completed this square and it seems that it was envisaged from the start of the square.[7] Building work proceeded slowly and it was not until 1733 that books began to be placed in the library.[8] The slowness of the work was due to the preoccupation with completing the residential buildings in Library Square during the 1720s. We learn that in 1735 'The Bursar is ordered by ye Provost and senr fellows to advance to Mr Hudson one hundred and twelve pounds on acct. of ye trouble he has taken and is herafter to take in settling ye Library.'[9] The heart of the library is the Long Room which was built to contain most of the book collection and to provide space for reading. At each end of the Long Room there is a three-storey pavilion. The Long Room was entered from the west pavilion. Underneath was an open arcade, with a wall separating Library Square from the Fellows' Garden. A gallery ran around the Long Room. The room is 64.5 metres long by 12.2 metres wide and was about 15 metres high, finished with a flat plaster ceiling. At each floor-level window (except at the stairs) in the Long Room an alcove capable of containing about 2,000 books was built. There are forty of these alcoves (or stalls as they are commonly called) and they provided semi-private and well-lit spaces for the readers. Each stall had bench seating in the middle and sloping desks projecting from the shelves for placing open books. There were no shelves under the desks.

The shape and layout of the Long Room allowed the best possible use to be made of daylight which was the only means of lighting until the 1960s.

---

5 *Journals of the House of Commons of Ireland*, Dublin 1796, vol. 3, p. 134 and p. 261.

6 Colvin, work cited in note 3, p. 36.

7 Edward McParland, *The buildings of Trinity College Dublin*. Reprinted from *Country Life* [1978] p. 3.

8 Board Minute Book, 20 Nov. 1733, MUN/V/5/2, records that the newly-appointed librarian, Mr Hudson, was paid £60 for placing books in the new library.

9 Borad Minute Book, 25 Mar. 1735, MUN/V/5/2.

The disadvantage was that the windows took up space which could have been used for shelving. In Wren's library at Trinity College Cambridge the stalls are lit by high-level windows with book shelves under them; but in Marsh's Library the windows are near floor level, the system adopted in Trinity College Dublin. Most illustrations of the Long Room made before 1900 show light streaming into the room. (Because of the need to protect the books from daylight the sun blinds are now kept down.) The books are shelved according to size and this, as well as making the best possible use of the storage capacity of the shelves, also provides a visually satisfying appearance of order. The 21 book stacks on the north side are identified with letters from A to W and those on the south side with letters from AA to WW. On one side of the stack (except for the two end stacks which are single sided) the shelves are lettered starting with *a* and on the other side starting with *aa*. The books on each shelf are numbered, thus allowing every book to be precisely located with its shelf mark (e.g. the first book on the shelves is A.a.1). The shelves were identified by numbers until about 1830 when the system was changed from letter-number-number to letter-letter-number when shelves were added to the stacks. It seems likely that this change took place when the sloping wooden desks, which took up the lower portion of the stacks (as can be seen in Malton's print of the Long Room), were removed to make way for more shelves. A concordance book survives (kept in the Department of Early Printed Books) which shows the old numbers with the new, and what were the new shelves. In each double sided stack six or seven new shelves were gained. This was achieved by dropping the first four or five shelves, which contained the folios and large quartos, towards the floor and then inserting the new shelves. This necessitated the renumbering of the entire stack. The decision to use a letter-letter-number system may also have been made to avoid confusion with the Fagel collection which used letter-number-number shelfmarks. The letter-number-number method of marking books was commonly used in eighteenth century university libraries and was used in Trinity College Cambridge and in Marsh's Library.

It has been mentioned that the library was not artificially lit until the 1960s. One of the competitors at that time for the new library commission (to be discussed later) asked: 'Is one to assume that the last sentence at the bottom of p. 21 [of the competition brief saying there is no artificial light in the Colonnade, Long Room, or the east pavilion] is purely an aside to arouse an atmosphere of academic obscurantism, or to indicate the Spartan stuff of Trinity College Scholars and Graduates, or to intimate that competitors are to do something about it?'[10] It may seem strange that in such a large build-

---

10 University of Dublin, *International competition for a new library building: Official answers to questions*, Dublin 1961, p. 17.

ing most of the spaces had no artificial light until the middle of this century. Because we are so dependent on electricity today we do not easily realize how well the Old Library functioned without artificial light. Apart from the winter when the library was closed at 3pm, there was usually enough light available to use the library for many hours each day. However, electricity and artificial light were gradually introduced into the west pavilion, permitting the reading room to be opened in the evening for the first time in January 1901.[11] On 24 March 1908 '... the new vacuum dusting machine was set to work in the Colonnade'.[12] Initially it was driven by an electric motor connected to the lamp circuit in the reading room but later a new wiring circuit was put in for it. The board was fearful of a fire in the library and hence it was wary of electricity and with good cause. In May 1914 the electrical wiring in the reading room caught fire but luckily no damage was done.[13] By 1914 there was electric lighting in the reading room, the librarian's room, and the entrance hall. Maintenance work was carried out to the electrical wires in 1917 and 1920 and an entry in the minute book noted: 'The recent burning of Rathmines Roman Catholic Chapel has drawn attention to the risks from electric wires.'[14] It is not surprising therefore that electricity in the Long Room was a late arrival. In 1950 the library committee discussed a proposal to put an electric heater in an alcove of the Long Room for the attendants to warm themselves, but due to the risk of fire they did not agree to the proposal.[15] The desire to protect the building from fire resulted in hose reels being installed in the Long Room in the 1870s and these were renewed in 1898. In 1901 an iron box was supplied for matches in the classing room ('In this box accidental ignition would be harmless').[16] Telephones and speaking tubes were used in the library. Telephones were installed by 1907, and an entry in the minute book mentions that repairs were made to the speaking tube from the classing room to the librarian's room in 1903, and a new tube was installed in 1920 between the classing room and the reading room. The speaking tubes were in use until about 1950.[17]

Sanitary conveniences in the library were primitive or non-existent until the early twentieth century. The minute book records that when the new reading room was opened in 1892 and the Colonnades closed in, a wash hand basin and urinal were placed at the south-west window; it became offensive

11 Library Committee Minute Book, 10 January 1901, MUN/LIB/2/7.
12 Ibid., 24 March 1908.
13 Ibid., 18 May 1914.
14 Ibid., 9 February 1920.
15 Library Committee Minute Book, 10 November 1950, MUN/LIB/3/3.
16 Library Committee Minute Book, 7 January 1901, MUN/LIB/2/7.
17 Ibid., 7 January 1903, 5-8 July 1907, 14-15 May 1920. Cyril Bedford, who worked in the library from 1942 until 1992, remembers the speaking tubes in use until the late 1940s.

and a pail was substituted for the urinal but it became such an unspeakable nuisance 'that finally in April 1899 the place had to be purged of the whole business'.[18]

The Copyright Act 1801 gave the library authority to claim a free copy of every work published in the British Isles. The consequence of this was a steady and increasing flow of books, creating the need for more and more shelf space and incidentally, prompting an anonymous hand to write 'alias, Packs of Trash' in the library memorandum book beside an entry recording the arrival of a consignment of books received under the Act.[19] By the early 1840s the stalls in the Long Room were full with about 90,000 books, and the library was receiving between 1,000 and 2,000 extra books a year. (Extra space had been found by removing the seats and reading tables in the stalls and using the space gained to build shelves.) In 1843 the assistant librarian suggested erecting bookcases under the windows in the gallery; each bookcase would hold 560 volumes and with forty windows (not allowing for the extra space at the ten middle windows) it was estimated that the gallery would hold 22,400 volumes. He had a sample bookcase erected for the board's visitation in 1844 and was given approval to erect two more.[20] Over about the next ten years the gallery was fitted out with these bookcases which provided book storage three shelves deep. This was achieved by means of a fixed inner bookcase and an outer one with shelves on either side which could be swung out on a pivot; at the central part of the building where the walls are thicker there were two cases on pivots making a depth of five shelves. Some of these cases are still in operation. In the 1840s and '50s the library was growing at the rate of about 2,500 books a year and it was estimated that the extra storage provided in the gallery would be full in 1857 with 25,000 volumes.[21]

A more radical solution to the book storage problem was needed. The board was forced to act when it was discovered that the roof was in poor condition. In November 1856 it asked John McCurdy, and Deane and Woodward to provide separate reports and suggest solutions.[22] McCurdy's solution was to replace the roof structure with iron trusses without disturbing the ceiling or slates; this solution also provided for book storage in the roof-space. Deane and Woodward's first proposal was to block up the gallery windows, run bookcases

18 Ibid., April 1899.
19 Library Minute Book, 18 August 1813, MUN/LIB/2/1.
20 Library Minute Book, 21 October 1844, MUN/LIB/2/4.
21 Ibid. Board visitation report 1853. The Minute Book (p.80) records that from 1843 to 1863 the number of printed books in the library grew from 94,832 to 142,335.
22 Details of the Board's deliberations on this matter are recounted and discussed by Anne Crookshank, 'The Long Room', in Peter Fox (ed.) *Treasures of the library; Trinity College Dublin*, Dublin 1986, pp 26-7, and in Frederick O'Dwyer, *The architecture of Deane and Woodward*, Cork 1997, pp 349-55.

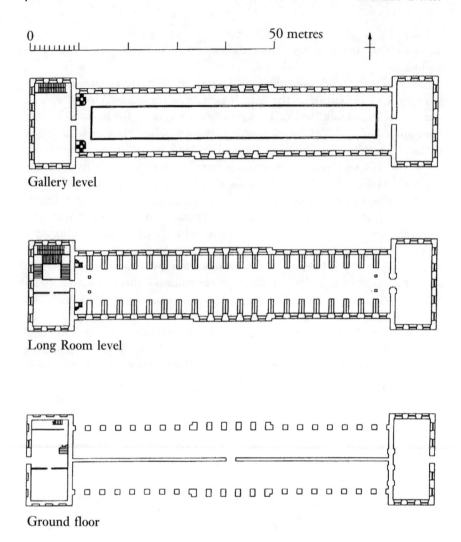

0   50 metres

Gallery level

Long Room level

Ground floor

Figure 1: Floor plans of the Old Library in 1732.
Note suggested arrangement of the main stairs in the West Pavilion.

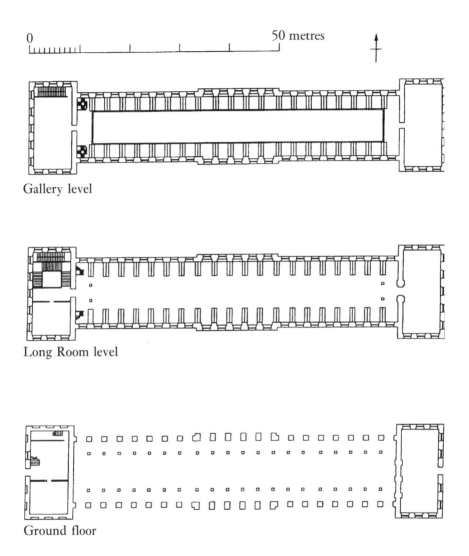

Gallery level

Long Room level

Ground floor

Figure 2: Floor plans of the Old Library after
the alterations were made by Deane and Woodward.

along the walls and provide lighting through the roof. Their final proposal to provide a new roof with a barrel vaulted ceiling sheeted in oak, with intersecting barrel vaults from the gallery, was accepted by the board (see figs. 1, 2). The building was protected with a canvas roof coated with tar (mixed with sand and alum to reduce the risk of fire) while the old roof was being taken down and the new one erected. The work was finished by May 1861. Such a radical change to an important eighteenth-century building would be unlikely to be contemplated today, but even in the mid-nineteenth century it must have required courage on the part of the board and the architects. The *Dublin Builder* reviewed the work favourably noting that to 'lengthen or widen or erect additions to the existing building, would necessitate a most material interference with the arrangement of other buildings in the proximity, and in fact may be pronounced an impracticability.'[23] Godfrey Pinkerton, writing for the *Architectural Review* in 1906, thought that the Long Room had been utterly spoiled by the alteration. Pinkerton had been helped on his Dublin visit by Sir Thomas Drew and one wonders if he was influenced in his opinion by Drew.[24] The cross-section (see fig. 3) shows the structural alterations that were made. Most of the weight of the roof was taken off the walls and carried by timber columns internally and granite columns under the library floor in the open arcade. About the same time the Rubrics, which joined the library at its north-eastern end, was detached by demolishing three of its bays.[25]

The gallery was almost full with nearly 23,000 volumes in 1859 before the roof was replaced. After the roof had been replaced the new structural arrangement allowed stacks in the gallery to be built at right angles to the wall and directly over the stacks at the lower level. As soon as the new shelves in the gallery were ready almost all the intake of new books were placed there. By 1887 the gallery was almost full with nearly 86,000 volumes, and again a new generation was faced with the problem of accommodating more books. The temptation to use the space under the Long Room for book storage proved too great to resist and by 1889 this was being considered, if not already decided. The proposal was to enclose the space by filling the arcades with windows and to provide shelving along the spine wall and between the windows laid out in stalls. The design was by Sir Thomas Drew. The proposal had the merit of being an economical solution to the book storage problem as well as providing space for a reading room, and was accepted by the board. But it was to change the appearance of the building and the character of the Fellows' Garden for the worse. As soon as the Colonnades were enclosed (in

23 *Dublin Builder* vol. 2 (1 February 1860) p. 196.
24 Godfrey Pinkerton, 'Some Dublin buildings – 2', *Architectural Review* (London) vol. 20 (1906) p. 111.
25 J.V. Luce, *Trinity College Dublin: the first 400 years*, Dublin 1992, p. 49.

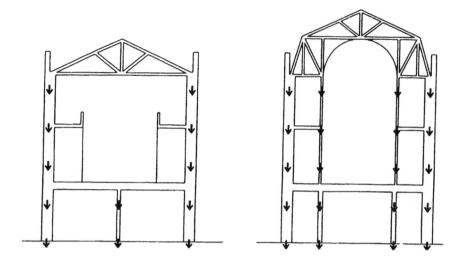

Figure 3: Diagrammatic cross-sections of the Old Library before (left)
and after (right) Deane and Woodward's alterations.
The arrows indicate the structural arrangements.

1892) a few stalls were erected between the windows and others added from time to time as the need arose. The attic of the west pavilion was shelved in 1896 for book storage.[26]

The need for space was again becoming urgent in the early 1900s and in 1910 the clerk of works was asked to report on the cost of flooring and shelving the roof-space in the east pavilion and by 1911 the board was discussing the necessity of building a new reading room, thus releasing the area in the Colonnades, used as a reading room, for book storage.[27] A few months later in February 1912 the board authorized the librarian, Dr T.K. Abbott, to consult Sir Thomas Manly Deane about building it.[28] Sir Thomas's proposals were ready in January 1913. They were presented on six sheets and showed three sketch designs for the new reading room. The first proposal showed an octagonal building to be placed in the Fellows' Garden, approached through a passage opening on the Library Square and going through the Colonnades at the library's mid-point. The building was to be two-storeys high with a flat roof and with an arcade and first-floor windows exactly matching those on the library. It would have provided a floor area of 432 square metres. Another pro-

26 Library Minute Book, 5 December 1910, MUN/LIB/2/7.
27 Ibid., 5 December 1910 & 20 May 1911.
28 Ibid., 24 February 1912.

posal was to use the same design but to place it between the library and the examination hall and behind the Lecky statue. (The Lecky statue was then in the green space mid-way between the library and the examination hall and near the line of the north façade of the library.) A third proposal was for a rectangular building to occupy the same site behind the Lecky statue. (Another proposal which was lightly pencilled on the drawing shows the octagonal building south of the east pavilion with its entrance on the east side. This idea was considered because the Provost, Dr A. Traill, refused to allow any encroachment on his garden, but no drawings have been found showing this idea developed.)[29] The front elevation of the building proposed to be sited between the examination hall and the library (the elevation was to be the same for both schemes) was carefully considered and one of the six drawings is devoted to a study of the front elevations of the chapel, dining hall, and printing house. The proposed elevation (with ideas taken from the pavilions of the west front of the college) shows a classical building with swag, venetian window, Ionic pilasters, balls and urns on a balustrade. Its roof ridge level was to be about 14 metres high coming level with about the middle of the second-floor library windows.

The Great War was soon to interrupt any further consideration of this building project, but room had still to be found for the growing number of books. Steel shelving was erected in the Colonnades by W. Lucy & Co., Oxford, from August 1913 until November 1915, and more steel shelving was put up in 1920.[30]

After the war the proposal to build a new reading room was again actively considered. Sir Thomas Manly Deane was asked to combine the reading room with a memorial to the Trinity men who had lost their lives in the war. The sketch designs (on two drawings) were ready in September 1920. The drawings show the design very much as it was finally built. The reading room was to be connected to the library by a sub-way, and would provide seating for 204 readers, two classrooms and lavatory accommodation for men and women. These drawings were approved and the minute book records: 'The Board resolved that the site between the Examination Hall and the library be granted for the erection of a Hall of Honour in memory of the Trinity men who died in the war with the view of associating it with a Reading Room for the library when funds permit.'[31]

Early in 1922 three rooms over the provost's stables were fitted out with shelving and the newspapers moved there.[32] Although the difficulty of find-

---

29 Drawings dated 3 January 1913, MUN/MC/36 & Library Minute Book, January 1913, MUN/LIB/2/7, p. 89.
30 Library Minute Book, 5 Aug. 1913, 10 Sept. 1915, 8 May 1920, MUN/LIB/2/7.
31 Library Minute Book, 21 June 1921, MUN/LIB/2/7.
32 Ibid, 16 January & 10 May 1922.

ing funds for the new reading room was a serious obstacle, Deane was asked to proceed with detailed drawings. It is quite clear from the set of twenty drawings that it was intended to build the Hall of Honour first, but the design for the rest of the building was well worked out. Costly materials were specified for the Hall of Honour, for example teak woodblock floor, black marble skirting, walnut doors, and Sicilian marble landing and stair treads. The design was based on the Magnetic Observatory in the Fellows' Garden built in 1838 by Frederick Darley. Some members of the board must have thought the Hall of Honour would never be built and in 1924 the idea of placing the war memorial tablets in the main entrance to the college was considered.[33] The Provost, Dr John Henry Bernard, set sail for Canada and the USA in 1925 with the view to getting funds for the building, but his trip had to be cut short after he caught bronchitis from the cold Newfoundland winds.[34] In the same year the library was given two army huts and space in the east wing of Campus House[35] for book storage, and it was decided to put in steel shelving there in 37 gallery stalls.[36] By January 1926 the college had collected £7,000 in subscriptions, enough to build the war memorial, and the board decided to set aside £2,000 a year, when there was a surplus, for the new reading room. In May Sir Thomas Deane was asked to invite tenders for the building work from P.J. Good and from G. & T. Crampton, and in April 1927 work started on the Hall of Honour.[37] All the pre-war drawings show the Lecky statue in its original position, but it was decided in May 1927 to move it to its present position between the library and the campanile.[38] In July 1928 the hoarding was removed from the Hall of Honour and a few months later on 10 November it was formally opened by the Provost, Dr Edward John Gwynn. An oration was given by the Vice-chancellor, Lord Glenavy, wreaths were laid, the names of the fallen were read out, and the last post was sounded.[39]

The subway from the library to the Hall of Honour had been built as part of the first phase of the project, and by May 1929 the London copyright agency book boxes were being received in the basement of the Hall of Honour before being brought through the subway to the library.[40] By 1935

---

33 A set of drawings bound together numbered 2 to 20 (dated 1923) with a survey drawing of the observatory (dated September 1922) and a drawing showing a proposal to put the memorial tablets in the main entrance to TCD (dated 29 February 1924), MUN/MC/42. A duplicate set, MUN/MC/203.
34 Library Minute Book, 13 June 1925, MUN/LIB/2/7.
35 Campus House was located in the Parade Ground at the east end of the College.
36 Library Minute Book, 30 April, 18 May, & 26 November 1925, MUN/LIB/2/7.
37 Ibid., 11 April 1927.
38 Ibid., 24 May 1927.
39 Ibid., 10 November 1928.
40 Ibid., 22 May 1929.

enough funds were available to start building the reading room, and excavation work began on 18 July 1935. Sir Thomas Deane had died in 1933 and the work of seeing the project through the building stage was taken on by Richard Caulfeild Orpen (1863-1938). The reading room was finished in 1937 and on 2 July of that year it was opened by the president of the Executive Council, Eamon de Valera. The *Irish Times* reported that the building cost £25,000 and had been fitted with 1,500 feet of steel shelving.[41] The reading room was opened to readers on 26 July after the books had been transferred from the old to the new reading room. The reading room had space for 160 readers (not 204 as previously estimated). Early in 1939 the space occupied by the old reading room was fitted with steel shelving at a cost of £2,243.

During the Second World War the college authorities were particularly anxious about the safety of the books and the library buildings. In July 1940 they placed the books of Kells and Durrow, and other important manuscripts, in a strong room and special cellar (to the north of the west pavilion and now used as a plant room) which had been built a year earlier.[42] In August 1940 the board decided to leave all the inner doors of the library unlocked to allow free movement through the building in case of fire.[43] The authorities' fears were well-founded as several important libraries in England had been completely destroyed or badly damaged by bombing during the war.[44]

Eamon de Valera was invited back to the college in 1957 to open the new manuscript room now housed in the Magnetic Observatory which had been adapted for this new use. The former manuscript room, which had moved to the ground floor of the west pavilion, was shortly after divided into two rooms and put into use as a delivery room and the deputy librarian's office.[45] This room was originally intended as a lecture room and had been used for this purpose until 1820.[46] The Magnetic Observatory was no longer required for its original purpose and the idea of using it as a periodical reading room and a staff reading room had been approved of by the library committee in November 1949.[47] It would have provided space for about thirty readers. The plan to convert it to a reading room was postponed and finally abandoned in favour of converting it to a manuscript room with space for read-

---

41 *Irish Times* (3 July 1937).
42 Library Minute Book, 6 July 1940, MUN/LIB/2/7.
43 Library Minute Book, 30 August 1940, MUN/LIB/2/7.
44 For example Birmingham Natural History Library was completely destroyed. The British Library and the University of London Library lost many thousands of books.
45 Library Minute Book, 3 June & 14 December 1957, MUN/LIB/2/7.
46 Library Committee Minute Book, 16 October 1953, MUN/LIB/3/3.
47 Ibid., 18 November 1949.

ers. The board agreed to this proposal in December 1954, in spite of Dr John Victor Luce's concern for the safety of the manuscripts in their new location.

On 21 November 1952 the first mention of a library extension as a solution to the need for more accommodation is recorded in the library committee minute book. At the meeting the librarian told the committee that in the previous year the library had received 12,000 new books (not counting periodicals and pamphlets) and that the existing shelving would be full in seven or eight years. He said that the overflow from the library was stored in six different parts of the college. This meeting discussed three possible solutions to the problem. 1) An extension to the library at right angles to the main building between Fellows' Garden and College Park. One floor could be used as lecture rooms and the other for the library. 2) Bookstores which would be capable of expansion in the Parade Ground (behind Westland Row). 3) A bookstore outside the college to be shared with the National Library. The members of the committee agreed that an extension to the library would be the best solution, and the board approved. Once it had been decided that an extension was needed the committee, in many subsequent meetings, discussed the problem of funding the building. Four possible sources of funds were identified: College graduates, large American foundations, the State, and the public. A lot of thought and care went into how these sources should be approached. Throughout the 1950s the provost and the library committee worked hard to obtain the funds needed. A film was made about the library and the public was encouraged to visit the library and make donations. The first contribution was made by Lord Iveagh and his daughters who gave £45,000.[48] In 1957 the appeal to graduates was made (11,000 copies of the appeal were printed).[49] The Provost, Albert Joseph McConnell, travelled to the United States to meet the heads of large American Corporations, and he entertained potential donors in the college; much of his efforts proved to be disappointing and frustrating. Dr McConnell had been to see officers of the Rockefeller Foundation in New York in December 1954. He had been well-received and was about to post a letter to John D. Rockefeller appealing for funds when he learnt that he had just given $20,000,000 (£7,142,000) for Anglican theological education in the United States.[50] The inference drawn from this by the provost and the board was that the Rockefeller Foundation was not interested in helping the library, a judgement which previous and subsequent correspondence proved to be sound. In the midst of all the frustration R.B.D. French must have helped to keep spirits up. Dr French was

48 Luce, work cited note 25, p. 162.
49 Librarian to Messrs Hely's Ltd, 28 June 1957, MUN/PH/BOX/145/15.
50 G.F. Mitchell to A.J. McConnell, 15 January 1955, MUN/PH/BOX/145/162.

a lecturer in English, editor of *Trinity*, and a noted composer of witty sketches for the Dublin University Players. He drafted most of the appeal-fund letters (including a very funny spoof one intended for an American graduate), wrote the script for the film *Building for books*, directed by Vincent Corcoran, and he wrote the booklet for the appeal, which was printed by the Three Candles Press and bound in hardback.[51]

While the work of securing funds for the library extension proceeded, and the brief for an international architectural competition was been written, another idea was earnestly pursued for a short time. This was a proposal to combine the resources of the National Library with the library of Trinity College. This proposal came out of discussions between the provost, and the director of the National Library, Dr Richard Hayes. The outline of the proposal was that the Government was to rent the area between the Fellows' Garden and the College Park and to build on this site a block to contain the National Library and the extension to Trinity library. The two libraries would be separated by a party wall and their contents would be distinct. It was envisaged that when the libraries became full, Trinity would not be expected to provide an additional site, but instead an external book store would be built. Dr Hayes met the Taoiseach, Seán Lemass, on 25 February 1959 to explain the proposals and a few days later he sent him a memorandum giving details.[52] The idea seems to have remained dormant for a year before being given active consideration again. Dr McConnell may have been a little sceptical of the proposal's chances of becoming a reality and he did not want to hold up the architectural competition. However, if the Government could say 'maybe' he intended getting the assessors to meet again to consider the new circumstance. Lemass asked the secretaries of his department and of the Department of Education to consider the proposal. After taking their advice the Government decided the idea had much merit, but was unwilling to proceed without first consulting the Catholic hierarchy. Lemass, therefore, sent a copy of Dr Hayes's memorandum (with some word changes) to the archbishop of Dublin, Dr Charles McQuaid, asking him for '… the benefit of Your Grace's advice.'[53] Just over a month after sending the letter the Taoiseach was requested at a day's notice to wait on the archbishop at his palace where he was advised not to proceed with the proposal. Lemass took the advice and that was more or less the end of this idea, but it did not stop Trinity College and the National Library co-operating. Lemass met Dr McConnell on 10 May 1960 to inform him of the Catholic hierarchy's advice

51 Robert Butler Digby French, *The library of TCD*, Dublin 1954.
52 National Archives, Dublin, 'Proposed Heads of Agreement between the Government of Ireland and Trinity College, Dublin', [February 1959], S13795 B/61.
53 National Archives, Dublin, Seán Lemass to Charles McQuaid, 31 March 1960, S13795 B/61.

and the Government's decision. The decision must have cleared the air and allowed Lemass to consider less controversial ways to help the college. At the meeting Lemass was told that the college had raised £200,000 for the extension and that another £250,000 was needed. Lemass said he would discuss with the Minister for Finance the possibilities of a state grant for the scheme.[54] A grant was sanctioned in October 1961. In October 1963 the Government further undertook to meet half the originally estimated cost of £640,000 and to meet interest and sinking fund charges in excess of that amount on the understanding that the total cost would not exceed £800,000.[55] In return for the grant the college was to make its library more accessible to the public and to agree to co-ordinate its acquisition programme with the National Library.[56] The Government's decision to make the grant drew criticism from Dr Michael Tierney, president of University College Dublin. He told a meeting of the Social Study Congress, organized by the Dublin Institute of Catholic Sociology, that the large grants given to a Protestant university which pretended to be suitable for Catholics could not be justified. He accused the Government of being under the influence of the Wolfe Tone cult in giving such large subsidies. The papal nuncio, Dr Sensi, and Dr McQuaid were in the audience.[57]

The brief for the architectural competition was published in 1960.[58] In drawing up the brief some of the committee wanted to play safe and ask for a neo-Georgian pastiche but it was finally agreed that the new building was to represent the twentieth century as characteristically as the Old Library represents the eighteenth century.[59] The brief gave details of the functions that were to be catered for, the staff that would be employed and suggested the accommodation required. The brief included mandatory conditions which were that: the extension to be at right angles to the old building in the position first decided in 1954; the main pedestrian access to be from New Square; the east pavilion to be the main access for the Old Library; the old and new libraries to be connected with a covered passage; no provision to be made for a car park; the cost limit to be £390,000 (although it was known that the cost would be much more – in fact the final figure was over £600,000 – this low sum was inserted to control the cost of the designs). The new library was to have storage for at least 1,200,000 bound volumes, which at the current rate of intake of 20,000 a year would cater for 60 years growth. The closing date

54 National Archives, Dublin, memorandum, 10 May 1960, S13795 B/61.
55 Ibid., 9 October 1963, S13962C/63.
56 Luce, work cited note 25, p. 166.
57 *Irish Times* (29 June 1964).
58 University of Dublin, *International competition for a new library building*, Dublin 1960.
59 Ibid., p.16 and Luce, work cited note 25, p. 164. Dr Luce was registrar for the competition and he gives a detailed account of how it was run, pp 162-7.

for entries was 21 March 1961. The board appointed the earl of Rosse (vice-chancellor of University of Dublin), Franco Albini (architect), Sir Hugh Casson (architect), Raymond McGrath (principal architect to the Office of Public Works), and K. De Witt Metcalf (American library consultant) to judge the competition. J.V. Luce was appointed competition registrar. Metcalf was unable to attend during the judging and was substituted by R.T. Esterquest (librarian of the schools of medicine and public health at Harvard University). The competition attracted 218 entries from 29 countries. There were 18 entries from Ireland. The entries fell broadly into three categories: the long rectangle, the cube, and multi-storey. Granite and concrete were the materials favoured by most of the competitors. The jury awarded first prize to Paul G. Koralek from Great Britain.[60] Professor Albini was not entirely satisfied with Koralek's scheme and, although he did not oppose the award, he did not vote. He thought the building should be moved south to keep the continuity along the Broadwalk between the College Park and the Fellows' Garden. Furthermore he did not think that the architecture harmonized with its surroundings. He thought the solution could, however, be 'unreservedly contemporary whilst at the same time, without making concessions to a "period" taste, it could have attempted that dovetailing with tradition which present-day architectural thought regards as one of its most immediate problems'.[61] Albini felt that Koralek could revise his scheme taking these observations into account.

The new library was built by G. & T. Crampton Ltd. over the years 1963 to 1967 at a cost of £609,153.[62] The work was interrupted first by a national building strike and then by a strike of building merchants. Eamon de Valera, who had opened the reading room in 1937 and the manuscript room in 1957, returned as president of Ireland to open the new library on 12 July 1967.[63] The library is now named after George Berkeley (1685-1753), philosopher and Trinity fellow, who as a young man may have played a part in conceiving the idea for a new library in the early eighteenth century. The main hall is named after Lord Iveagh who generously opened the appeal fund. Most contemporary architectural critics judged the building an important contribution to modern architecture, a judgement which has proved to be good.

60 University of Dublin, *International competition for a new library building: decisions and report of the jury of award*, Dublin June 1961, pp 5-6.
61 Ibid., p. 14.
62 Patrick Delaney, 'Trinity College Library', *Architectural Design*, v. 37 (Oct. 1967) p. 468.
63 De Valera was well disposed towards Trinity College and it was his Government who decided in 1947 that it should receive an annual grant of £35,000 (James Lydon, 'The silent sister: Trinity College and Catholic Ireland', in C.H. Holland ed., *Trinity College Dublin and the idea of a university*, Dublin 1991, p. 42.)

When, in 1801, the library became entitled to a copy of every book published in the British Isles, the flow of books into the library inevitably led to an insatiable demand for shelf space. The increase in student numbers from under 600 in the late eighteenth century[64] to over 10,000 today has put ever-more demands for library services and reading space. The college authorities have had to cope with these demands and provide solutions where solutions must have sometimes seemed impossible. The intelligent management by the board and the wise choice of architects have ensured that Burgh's masterpiece has not been damaged by alterations. It might have been better if some of the alterations had not been done; for example, the enclosing of the Colonnades, and the stairs in the middle of the Long Room which interrupts the sense of space. On the other hand Deane and Woodward's barrel vaulted ceiling in the Long Room was a truly inspirational solution to the problem of the decaying roof, and the need for more shelf space. There have been some near misses too: a proposal (probably about 1930) to build a single-storey addition all the way along the south of the Old Library would have utterly spoilt the building.[65] From the 1860s, when the Old Library was finally detached from other buildings in Library Square, the view that it should stand alone has prevailed, despite a proposal by McCurdy and Mitchell for a reading room linked to the library and the examination hall by an arcaded passageway,[66] and a proposal by Thomas N. Deane to link the library and the museum with an arcaded bridge.[67] Links there must be, however, but they are below ground connecting the Old Library to the 1937 Reading Room and the Berkeley Library.

Paul Koralek's firm was also chosen to adapt the east pavilion to cater for both tourists and students. The primary aim of the remodelling was to provide a library shop. At the same time there were worries about the weight of visitors on the west staircase[68] – such a one had recently collapsed in Slane Castle – and so it was decided to construct a concrete staircase in the east pavilion. Half the Fagel library had to be displaced to make room for this new stairs. A special Department of Early Printed Books was also constructed in the upper floors of the pavilion.

The desire to cater for increasing numbers of visitors to the library has been realized in recent years by adapting over half the area of the Colonnades for use as a shop and exhibition space. Although this work may please many

64 Eda Sagarra, 'From the pistol to the petticoat? The changing student body 1592-1992', in Holland, work cited note 61, p. 112.
65 Drawing, MUN/LIB/MC/47.
66 Drawings, MUN/LIB/MC/92, 92A & 92B.
67 Edward McParland, 'The College buildings', in Holland, work cited note 61, p. 174.
68 In 1906 the west stairs was pronounced safe after it was tested by placing 20 men on the half landing; Library Minute Book, 13 January 1906, MUN/LIB/2/7.

tourists the sad outcome was that thousands of books had to be removed to the book repository in Santry. In the space that was left for books as much storage as possible was provided by building a mezzanine floor and using mobile book stacks. This work was designed by Arthur Gibney and Partners.

The need to provide more space for an increasing number of books and readers is as pressing now as it ever was and building work has started on a new library on the campus to cost about £16 million. The new building is designed by McCullough Mulvin and Keane Murphy Duff.

A Guide to the Manuscript Sources in TCD for the History of the Library

JANE MAXWELL

The manuscripts department in the library of Trinity College Dublin is renowned for its diverse collection of holdings on subjects including the Irish language, Egyptian books of the dead, continental travel, Latin, the middle ages, ancient rebellions and modern Irish literature. But it is also home to a large collection of material specifically pertaining to, and usually produced by, the college itself. These materials are described as muniments, a word which implies documents which defend or secure the rights and privileges of the institution which produces them. However in Trinity College the word muniment is used in a wider sense meaning simply the records of the university. The college muniments were transferred from the muniment room in the provost's house to the care of the library in the early 1970s where they were catalogued by Margaret C. Griffith. The library muniments, mainly transferred from other parts of the library, are accessible to the researcher, as are the other muniments, except when they are less than 30 years old, if they are uncatalogued or if they are deemed to be sensitive. Thirty-two volumes of catalogues of the college muniments are available in the manuscripts department and copies of some of these are in the National Register of Archives in London. The researcher should not be misled by the apparently homogenous layout of several of the muniments catalogues, and must remember that a series title does not always reflect the variety of material therein, particularly in the earlier volumes of a series. *Caveat lector.*

There is also non-muniment or manuscript material that relates to the library and this is usually subject-indexed in such a way as to be easily accessed by the researcher. Here will found MSS 2770-4 (all MS references are to TCD Library), the papers of the Vice-Chancellor Archbishop Lord John George Beresford (1773-1862) concerning Irish university affairs, or MS 2640, the account book of Roger Parker, a sixteenth-century steward or butler, which has at least two references to the library. There are also items like MS 3681, an 'alphabetical book of payments made for the College 1904-10', which records the college payment for railings to protect the library monuments from bicycles and also for wiring to power the book dusting machine.

Approaching a study of the history of the library through the librarians'
papers will yield little. For many years the office of librarian was tacked on
to the responsibilities of other academic offices. John Barrett, who first became
librarian in 1791, was professor of oriental languages, of Greek and of Hebrew
as well as being vice-provost and registrar. He left his account of the early
history of the college, MS 3510, with no reference to the library at all. There
is some library interest to be found among his other papers, MSS 2368-78,
especially MS 2374 where booklists of 1681-1811 have been placed possibly
because Barrett was using them. As librarian Barrett made the first serious
attempt to put the pre-nineteenth-century muniments in order. The correspondence (MS 2214) of Dr James Henthorn Todd, who was librarian from
1852-1869, having first served as an unpaid assistant, contains disappointingly
few references to the library. He held the chair of Hebrew while he was librarian, as well as being senior lecturer, bursar and registrar, and he was a noted
Irish scholar. It was during his tenure that the library began to address the
more complex cataloguing needed to deal with the influx of books following
the Copyright Act in 1801. Librarians' papers or assistant librarians' papers,
not necessarily pertaining to the library, include those of A. de Burgh, T.K.
Abbott, H.W. Parke, and J.G. Smyly.

Provosts' papers provide a little more colour, although in the case of John
Henry Bernard, provost from 1919 to 1927, the library did not loom large
among his concerns. His papers are MSS 2381-93. Humphrey Lloyd, who
was provost from 1867 to 1881, compiled records (MSS 1937a, 3487) which
refer briefly to the manuscripts, catalogues and library expenses. Vice-provost
Thomas Prior's board diaries from 1817 to 1838, MSS 3367-9, contain some
personal records as well as several references to the library, in his board memoranda, which do not appear in the board minute books, MUN/V/5. Other
officers who kept personal board notebooks include provosts Elrington, Traill,
and Mahaffy, vice-provosts Carson and Goligher, and librarian Todd.

LIBRARY MUNIMENTS (TCD/MUN/LIB):
A RÉSUMÉ OF THE CATALOGUES

MUN/LIB/1/1-50: *catalogues, book lists, accession registers:* this series relists the
earliest library catalogues already recorded in Thomas K. Abbott's *Catalogue
of the manuscripts in the library of Trinity College Dublin*, Dublin and London
1900, and its unpublished continuation. A study of the early catalogues of the
library is best approached after consultation of the introduction by former
keeper of manuscripts, William O'Sullivan, to Marvin L. Colker's *Trinity
College Library descriptive catalogue of the mediaeval and renaissance Latin manuscripts*, Aldershot 1991. It is in this series that the reader will search for evi-

dence of seventeenth-century Archbishop James Ussher's ownership of books (see also MUN/LIB/6/10; MS 790).

MUN/LIB/1 also has some details on other collections which were donated to or purchased by Trinity College: Sir Jerome Alexander's library (see also MUN/LIB/10/2), the Bath library (see also MUN/LIB/10/1, 2), the Claudius Gilbert library, the Palliser, Willoughby (see also MUN/LIB/6/9) and Lecky libraries. Here also is material concerning the Fagel library which is one of the library's many treasures (see also MUN/LIB/11, 12, 15). This was the library of the pensionary or chief minister of Holland, Hendrik Fagel, which he sold under financial pressure in 1802. Accounts of the arrival and contents of these various libraries can be found in the published histories of the college.

MUN/LIB/1/27 (MS 1707), catalogue of pamphlets, *c.*1830.

MUN/LIB/1/27a (MS 2932), pamphlets from Bishop Stearne's library which were deposited in the college, 1741.

MUN/LIB/1/27b, theological pamphlets, *c.*1840-1895.

MUN/LIB/1/32-35b, list of presentations, 1837-1968.

MUN/LIB/1/36, catalogue of scientific books, 1849.

MUN/LIB/1/37, notes for a catalogue of incunables, *c.*1870.

MUN/LIB/1/43, catalogue of copyright books, 1879-?1887.

MUN/LIB/1/51-8, covers manuscripts catalogues, including Samuel Foley's seventeenth-century manuscripts catalogue and an annotated version of a catalogue printed in 1697 by Oxford professor Edward Bernard; the catalogues of John Lyon (1702-90, canon of St Patrick's Cathedral), Dr John Madden, Bp John Stearne and the historian Henry J. Monck Mason (1775-1859). Those by Lyon and Monck Mason are our main historic catalogues.

MUN/LIB/1/59-67, 67a-e, 68, 68a-e are catalogues and book lists of manuscripts including John O'Donovan's and Theophilus O'Flanagan's Irish catalogues, and annotated versions of published catalogues of specific collections; for example librarian Josiah G. Smyly's work on the Greek manuscripts and James Hardiman's work on maps. MUN/LIB/1/68a is a catalogue of papyri which were delivered to Trinity College in August 1840. The hieroglyphic papyri, along with some cuneiform tablets, are the most ancient material in the library. This catalogue gives a brief detail of each item and its measurements. It mentions two rolls belonging to the Royal Irish Academy.

MUN/LIB/1/68aa, 68ab, notes by Sir T.W. Haig on our oriental manuscripts which even today remain inadequately catalogued.

MUN/LIB/1/69, 69a, 70-93, 94, catalogues and book lists of printed books which include legal deposit books and periodicals accession registers. MUN/LIB/1/70-77 are registers of legal deposit books.

MUN/LIB/2: *library minute books:* these are not as cohesive a series as the title implies. They were originally called 'journal books' (see MUN/LIB/2/6 p. 5

and MUN/LIB/2/2 fol. 18v), and are very detailed in the description of the upkeep and running of the library and on the accessioning of books.

MUN/LIB/2/1 (1785-1816) is almost entirely about books; purchasing, binding, cataloguing and shelving. There are bookbinders' receipts at the back. It begins with receipts of money for the purchase of books in 1774 and 1807. It continues in 1785 with 'Memo of books rec'd for the library' giving the date, title and source of the books, and includes manuscripts. Other details recorded include the completion of the manuscripts catalogue and details of books sent to binders for which the classing number or shelf locations are sometimes given. This volume also includes stationery requirements. Edward Barwick, who was employed as a cataloguer (see MS 2374/39), made entries in this book. He listed the contents of the parcels of books as they came in from publishers. The tedium this involved was relieved somewhat by Barwick's expressing his opinion of the material he was handling: 'Wed Aug 18 1813 Arrived 2 large parcels of books (alias packs of Trash) from Stationers Hall'. This was not the only way he diverted himself at work (see MUN/LIB/2/6).

MUN/LIB/2/2 (1817-27) is also almost entirely concerned with books although it does mention a few small details such as the removal of seats from the Fagel library and refers to the annual board visitations in October. There are some letters from publishers between the pages.

MUN/LIB/2/3 (1834-42) includes a very detailed account of the arrest of one Harmon, a book thief, in circumstances that to modern sensibilities look very like entrapment. This volume contains the assistant librarian's reports on the numbers of books and manuscripts in the library. Here also begins the reporting of details of the day-to-day maintenance of the library such as employing cleaners and the duties of the porters.

MUN/LIB/2/4 (1843-87) is much more detailed. It is a record of the annual visit to the library by the board of the college, subsequent board resolutions and other matters arising from these visits. The record then changes to become a statement of the counting of the number of books in the library at the beginning of each academic year.

MUN/LIB/2/5 (1887-1902) begins like a personal work diary of the Revd. Thomas Kingsmill Abbott, librarian (and professor of Hebrew and of Biblical Greek from 1887-1913), and there are many letters to Abbott stuck into it. The volume is called 'Library Notes' and as such belongs properly with MUN/LIB/4/3 below. It is roughly indexed.

MUN/LIB/2/6 is a small collection of loose papers, bound arbitrarily into a volume, recording books lent, lost and stolen *c.*1820, and there is also a letter from librarian John Barrett which accompanied the annual accounting in 1817. This volume also records the books stolen by Barwick, the superintendent of the new catalogue, who resigned 1816. There is also a list of books recommended for purchase and an inexact list of the Irish manuscripts received from Sir John Sebright. Sebright's grandfather bought Edward Lhuyd's collection of Irish manuscripts which Sir John inherited. Edmund Burke persuaded Sir John to present it to Trinity College in 1786 (see also MUN/LIB/10/1).

MUN/LIB/2/7 (1895-1958) is the first of this series which actually bears the title 'Library minutes' and it is a more formal record. This is a remarkably detailed record of the care, maintenance and procedures of the library. It goes so far as to name the curate to whom one of the library staff was to be married as well as the time and location of the ceremony.

MUN/LIB/3: *library committee minute books, 1845-84, 1943-60*: there is less variation in style and content in this series than in the previous one. The minutes give an account of the progress of the Printed Catalogue but very little is recorded about the day-to-day operations of the library. The volume containing the minutes from 1885 to 1942 is missing. There are no details of the books which were being purchased; they are referred to as being listed elsewhere in an order book. MUN/LIB/3/2 contains regular reports by Henry Dix Hutton on the progress of the Printed Catalogue. The proceedings of the library committee were reported in the press in the days before television (see MS 2862 p. 5).

MUN/LIB/4: *diaries and memo books of librarians and staff*: MUN/LIB/4/1 is the notebook of a porter, William Benson, covering 1799-1825, and as such is one of the few records the college holds for this level of employee. It is very much in the nature of a private commonplace book; apart from a list of readers, it notes when and why the library was closed, the whereabouts of particular books, weather reports and information concerning the curing of toothaches and the killing of flies.

MUN/LIB/4/2 (*c.*1860) includes rules for the compilation of the Printed Catalogue with 'extracts from the minutes of the evidence before the British Museum's commissioners' illustrating what confusion arises from poor cataloguing practices.

MUN/LIB/4/3 (1867-96) is mostly concerned with staffing arrangements. This volume is entitled 'Library Notes' but does not appear to have been kept as a daily record as were MUN/LIB/2/7 or MUN/LIB/4/8. Rather it appears to be a chronological list of details on staffing issues extracted from another source. The final entry, an added single item from 1928, records that the last duty of one Davidson, hours before he died at the age of 78 years, was to put the Book of Kells on display in the morning.

MUN/LIB/4/4 is a notebook, belonging to library employee S.E. Brambell, which contains a short list of books with their shelf-marks. This is followed by notes from reading on the history of the early christian manuscripts in the library and on the history of the library itself and a record of the number of books replaced by newer editions in the late 1890s.

MUN/LIB/4/5 (*c.*1880-9) contains the unknown owner's bibliography on the Book of Kells and a bibliography on the history of the library.

MUN/LIB/4/6-7 (1889-1917) lists books and shelf-marks.

MUN/LIB/4/8 begins in 1889 with a note of Alfred de Burgh's joining the library. From 1890 to 1894 it restricts itself to noting when staff were absent or when the library was 'counted', but in 1895 there is a sudden burst of eloquence beginning with the 'Biggest snowstorm for over 30 years'. It continues with the most minute details, up to 1917, of the daily operations of the library from posting manuscripts to England for use there, to the first time the library is closed for St Patrick's Day (1903); from the state of the librarian's health to the November day which was so dark that the librarians had to sit by the windows to work. The volume appears to have been entered up in a number of hands, chiefly that of Alfred de Burgh. He seems also to have been responsible for MUN/LIB/2/7 which records more or less the same information.

MUN/LIB/4/9-19 are the diaries of Alfred de Burgh and Joseph Hanna. De Burgh joined the library staff in 1889 and served as senior assistant librarian from 1896 to 1929; Hanna continued from 1930 to 1937. The diaries record some details of library maintenance, board decisions, staffing, loans, deaths, weather, sale of waste paper, the first use of a mowing machine in 1925. These records go up to 1937 but the volumes are little used.

MUN/LIB/4/21 is the taped reminiscences, in 1967, of Dr Hazel M. Hornsby who joined the library as library assistant in 1934 and was chief cataloguer from 1959 to 1967. TCD TAPES 141-6 are other taped recollections of the library.

MUN/LIB/5, 5a-5e *(1854-1958) binding and other records*: MUN/LIB/5/1-13 (1854-1916) contain book-binding accounts with, among others, M.A. Bigger, Galwey & Co. and A. Thom.

MUN/LIB/5a (1854-1957) is another series of binding records which goes into considerable detail about the books being sent for binding.

MUN/LIB/5b-c (1855-1934) are booksellers' invoices/receipts.

MUN/LIB/5d (1870-1928) are invoices for English periodicals.

MUN/LIB/5e/1*, 1-24 (1839-1958) are library account books including accounts with various binders and booksellers. There is another binding account book at MUN/LIB/8/12 (1850-7). Also in MUN/LIB/5e are the librarian's audited expenditure accounts, covering such things as purchases, bindings, subscriptions, overtime and salaries (1854-1958). There are further informal cash account books in this series also including salary books, petty cash books (see also MUN/LIB/6/24) and incidentals accounts. MUN/LIB/5e/18-19 (1932-51) are analysis books which summarize accounts with various suppliers of books and periodicals, and give a breakdown of expenditure on library materials including, in 1962, '£2 for cigarettes etc'. MUN/LIB/5e/22-4 (1929-51) refer to books bought in France, England and America.

MUN/LIB/6, 6a, 6b: *records of book use*: this series contains admissions signature books, 1737-1963, registers of readers 1821-68, loans 1684-1869 (incomplete), staff borrowings and, at MUN/LIB/6/17a, light reading loan book for 1857-69, which shows the Revd Dr T.K. Abbott (librarian 1887-1913), already a graduate and fellow, borrowing the distinctly unacademic sounding *Rose, Blanche and Violet* in 1859.

MUN/LIB/7 *(1861-present)*: *records of manuscript use.*

MUN/LIB/8: *records of the Lending Library*: this series includes catalogues of books, 1830-94, and borrowers' books, 1762-1929. There is also an account of the sales of the printed catalogue of this library and a binding account book (1850-7). MUN/LIB/8/26 is an account book which begins with a table revealing the number of persons admitted to the library each year, the number of volumes borrowed and the number of people reported for not returning books on time. It continues with a breakdown of money spent on the lending library and ends in 1853 on an indignant note, rich with underlinings, detailing a change in the methods for selecting books to be purchased. The fellows, professors and students were canvassed for their opinion on this matter and, from the resulting list of suggested books, 'not one single book' could be sanctioned by the librarian. As a result only £8 was spent on the lending library that year.

MUN/LIB/9, *miscellaneous* (a title which often implies difficulty in recognizing an item as belonging to a series). It includes a volume of statutes.

MUN/LIB/9/1 is a staff roll, 1861-6; there are also records of foreign publications, 1843-1950 (incomplete), periodicals and pamphlets; there is a volume of memoranda on various library issues, 1890-1925, library visitors books (see also MUN/LIB/29) and a book of newspaper cuttings, 1899-1927.

MUN/LIB/9/15 is a collection of letters extracted, as being interesting autographs, from the library correspondence, 1899-1933; MUN/LIB/9/18 is correspondence, from 1869 to 1882, which reveals the amount of work which had to be undertaken by the assistant librarian, Thomas French, to facilitate the mostly overseas researchers who wished to glean information from the library manuscripts. This was remote access nineteenth-century style.

MUN/LIB/10, *miscellaneous material relating to the library* up to 1799 including receipted bills extracted from MUN/MC/4 (bursars' vouchers series), accounts, correspondence and memoranda.

The catalogue of MUN/LIB/10/1 relists all early book lists which had already appeared in manuscripts catalogues before the MUN/LIB prefix but which rightfully belong in this series. MS 1945 is a collection of early book lists, probably mainly seventeenth century, but MS 1945/6 is in the hand of eighteenth-century professor of divinity, vice-provost and book collector Claudius Gilbert, and MS 1945/13a is a list of the Irish manuscripts in the Sebright library in 1786 in the hand of Theophilus O'Flanagan.

MS 2160a includes seventeenth-century book lists and accounts for books purchased from named sellers. The booksellers' receipts give a good picture of the college's purchasing activities. MS 2160a/10 is partly in Ussher's hand and MS 2160a/11,13,16 and 17 are partly in the hand of Luke Challoner, one of the charter fellows and vice-chancellor from 1612 to 1613.

MS 2374 is a collection of John Barrett's papers which contains early book lists and which has been already mentioned earlier in this essay. It also includes a list of pamphlets and a list of the German books of J.D. Martini, professor of German, 1789-97.

MUN/LIB/10/2 *(1610-1800)* has most of the loose papers on library finances from the seventeenth century; details of books loaned, lost and stolen in the 1600s; the appointment of John FitzGerald as keeper of the library in 1619; records of the binding of some of Ussher's books and others; material regarding the Bath library, the Alexander library; books sent to Dunsink Observatory in 1782; receipts for book purchases, stationery, cataloguing, subscriptions, staff and library maintenance costs in the eighteenth century.

MUN/LIB/11 *(1800-99) library accounts*: accounts with binders and booksellers, ironmongers, carpenters, shippers, furniture makers; the costs associated with the Fagel library (binding, cataloguing, staffing); maintenance accounts, cataloguing, porters' salaries, book carriage; book colouring (turning a black and white picture into a coloured one in the days before colour printing); cataloguing the Irish manuscripts (which includes receipts for payments to the Irish scholar Professor Eugene O'Curry of Newman's University); copyright agent fees; the Lending Library; subscriptions; staffing; installation of a 'speaking telegraph'; coal allowances for the reading room; carpeting the library and a seal for gilding books.

MUN/LIB/12 *(1802-1909) miscellaneous papers*: this includes the diary of Thomas Elrington, provost 1811-20, concerning the transport of the Fagel library from London (there is a copy of the sale catalogue of the Fagel library at MS 1701); library regulations 1817 and 1853; a draft for revised statutes concerning the library, 1803; some material relating to legal deposit; the pay and duties of staff; finance; maintenance; periodicals; pamphlets; the Royal Geological Society of Ireland, 1895-1908 (see also MSS 2784-5); the numbers of books in the library and the number of missing books. MUN/LIB/12/56 is an undated address by the librarian to the Library Association members, and MUN/LIB/12/59 are notes from reading by Provost Alton on the history of TCD library. There is some overlap between the kinds of material in this series and the previous one.

MUN/LIB/13 *(1800-99) correspondence*: (See also MUN/LIB/9/15,18; MUN/LIB/15,16; MUN/LIB/28; MUN/LIB/35; MS 1931.)

MUN/LIB/14 *(1900-51) invoices and receipts*: from booksellers, and some subscriptions to journals.

MUN/LIB/15 *(1878-present) miscellaneous loose papers*: this series contains material on a very wide range of subjects and it is being continuously augmented. Much of it is as yet unavailable for consultation. It covers, among other things, staffing, library fund-raising, cataloguing, committee papers, issues of space, censorship, the Fagel library, numbers of readers, facilities, the Book of Kells and the 1641 depositions (MSS 809-41).

MUN/LIB/16: twentieth-century incoming correspondence arranged alphabetically by correspondent. It is not yet available for consultation.

MUN/LIB/17 *(1848-1954) library reports (incomplete)*: these reports give the numbers of printed books and manuscripts in all the reading rooms, and the number of books bought, donated, catalogued or lost. Every now and then other information is given: a complaint about lack of space by librarian J.H. Todd in 1853, or a note of the reduction of the number of book losses from the Long Room as a result of changing the system of keeping dockets in 1892. For the 1950s there is a 'state of the library' document from the librarian, H.W. Parke.

MUN/LIB/18 *(1855, 1857-9, 1886-1950) counting sheets*: these are large sheets on which is recorded the number of volumes of different library materials in the college. The first four are concerned only with the Long Room but later ones cover the Fagel library, the East Room and the Reading Room.

MUN/LIB/19 *(1835-1946) number books and counting books*: these volumes record the number of books in the Long Room, shelf by shelf. They indicate how many books are on each shelf, where there is shelf space still remaining, and what books have gone missing. Eighteen thirty-nine was a bad year for losses with 126 volumes being stolen, 70 of which were recovered in pawn offices. Some volumes note where the books are too high for the shelf or where specific books needed rebinding.

MUN/LIB/20 *(1839-1965) registers of publications received (alphabetically by author)*: for registers of publications recorded under names of publishers and under legal deposit see MUN/LIB/1/70-8 (1935-68) and MUN/LIB/9/7 (1901-08). MUN/LIB/20/17 is a miscellaneous book containing summaries of the contents of book boxes from the copyright agent in London, 1885-1958.

MUN/LIB/21 *(1849-69) lists of periodical accessions.*

MUN/LIB/22 *(c.1850-1936) claiming material under the copyright acts*: this comprises mostly of letters to and from the copyright agency.

MUN/LIB/23 *(1886-1988) material connected with the admission of readers*: this includes reader admission forms and declarations, and also statistics for the Lecky library, 1973-1988. There is a small pass permitting Maud Gonne to consult books on architecture and embroidery in 1910.

MUN/LIB/24 *(1914-52) printing and binding accounts* (See also MUN/LIB/5.)

MUN/LIB/25 *(late nineteenth, early twentieth century) bank pass books, statements.*

MUN/LIB/26-38, are mostly unsorted, uncatalogued twentieth-century materials which are not available for consultation.

MUN/LIB/26, *Friends of the Library*: minutes, membership, finances, correspondence, *Long Room* editorial papers.

MUN/LIB/27, exhibitions.

MUN/LIB/28, *library shop correspondence.*

MUN/LIB/29, *Long Room visitors books* (See also MUN/LIB/9/12).

MUN/LIB/30, *making of the 1992 Faksimile Verlag Book of Kells facsimile.*

MUN/LIB/31, *staff societies, conferences.*

MUN/LIB/32, *librarians' files on automation and buildings.*

MUN/LIB/33, *research-floor librarian's papers* and material relating to *Long Room*, the journal of the Friends of the Library.

MUN/LIB/34-5, 38, *papers of the keepers of manuscripts.*

MUN/LIB/36, *cataloguing department material.*

As more records are transferred to the library and as new areas of responsibilities are formally created and old ones are discontinued or amalgamated this series of TCD/MUN numbers will increase.

Apart from the specifically library generated muniment material there are other muniment collections which may bear upon the subject of the history of the library.

MUN/V[olume]: the oldest volume still existing among the records of the college is the so-called 'Particular Book' (MUN/V/1/1); this has a list of books and manuscripts in the library in 1601. Other items in the MUN/V series include the board registers or minute books, MUN/V/5 and their indexes, MUN/V/5b. MUN/V/5a is a series of registrar's rough board notebooks. Other board records are MUN/V/6, the companion books, which are scrapbook type collections of documents associated with board business. MUN/V/7 are board letterbooks. MUN/V/57 are the bursars' quarterly accounts in which the first reference to the library was the payment in 1722 of Sir Jerome Alexander's annuity. These are quite detailed records of college-wide payments and include the librarians' salary. MUN/V/63 are college salary books. The MUN/V series also contains the Book of Benefactions, MUN/V/1/2.

MUN/MC is a collection of maps, plans and photographs of the college and includes plans and drawings of the library. There is an undated drawing of the Old Library staircase by Richard Cassell, a design by Thomas Drew for enclosing the colonnades in 1889, plans for the 1937 Reading Room and War Memorial by Sir Thomas Deane, 1913-1920. There are very detailed plans for the Berkeley Library which are as yet unavailable for consultation, as well as unexecuted plans for extensions in 1961, and underground storage in 1928. The photographs include those taken in 1969 during the reconstruction of the west pavilion of the Old Library.

MUN/P/1, *general and miscellaneous papers*: this series contains very little of interest to the history of the library, although it includes a note of a salary to a seventeenth-century keeper of the library and an eighteenth-century petition from a porter.

MUN/P/2, *college buildings*: this is a very important series for studying the physical history of the library as it includes tradesmen's bills, estimates and correspondence, 1596-1963. The first reference to the library among these records is to plastering being carried out in 1703. It also documents the building of the Old Library, 1712-1732, and the work on the Fagel library in the early 1800s. There is a report on the desirability of enclosing the colonnade in 1889. Also included is an early twentieth-century idea for an underground bookstore (see also MUN/LIB/15; MUN/MC); an undated complaint about the state of the reading room; material concerning the upkeep of the fabric of the buildings; and proposals for use and physical development of the library. The later material relates to the 1937 Reading Room and to the Berkeley Library.

MUN/P/3 *(1880s) bursars' incoming correspondence*: there is one item of relevance here (MUN/P/3/618) – a letter from Henry Dix Hutton about the catalogue, 1882.

MUN/P/4 *(pre-1685-1917) bursars' vouchers for services and purchases*: this includes references to the moving of books and furniture into the new library in 1732 and 1801 (MUN/P/4/36/17; 78/16); library busts in 1746 (MUN/P/4/50/25); and mentions a fire in the library in 1720 that cost £3 8s. 8d. for 'men wth ye Ingon and buckets, 12 boys who brought water, drinks for the assistors and ye under sexton yt rang ye Church bell' (MUN/P/4/25/18). The vouchers also record dealings with booksellers, binders and stationers, and detail the costs for mounting and cataloguing the Egyptian papyri.

MUN/P/7, *bursar's quarterly accounts*: these are receipts from various sources and records of disbursements to various persons. Included are a few library expenses beginning in 1613 with a quarter's salary for the library keeper and ending in 1744 with a payment for a woman attending the library. This series is continued in the MUN/V/57 series. The bursar's balance book which records the college's audited income and expenditure account for 1872-83 is at MUN/V/75/4.

MUN/P/8, 8a *(1771-1817) bursars' annual abstracts*: various summary accounts including library building accounts. MUN/P/8a is similar but less detailed.

MUN/P/14 *(1798-1838) steward's quarterly house accounts*: includes payments to staff in the library. MS 3683 is the bursar's balance book for 1872-83, an audited college income and expenditure account which includes library expenses.

MUN/P/52 has some material on the architectural competition for the Berkeley Library which is not yet available for consultation.

Apart from the muniment series there are items among the holdings in the manuscripts department which may interest the student of the history of the library. It is neither possible nor necessary to attempt an exhaustive listing here. A survey of the essays in this book will give a reasonable picture of the range of issues covered both by the records held in the library and elsewhere.

The early statutes of the library are to be found in MSS 1938, 1956, 2017. The statutes compiled by Archbishop Laud, were based on those of Provost Bedell, which do not appear in the printed editions of the statutes of the library. MS 4970 is a copy of the Laudian statutes with an index and is followed by the library and chapel statutes.

MS 2682a is the introduction to an index to John O'Donovan's catalogue of the Irish manuscripts made *c.*1870. The index itself is gone, but the introduction provides information on and pictures of Dr J.H. Todd and John O'Donovan. It also contains a brief account of the making of the catalogue by O'Donovan, who began work on the catalogue under the direction of Todd, and Professor Eugene O'Curry of Newman's University. MS 2865 is a catalogue of the Revd J. Johnstone's Icelandic manuscripts subsequently acquired by the library. MS 2932 is a 1903 catalogue of Bishop Stearne's pamphlets which were to be given to the library. MS 2862 is a press-cutting of T.K. Abbott's reply to the statement in the Trinity College Commission's report about the cataloguing of Irish manuscripts. Bishop William Reeves, through whose efforts the Book of Armagh was secured for this country, has left some correspondence at MS 2903, which bears on library, specifically manuscript, issues. MS 2903/48 a biographical sketch of the Revd John Lyon.

For information on the origins of the Lecky library there is MS 1931a, the correspondence between Alfred de Burgh and Catherine E. Lecky concerning the donation of W.E. Lecky's books to the library. Part of MS 10048 are Theodore Moody's files as senior lecturer concerning the day to day running of the Lecky library. These are not yet available for consultation.

Of much more recent interest are MSS 9794, 9795/1, which are materials of R.B.D. French pertaining to the library in the 1950s. French (1904-81) was senior lecturer in English and information officer in Trinity College. Press-cuttings collected by French dating from the late 1950s to the late 1960s cover all the press reporting of the library appeal for funds which preceded the building of the Berkeley Library. The film *Building for Books*, which was made to support this appeal, is TCD VIDEOTAPE 2.

But even the most thorough search through the library records cannot be expected to give a full understanding of the events in the history of the library. In a letter dated 1789 and reproduced in part in Constantia Maxwell's, *A history of Trinity College Dublin 1591-1892* (Dublin 1946, p. 141), the writer, a student in the college, refers to a boy being shot in the library by a gentleman at whom the unfortunate youngster had thrown snowballs. The absence of any record of such an event in the minutes of either the library or the board is an interesting omission which should temper the enthusiasm of whoever might wish to write the definitive history of Trinity College Library.

John Madden's Manuscripts

WILLIAM O'SULLIVAN

Although T.K. Abbott notes in his introduction to the *Catalogue of the man-uscripts of the library of Trinity College Dublin*, Dublin 1900, 'A most impor-tant addition to the Library was made in 1741, by Bishop Stearne's bequest[1] of the MSS formerly belonging to Dr. John Madden', there is nowhere in the index an entry for Madden or any reference to him in the catalogue descriptions. Some of his work is ascribed to other scholars, like MSS 654-6 to Daniel Molyneux, the Ulster king of arms, and Madden's most impor-tant personal collections for Irish monastic history and genealogy go unat-tributed to anyone. The catalogue of his manuscripts in his own hand (MS 653, ff. 68-78v), although headed 'The catalogue of my M.S. 1700' is cred-ited to Stearne, who wrote in just a few extra entries. Of the major contrib-utors to the college collection Madden is the least known and acknowledged, and yet his catalogue was published under his name in Oxford in 1697.[2] Many of his manuscripts are entirely in his own hand and it appears frequently in others, but it was only by close perusal of his genealogical notes that I was at last able to ascribe the mysterious anonymous hand to him.[3]

John Madden's grandfather, Thomas, was the first of the family to come to Ireland. His son John had an estate at Maddenton, County Kildare,[4] but married in 1636[5] Elizabeth Waterhouse, the heiress of Manor Waterhouse, a

---

1 Stearne's manuscripts reached the library in 1741. He died in 1745.

2 *Catalogi ... manuscriptorum Angliae et Hiberniae*, Oxford 1697, vol. 2 part 2, pp 57-60.

3 MS 1217, ff. 244-244v, 246-7; MS 1216, f. 81. All the manuscripts cited below belong to Trinity College Dublin, except where otherwise indicated.

4 Very convenient for the Curragh, it was much used by the duke of Ormonde for 'refresh-ment' in the early 1660s (*HMC, Ormonde MSS*, new series, London 1904, vol. iii, pp 136, 151). Another Maddenton in County Monaghan, where the family lives now, has been renamed Hilton Park.

5 Madden pedigree in *Burke's family records*, London 1976, pp 766-8. This is also the source for other biographical details below where no other source is cited. Incidentally Elizabeth's mother was great-aunt to Theophilus, Baron Newtownbutler (d.1723), whose name appears over his books in gold letters in the Long Room and whose poem book, MS 879, is much valued.

finer property in County Fermanagh. The 1641 rebellion drove the family back to England, and both our John (in 1649) and his elder brother Thomas (in 1646) were born at Enfield, Middlesex. With the peace they were back in Ireland. Their father died in 1661. Thomas went to school in Enniskillen, John in Dublin.[6] Thomas entered TCD in 1663 and went on to study law at the Inner Temple, London. While in England he visited the countess of Bath, the widow of a former fellow of the college and close friend of Archbishop Ussher. He was successful in persuading her that she ought to commemorate the late earl by a donation of £200 for books for the college library.[7] The splendid folios thus acquired are handsomely decorated with the countess's arms, and one of the 'Old' library rooms was known as the Bath Library. Thomas died in 1677.

John Madden describes MS 659 without any reference to his brother's part in it. The notebook begins with a pasted-in engraving of the Madden arms with underneath the legend: 'Thomas Madden of the Inner Temple Esq., descended of the Maddens of Maddenton in Wiltshire, who are now seated at Rousky Castle in the co. of Fermanagh in the kingdom of Ireland.' Thomas had copied into it a number of Latin poems, particularly some of Richard Crashaw's *Epigrammata sacra*, Cambridge 1634. Later John used it to enter his lists of Irish lord chancellors and judges.

John entered the college in 1670 and graduated MB in 1674 and, despite his elder brother's death in 1677 and his consequent inheritance of the family properties, continued with his medical career, becoming MD in 1682.[8] He was elected a fellow of the College of Physicians in 1684 and was to be president in 1694, 1697 and 1700. In 1680 he married Mary Molyneux, the grand-daughter of Daniel, the Ulster king of arms and one of the earliest Irish antiquaries, but perhaps more importantly sister of William and Sir Thomas Molyneux, who were at the centre of the intellectual life of Dublin. William was the founder in 1683 of the Dublin Philosophical Society, established for the advancement of scientific studies. It was the Irish counterpart of the Royal Society, founded some 20 years earlier. Some of the papers read to the Dublin society were published in the *Transactions* of the London society, but many more remain in manuscript. Madden joined the Dublin society in 1684, but no papers he may have read have survived, though he does appear with other doctors as an observer in a medical experiment.[9] The

6   G.D. Burtchaell and T.U. Sadleir, *Alumni Dublinenses*, new edition, Dublin 1935, p. 544.

7   MUN/LIB/10/13-16

8   Work cited note 6, p. 543.

9   K.T. Hoppen, *The common scientist in the seventeenth century: a study of the Dublin Philosophical Society, 1683-1708*, London 1970, pp 44-5; 'The papers of the Dublin Philosophical Society, 1683-1708: introduction and index' to a publication in microfiche, *Analecta Hibernica* vol. 30 (1982) p. 207.

only extant membership list of the society is to be found in one of his note-books.[10]

His manuscripts, however, clearly demonstrate that his tastes lay in anti-quarian studies rather than in the New Learning. His main interests were in genealogy and in continuing the work initiated by Sir James Ware into the history of the religious houses in Ireland in his *De Hibernia et antiquitatibus ejus* ... , London 1654. Until their sale to Lord Clarendon, lord lieutenant in 1686, Ware's manuscripts were still in Dublin in the hands of his son, Robert, and Madden made many copies and notes from them. One of Ware's manu-scripts, a notebook kept in London in the 1650s, he did not return. It is now MS 664. Like Ware he also worked extensively on the Irish public records. However, his herbarium, the earliest Irish one to survive, with the plants iden-tified in his own hand, remains as evidence of his scientific interests. It is likely that at least some of the plants were collected at Manor Waterhouse,[11] because, despite his antiquarian studies and his medical career in Dublin, he had important duties as a considerable landowner in County Fermanagh. His estate there was surveyed in 1688 by George Black and the resulting map incidentally shows the extent of the improvements he had already carried out in the park at Manor Waterhouse: formal gardens near the house and long straight tree-lined avenues with circular openings at the crossings in the French style.[12] The grounds were however to be further developed by his son and heir, the Reverend Samuel Madden, who favoured the new poetic-roman-tic style, into one of the show places of the country.[13] Samuel is better remem-bered as 'Premium Madden' for his successful proposal that the best students at the Term Examinations should be awarded prizes, a scheme he later extended into the Royal Dublin Society, of which he was one of the earliest and most active members.[14] Another son, Thomas, following in his father's footsteps, studied medicine and became the college lecturer in anatomy in 1730, his uncle, Sir Thomas Molyneux, being professor of physic at the time.

When the troubles broke out again with the deposition of James II, John Madden fled to England and was attainted by the Patriot Parliament in 1689. He has left us two alphabetical lists of the protestant refugees in England.[15] His first wife died in 1695 and he then married Frances, daughter of Nicholas

---

10 MS 655, ff. 48v-9.
11 E.C. Nelson, 'A late seventeenth century Irish herbarium ...', *Irish Naturalists Journal* vol. 20 (1981) pp 334-5.
12 MS 1208, no. 82, reproduced in part in E. Malins and the Knight of Glin, *Lost demesnes*, London 1976, p. 44.
13 Ibid., p. 43.
14 J.W. Stubbs, *The history of the University of Dublin*, Dublin 1889, p. 198; H.F. Berry, *A history of the Royal Dublin Society*, London 1915, p. 53.
15 MSS 847, 1449.

Bolton and great grand-daughter of Sir Richard Bolton (d.1648), lord chancellor. She was to inherit the Madden manuscripts. John Madden's will is dated 21 August 1703; he died on October 19 and the will was proved on November 6.[16] The widow sold the manuscripts to John Stearne, dean of St Patrick's. He became bishop of Clogher in 1717, vice-chancellor of the university in 1721, and one of its most considerable benefactors.[17] The sale took place before 22 May 1708 when Stearne noted his loan of some manuscripts to Dive Downes, the bishop of Cork. He still had them on 14 July 1741 when Walter Harris borrowed five, including a volume of the Depositions relating to the 1641 rebellion.[18] In between those dates there are notes in Madden's catalogue of loans to Harris and to Thomas Carte, who cites the manuscripts in his life of Ormonde.[19] Sometime during the summer of 1741 Stearne must have decided on his gift of the manuscripts to the college because John Exshaw's work on the rebinding of the Depositions was finished by November 6 in that year. This was certified by John Lyon, a Dublin antiquary, who had recently been appointed a minor canon of St Patrick's Cathedral and who in that month became assistant in the library with charge of the manuscripts until he had completed his catalogue of them.[20] The college knew that, like the printed books, the manuscripts had to be rendered worthy of their place in the glorious 'New' library. Lyon's work on the Depositions may have generated the notion that in him the college had found the right man and he was very likely a friend of its benefactor, Stearne.

Madden's printed catalogue describes the Depositions as arranged in two volumes: 1645/6 containing the examinations 'for most part of Munster, Ulster and Conaught', and 1646/7 the examinations 'of the province of Leinster, many of which consisting of diverse sheets of paper are narratives of the progress of the rebellion in the several parts of the kingdom of Ireland'.[21] The rebinding took place after Lyon had rearranged the material by counties into 31 volumes. Having thus destroyed the latest archival state

16 F.S. Bourke (1895-1959), FRCPI and president of the Irish Bibliographical Society provided me with a copy of Madden's will and encouraged me to undertake this study. I should like, however belatedly, to dedicate this essay to his memory.

17 *Dictionary of National Biography.*

18 MS 653, ff. 69v, 72, 75.

19 Ibid., ff. 74v-5.

20 W. O'Sullivan, 'The eighteenth century rebinding of the manuscripts', *Long Room* vol. 1 (1970) p. 21; Register of the Board, 1 Dec. 1742, MUN/V/3. While the manuscripts must have been kept in his Dublin house, his library was in Clogher, whither the Board dispatched the librarian, William Clement, on 21 July 1742 (MUN/V/3), to choose the books needed for the college library and on Aug. 24 Thomas Reilly, the carman, presented his bill for taking empty boxes and bringing them back filled with books (MUN/LIB/10/153a).

21 Work cited note 2, p. 58.

of the Depositions,[22] Lyon turned his attention to the Ussher manuscripts which had been moved into the 'New' library on 14 April 1732.[23] Here he operated in an equally high-handed manner breaking up Ussher's notebooks and reassembling the material according to his notions of subject. Of course this was only a small part of his work in reordering the whole college collection of manuscripts by subject in their new cupboards A-E.[24] He ignored the existence of the previously published catalogue of 1697, already in the hands of scholars, and provided no concordance between the old and the new shelf-marks. This continued to plague inquirers for the next 150 years. Finally Abbott, in superseding Lyon's system with a new numbered sequence in 1900, provided a concordance of the numbers in the old published catalogue with his own.

In November 1742, certifying Exshaw's work on the binding, Lyon noted that the college manuscripts were done and only the Alexander and Stearne manuscripts remained to do. These he arranged in cupboards F-G. His work of reordering and overseeing the rebinding came to an end in March 1744.[25] The board paid him £40 for his cataloguing of the manuscripts and the pamphlets in the last quarter of 1747.[26] However, a grateful college was not yet content and in 1751 he was made a doctor of divinity and on 10 May 1755 he received another £40 for completing his work on the charters in the manuscripts room. This forms an integral part of his catalogue of the manuscripts, which is basically a moderately expanded shelf-list.[27]

The Depositions are undoubtedly seen as the most important element of Madden's collection. Among the college manuscripts they come second only to the Book of Kells in Irish popular mythology. They have provided a major historical battleground for Ireland's deeply divided politics since their creation in the '40s and '50s of the seventeenth century. In 1941 the Irish Manuscripts Commission, having undertaken a transcript, shrank from publication, preferring to let sleeping dogs lie. Recently Professor Aidan Clarke has made a most painstakingly close analysis of the several stages in their composition, since these examinations into the losses and atrocities of the rebellion were taken under a sequence of commissions.[28] He seems, however, to have been unaware of Madden's ownership or of the arrangement described in his catalogue, most likely created for Professor Clarke's final stage, when

22 MUN/LIB/10/43.
23 Lyon's account for locks and keys, 11 Sept. 1742, MUN/LIB/10/154.
24 Work cited note 20, p. 27.
25 Ibid., p. 28.
26 MUN/V/57/3.
27 MUN/V/3.
28 A. Clarke, 'The 1641 Depositions' in Peter Fox ed., *Treasures of the Library, Trinity College Dublin*, Dublin 1986, pp 111-22.

the Depositions were used to service the Cromwellian courts' judgments on the atrocities committed by the losing side. A further complication in what is an archival quagmire is a volume of indexes, which contains two roughly alphabetical lists of persons: the first containing references to the individual papers numbering over 400, the second, with references numbering over 4,200.[29]

Stubbs records that the Depositions had earlier belonged to Matthew Barry, clerk of the Irish privy council, and had been 'sold along with his books' to Madden.[30] MS 830, f.124, contains the following title: 'Mr. Matthew Barry's booke of examinations taken by order from the Councell board in the yeares 1641: 42: 43: 44: 45 & 46. Returned to the office 17 November 1654' (that would have been after the court proceedings), and f.125 has the following information: 'Received at the Board at the hands of ... Henry Jones Lord Bishop of Meath and Henry Brereton clerk the 19th day of December 1662, [signed] Ma. Barry'. Matthew came of a rising Dublin merchant family. One of his cousins became Lord Barry of Santry. Matthew is described as having been trained up in the office by Sir Paul Davys, the perfect civil servant.[31] Appointed in 1630, he had continued to serve under Strafford, under the Commonwealth, until finally Ormonde rewarded him with the secretaryship of state in 1661. His son William had, however, already received the reversion of the clerkship in the previous year, so in 1661 he would have been the clerk when Matthew received the reversion of the office. Subsequently in 1672 Sir William, as he had meanwhile become, his brother John, later Sir John, and Matthew were appointed jointly to the clerkship. Sir William would certainly have been out by 1681 when he became chief justice of the king's bench, and Sir John became secretary of state in 1678, so Matthew might then have been in a strong position to take home the Depositions when he felt so inclined. It was fortunate that he did as fire destroyed the council office and all its records in 1711. Apart from a gap under James II, Matthew continued as clerk until his death in 1696. Meanwhile in 1678 he had also become clerk of the pipe exchequer jointly with his son Joseph, passing the office in 1693 to his son Paul, who was succeeded in turn by his son Paul in 1722. When Thomas Carte came to Dublin in pursuit of the Barry papers for his life of the first duke of Ormonde, he contacted the grandson, who in turn directed him to Stearne.[32] He was not in Dublin at the time, so Carte had to

29 MS 841.
30 Stubbs cited note 14, p. 178.
31 Work cited note 5, pp 69-71; R. Lascelles ed., *Liber munerum publicorum Hiberniae*, London 1852, vol. II, p. 83. For the careers of the Davys family consult J.L.J. Hughes ed., *Patentee officers of Ireland, 1173-1826* (Irish Manuscripts Commission), Dublin 1960, and F.E. Ball, *A history of the county Dublin*, Dublin 1906, part 6, pp 29-33.
32 Bodleian Library MS Carte 227, f. 24.

make a second visit in 1733-4 to work on Stearne's 'valuable collection, among which six volumes of Mr Matthew Barry's, Dr Madding's manuscripts'.[33] He used the Depositions, which he described as being 'in two or three large volumes in folio'.[34] Elsewhere he writes of using 'many other papers brought by Mr Barry out of Sir Paul Davys' office'.[35]

Reading that as simply meaning the council office, where Sir William followed his father, may account for another element in the Stearne/Madden manuscripts, but one which is not represented in the catalogues. These are Sir William's papers, partly personal: MSS 646-7, 649, 703/1. Of these, 649, containing copies of the proceedings in the Court of Castle Chamber in the early years of Charles I, according to a note in it, was first borrowed from Sir Theophilus Jones in 1666 and afterwards given by Sir Theophilus as a New Year's gift. The presence of these manuscripts in the collection would seem to be most readily accounted for if they formed part of the sale by Barry to Madden. Sir William had died in 1687. Early in his career he had been a legal adviser to the college and its tenant on lands in Limerick and Tipperary, frequently in arrears. On 21 August 1665 he borrowed Ussher MS BBB 57 from the college, and it finally returned with the Madden/Stearne manuscripts in 1741 and is now MS 845/3.[36] Another Ussher manuscript that returned at the same time, MS 593, is part of a transcript of the Book of Howth, a small part remaining in MS 584, ff. 1-74, which is in the same hand as pp 58-182 of 593. The text is annotated in Ussher's early hand. It no longer follows the order of the original. MS 584 was rebound by Exshaw in 1742, but not apparently MS 593.

The Court of Wards and Liveries, a source of considerable revenue for the crown and an instrument for the advancement of the state church, was put on a firm footing in 1622. Sir Philip Percivall was appointed registrar. News of his death reached Sir George Lane in exile with the king in Bruges in 1657. He produced letters under Charles I's privy seal giving him the reversion and he was accordingly appointed. The operation of the court effectively came to an end with the rebellion in 1641 and it was formally abolished in 1662.[37] Under Strafford a record office for the court was set up in the King's Inns, but only a single volume remained in official custody in the Public Record Office in 1922.[38] Until that office was established in 1867 the older records were for the most part kept in the Bermingham Tower of Dublin

---

33 T. Carte, *An history of the life of James duke of Ormonde*, London 1736, vol. I, p. iii.
34 Ibid., p. 177.
35 Ibid., vol. II, p. 291.
36 MUN/P/23/443, 595; MUN/LIB/10/12.
37 Lascelles cited note 31, vol. II, p.35.
38 H. Wood, *A guide to ... the Public Record Office of Ireland*, Dublin 1919, p. 265.

Castle. Lane, afterwards Viscount Lanesborough, became keeper there in 1663 and clearly Madden's patron in his researches into the records.[39] MS 671, entirely in Madden's hand, contains a series of extracts mostly from the early pipe rolls, but opens with a survey in Latin of the survival of different categories of rolls made for Lane. That Madden used the wards records is evident from a list of his sources in MS 1217. Probably no great care was taken of the records of a defunct court and Madden most likely received from Lane the five volumes in the collection (MSS 643-5, 648), which are now all that survive of the records of that court.

What inspired Madden's interest in the history of Irish religious houses is unknown. It was, perhaps, a desire to emulate Sir William Dugdale's monumental *Monasticon Anglicanum* (London 1655-73), reinforced by working through Ware's manuscripts. The principal source quoted in his monasticon (MS 579) was, however, the public records in the Bermingham Tower, though he also extracted the inquisitions into the dissolved houses in the chief remembrancer's office (MS 656). A copy of MS 579 was made for Archbishop William King, probably when the manuscripts were in Stearne's hands, and this is now with the rest of his library in Cashel. This in turn was copied by Walter Harris, who however, according to a note in Madden's catalogue (MS 653, f.78v), borrowed Madden's original for comparison in 1733. Harris's copy, now volume XIII of his manuscripts in the National Library of Ireland,[40] which has been mainly used by scholars, is headed 'King's collectanea' and as a result, until very recently, the credit for Madden's work has gone to the archbishop.

Most commonly in demand by readers of all Madden's works have been his genealogical compilations, which often provide the only readily available information on the hundreds of English families settled in Ireland, particularly of course for the seventeenth century. But his researches stretched back into the middle ages and also include some of the native Irish families. Sir William Betham (1779-1853), the Ulster king of arms, had copies made and John O'Hart (*Irish pedigrees*, New York 1923), printed Madden's indexes to his three best-known genealogical manuscripts.

The growth and extent of the Madden/Stearne collection present problems, basically how much did Stearne contribute? Comparing the manuscripts listed by Madden in 1700 with the printed catalogue of 1697 there are five extra entered in Madden's hand and eight in Stearne's among the folios, and five in Madden's hand among the quartos. This still leaves a large number of manuscripts entirely unaccounted for, since they occupied the whole of cupboard F and the first two shelves in cupboard G, as Lyon, who disposed

39 Lascelles cited note 31, vol. II, p. 78.
40 *Analecta Hibernica* vol. 6 (1934) p. 397.

them, makes clear, apart from a few later accessions.[41] Some of those not catalogued by Madden are entirely in his hand or have his notes in them: MSS
579, 614, 671, 674, 698, 804, 843, 847 + 1449, 1213-15, 1438. Similarly a few
are in Stearne's hand: 682, 685-6, 712 part 1, and he notes in the Madden
catalogue that 554 was copied at his expense. After that it is a matter of the
tastes of the two men: the records of convocation, the chapter acts of St
Patrick's Cathedral, Dublin, where Stearne was dean, books which seem to
be wholly or partly in the hand of his close friend, Archbishop King, sermons
and divinity commonplaces are more likely to have belonged to Stearne,
whereas heraldry and antiquarian studies and books useful for genealogy are
more likely to have been Madden's.

Stearne's entries in Madden's catalogue include four of the medieval manuscripts: 178, 314, 427, 657 and there are two more among those not entered:
667 and 689. Those certainly Madden's are 17, a Hebrew Psalter; 72, a sixteenth-century copy of a middle English Psalter; 94, the Book of Hours from
Bective Abbey, County Meath, perhaps to be connected with his second marriage to Frances Bolton, whose family had lived in the abbey before the 1641
rebellion;[42] 678, a middle English version of Thomas a Kempis' 'Imitation of
Christ', in the hand of Stephen Dodesham and formerly in the Charterhouse
of Sheen;[43] 525, the fifteenth-century chartulary of the Dublin monastery of
All Hallows, which was on the site of the college; and 606-7, two fourteenth-
century copies of the English statutes. Madden also owned a quarto Latin
Bible and there is one in the Madden/Stearne collection (MS 37), but it is
too tall to be described as a quarto. However, he switched the octavos of his
printed catalogue to quartos in his manuscript catalogue. He also owned the
sixteenth-century 'Book of the De Burgos', MS 1440, partly in Irish. MS
1438 is an Irish-Latin dictionary in his hand, presumably of his own composition, based on the recently published Irish Bible, perhaps as a help towards
learning to read the language. This might also suggest that MS 1439, an
important copy of Geoffrey Keating's 'Foras Feasa', written by Sean mac
Torna O Maolchonaire, belonged to him rather than to Stearne. It does not,
however, appear in his list of sources in MS 1217, though that has a puz-
zlingly obscure reference to an Irish manuscript.[44]

Besides the probable loss of his Latin Bible (quarto 6), two others of
Madden's manuscripts are missing. Folio 13, the journal of the Irish House of
Commons, 1613-15, a copy that had belonged to Edmond Medhop, the clerk

41 MSS 707, 715-16, 743, 760, 821, 887.
42 J. Lodge, The peerage of Ireland, ed. M. Archdall, Dublin 1789, p. 141.
43 A.I. Doyle, 'Stephen Dodesham of Witham and Sheen', in P.R. Robinson and R. Zim eds.,
    Of the making of books, Aldershot 1997, pp 111-12.
44 MS 1217 f. 1v.

of the parliament, is now in the Armagh Public Library still bearing its Madden number. It also contains the bookplate of the Dublin bookseller Michael Ignatius Dugan, who bequeathed his manuscripts to John Lodge, deputy master of the rolls, whose collection was bought for the Armagh Library by William Reeves, afterwards bishop of Down and Connor, in 1865. Folio 17 was William Farmer's 'Irish chronicle', 1612-15. This was printed by Lodge in his anonymous *Desiderata curiosa Hibernica* (Dublin 1772, vol. I, pp 151-326) and as frequently happened in those days manuscripts sent to the printers did not return. Some of Walter Harris's papers are also in Armagh and these two manuscripts were probably among his unrecorded borrowings from Stearne. Another Armagh manuscript, Robert Ware's 'Antiquities of Dublin', is noted by Reeves to have been bought by Dugan at Harris's sale. Harris married Robert's granddaughter and died in 1761; Dugan died in 1768.[45] Another manuscript in Madden's hand, unrecorded in his catalogues, is a copy of the roll called 'Reportorium viride'. Marked 'No. 31' it is kept with the original in the archives of the archbishop of Dublin, now in the Representative Church Body Library.

MANUSCRIPTS ARRANGED IN MADDEN ORDER

Abbott	*Lyon*	*C.M.A.H.*	*Madden Folios*
806	F.1.20	1640	1
807	F.1.21	1641	2
840	F.3.11	1642	3
672	F.3.15		
843	F.3.17	1643-4	4-5
844	F.3.18		
809-41	F.2.2-		
	F.3.10,12	1645-6	6-7
846	F.3.28	1647	8
857	G.1.9	1648	9
804	F.1.18	1649	10
864	F.1.19	1650	11
617	G.1.6	1651	12
Armagh Public Library		1652	13
669	F.1.13	1653	14
1219	G.1.15	1654	15
1220	G.1.21	1655	16
		1656	17
673	F.3.19	1657	18

45 Arthur Vicars ed., *Index to the prerogative wills of Ireland, 1536-1810*, Dublin 1897, p. 147.

Abbott	Lyon	C.M.A.H.	Madden Folios
593	F.4.4	1658	19
849	F.4.11	1659	20
1221	G.1.7	1660	21
856	F.4.9	1661	22
1213	F.3.23		23
1215	F.3.26		24
1214	F.3.25		25
			Quartos
678	F.5.8	1662	1
72	F.5.19	1663	2
851	F.4.14	1664	3
866	F.4.16	1665	4
652	F.4.20	1666	5
656	F.4.25	1667	6
654	F.4.23	1668	7
653	F.4.22	1669	8
1218	F.4.15	1670	9
659	F.4.28	1670	10
1217	F.4.18	1670	11
655	F.4.24	1671	12
666	F.5.2	1672	13
525	F.4.29		14
664	F.4.30	1673	15
			16
94	F.5.21		17
1440	F.4.13		
607	F.6.6	1674	
606	F.6.5	1675	

ADDITIONS TO THE MADDEN FOLIOS IN STEARNE'S HAND

1216	F.3.27		26
842	F.3.16		27
657	F.4.26		28
178	F.4.6		29
554	F.1.8		30
613	F.1.5		31
615	F.1.4		31
616	F.1.1		31
505	F.4.7		32
314	F.5.7		33
706	G.1.20		34
525	F.4.29		35

PROBABLE OR CERTAIN ADDITIONAL MADDEN MANUSCRIPTS IN LYON ORDER

Abbott	Lyon	Reasons for attributions
646	F.1.2	Davys
643	F.1.3	Wards
614	F.1.6	Madden's hand
647	F.1.7	Davys
643	F.1.9	Wards
1438	F.1.11	Madden's hand
645	F.1.12	Wards
670	F.1.14	Genealogy
579	F.1.15-16	Madden's hand
808	F.2.1	? Davys
671	F.3.13	Madden's hand
648	F.3.22	Wards
1213	F.3.23	Madden's hand
1214	F.3.25	Madden's hand
1215	F.3.26	Madden's hand
644	F.3.29	Wards
644	F.3.30	Wards
649	F.4.1	Davys
674	F.4.2	Madden's hand
847 (1449)	F.4.3	Madden's hand
848	F.4.10	Thynne's ambassadors
856	F.4.12	Heraldry
698	G.1.3	Madden's hand
618	G.1.4-5	Dugdale's summons
699	G.1.8	Charles, Lancaster herald
703	G.1.16	Davys
	G.2.7	Madden's herbarium

Lost and Found: A Stray of the Thirteenth Century from Trinity College Library

BERNARD MEEHAN

The movement of books in and out of collections forms a compelling subject for the student of medieval and early modern libraries. Losses and survivals from the early days of Trinity College Library can be traced to a considerable extent through the early catalogues, which have, on the whole, been preserved carefully among the records of the library.

The greatest single collection of manuscripts and printed books to come to the library had been built up by James Ussher, archbishop of Armagh (d.1656). Ussher's library, which was bestowed on the college by Charles II in 1661, contained around 10,000 volumes, and included some important decorated medieval manuscripts, such as the twelfth-century Winchcombe psalter (TCD MS 53) and a volume by the thirteenth-century historian and artist, Matthew Paris (TCD MS 177).[1] Ussher's collection had suffered serious depletion on a number of occasions before 1661, and further losses occurred after that date. Lists added to Samuel Foley's 1688 catalogue of the college manuscripts (MS 7/1)[2] contain, on folio 1r, a list of 'Manuscripts wanting in the College Library the 31th [sic] of March, 1702'. In this list, several shelfmarks were subsequently deleted, presumably because the manuscripts in question had been found. Others came to light when Canon John Lyon began his cataloguing work in 1741, and are marked as having been found in that year or the subsequent year. Beside the 1702 list, Lyon added a note of 'Manuscripts wanting in 1742'. That later list includes the Book of Ballymote and the Book of Lecan, both now in the Royal Irish Academy, and 'Quatuor Evangelia Graece 12°', now in the Schøyen collection, Oslo. The 1702 list does not, incidentally, include two leaves from the Book of Kells, folios 335 and 336, which had been noted as missing in the sixteenth century but were found in 1741.[3]

---

1 B. Meehan, 'The manuscript collection of James Ussher', in ed. P. Fox, *Treasures of the Library, Trinity College Dublin*, Dublin 1986, pp 97-110.

2 William O'Sullivan, introduction to Marvin L. Colker, Trinity College Library Dublin. *Descriptive catalogue of the mediaeval and renaissance Latin manuscripts*, 2 vols., Aldershot 1991, vol. 1 pp 26-8.

3 B. Meehan, *The Book of Kells: an illustrated introduction to the manuscript in Trinity College Dublin*, London 1994, p. 92.

The first volume to be noted as missing in the 1742 list is 'A 49 Biblia Sacra Latine 8°'. An unexpected opportunity to identify this stray from the library was presented in 1996, when a small, mid-thirteenth-century English or French bible was brought to the library's conservation laboratory for repair from its present location at St Columb's College, Derry. The bible measures in the region of 130 x 86 mm and contains 572 leaves. It has modest decorated initials on several leaves, and the opening of Genesis is marked by an elaborate initial *I* which runs the length of the page and depicts seven scenes from that book, as well as the Crucifixion at the base of the letter.⁴ The shelfmark 'A. 49' appears at the top of the present leaf I/3,⁵ corresponding to the reference in Edward Foley's catalogue of the college manuscripts made *c.*1688 (MS 7/1 folio 19v): 'Biblia sacra ex versione S Hieronymi. 8° membr.', and to the rough copy of his catalogue (MS 7/3 folio 8v): 'Biblia sacra ex versione Hieronymi 8° membr'. Using Foley's compilation, A. 49 was listed as no. 248 in Edward Bernard's printed catalogue of 1697.⁶

Older shelfmarks on leaf I/3, on either side of 'A. 49', were crossed out when they became redundant. To the left is 'G. 4.'. This can be identified with the shelfmark G.1.4 from the catalogue of the college's manuscripts produced *c.*1670, where again it is described as 'Biblia Sacra ex versioni Hieronymi' (MS 7/2 folio 24r). The shelfmark 'FFF 20' to the left of 'A. 49' identifies the manuscript unmistakably as one from Ussher's library. While the catalogue of Ussher's manuscripts has not survived, it seems certain that it was compiled by Sir James Ware,⁷ and the form and hand of the shelfmark are consistent with, for example, 'FFF 33' on the present TCD MS 306, or 'FFF 43' on the present TCD MS 309.

A fourteenth-century inscription at the foot of leaf I/4, repeated on leaf XVI/24, adds to the interest of the manuscript. It makes it possible to trace the ownership of the book in the fourteenth century, indicates that it was in Irish hands by that date, and demonstrates a degree of literacy among the secular clergy of the time. The inscription records that a certain Master Peter Parys was leaving the manuscript on his death to a certain Lord John Spenser, with the wish that it should continue to pass from one secular priest in Ireland to another. The recipient was to provide alms for the poor and prayers for

4   I am indebted to Anthony Cains for bringing the manuscript and inscription to my attention and for making available his conservation notes and materials on it. The permission of St Columb's College, Derry, and Mrs P. Grant to publish this note is also gratefully acknowledged.

5   The manuscript has not been foliated. Folio references are to the gathering ('I') and the position of the leaf within that gathering ('3').

6   Edward Bernard, *Catalogi librorum manuscriptorum Angliae et Hiberniae*, Oxford 1697, vol. 2 pt. 2 p. 21.

7   O'Sullivan (as note 2), pp 22-3.

the soul of Peter Parys. The names Parys and Spencer are not uncommon in the records of late medieval Ireland. While it has not been possible to trace the individuals in question, occurrences of the names in counties Meath and Louth in the early fourteenth century suggest the possibility that the manuscript circulated in the area and that Ussher acquired it during his time as bishop of Meath between 1621 and 1625.[8] The manuscript may perhaps be added tentatively to William O'Sullivan's list of surviving medieval manuscripts with connections to county Meath.[9] (The appendix to the present article contains a transcription and translation of the inscription, the work of my colleague Stuart Ó Seanóir.)

An amusing ownership inscription, in a sixteenth-century hand, occurs on the first leaf of gathering VII: 'hic liber est meus Testis mei est deus si quis mihi non credit'. (This book is mine. God is my witness, if anyone does not believe me).

The bible came to St Columb's College as a gift of Sir Edward Reid in 1901, along with a number of other volumes. Where it spent the years between the eighteenth century, when it was in Trinity College Library, and Reid's acquiring it remains unknown.

APPENDIX: OWNERSHIP AND TRANSFER INSCRIPTIONS ON
FOLIOS I/4 AND XVI/24, TRANSLATED BY STUART Ó SEANÓIR

[I]stum librum legavit .M. Petrus Parys domino Johanni Spenser
Master Peter Parys left this book to Lord John Spenser

Quem relinquet post mortem eius magistro aut bacallario
Let him leave it after his death to a master or bachelor

Artium aut honesto sacerdoti seculari de terra hibernie
of arts or an honest secular priest of the land of Ireland

predicatori aut disposito ad predicandum. Et recipiens
being a preacher or disposed to preaching. And receiving

8   There is a charter of the widow of one Roger le Spenser concerning a grant of land at Duleek, County Meath, 27 January 1310: see ed. J. Mills and M.J. McEnery, *Calendar of the Gormanston Register*, Dublin 1916, pp 50-1. On 23 April 1312, at court in Drogheda, one John Paris, charged with murder, claimed to be a clerk: see ed. H. Wood, A.E. Langman, M.C. Griffith, *Calendar of the justiciary rolls Ireland 1308-1314*, Dublin 1956, pp 239-40. I am very grateful to Dr James Lydon for these references and to Dr Lydon and Dr Bernadette Williams for discussion of the inscription.
9   William O'Sullivan, 'Medieval Meath manuscripts', *Rioght na Midhe* (1986) pp 3-21, and 'Additional Medieval Meath manuscripts', *Rioght na Midhe* (1987) pp 68-70.

eundem distribuet post eiusdem receptionem pauperibus iijs
the same let him (after its receipt) distribute 3 s[hillings]

iiijd atque orabit pro anima dicti petri. Et sub hiis con/
4d to the poor and he will pray for the soul of the said Peter. And by these

/dicionibus transibit ab uno seculari sacerdote ad alterum.
conditions it will pass from one secular priest to another.

Legal Deposit, 1801–1922

VINCENT KINANE

'Interference with the Copyright Privilege now, would leave Ireland without any comprehensive collection, representing the actual facts of publication rather than the judgement of individual librarians or committees.' Thus states a Trinity College memorandum sent to several peers during the debates in parliament prior to passing the Copyright Act of 1911, when the college's legal deposit privilege of 110 years standing was yet again under threat. This mature appreciation of the responsibility engendered by the privilege is in stark contrast to the reception of the intake in the early years of the nineteenth century. The library minute book on 18 August 1813 records the arrival of two large parcels from Stationers' Hall in London; a cynical hand added the note 'alias packs of trash'.[1]

Legal deposit obligations were rooted in the needs of government to curb the publication of seditious and blasphemous literature. It had nothing to do with enriching learned libraries, or safeguarding the national literature. In England when the Press Licensing Act lapsed in 1695 so too did copyright protection in literary works, as also the legal deposit requirements. In the early eighteenth century, under pressure from the book trade, legal protection was reinstituted by the Copyright Act of 1709 (8 Anne c.19). Legal deposit obligations were also included in the act, now not for censorship purposes, but something akin to a stamp duty for the registration of copyright.[2]

Throughout the eighteenth century Ireland had no copyright law and no consequent legal deposit requirements. This changed in the aftermath of the Act of Union, when it became necessary to regularize the copyright position within the Kingdom. The Copyright Act of 1801 (41 Geo.III c.107) extended copyright protection to Ireland, and, as a clause in the act, Trinity College

---

1 TCD Library, Memorandum with a view to the debate in the House of Lords, 20 Nov. 1911, MUN/LIB/22/19/11; Library Minute Book, 18 Aug. 1813, MUN/LIB/2/1. (Hereafter all MSS refs. are to TCD Library).
2 R.C.B. Partridge, *The history of the legal deposit of books throughout the British Empire*, London 1938, pp 3, 31, 33-4.

and the King's Inns were nominated as legal deposit libraries in Ireland, bring-ing the number of privileged libraries to eleven.

There is no evidence that Trinity's authorities lobbied to have it so des-ignated. In fact at that date none of the eleven legal deposit libraries in the British Isles benefited much from the privilege. The publishers made little effort to register their works at Stationers' Hall and fulfil the consequent legal deposit requirements. Thus Cambridge University Library got only 25 of the 400 or so works published in London in 1804 and the Bodleian at Oxford received almost none.[3] There were, however, rumblings from 1805 onwards against this state of affairs, especially at Cambridge. In 1807 Edward Christian published one of the seminal pamphlets in the debate, *Vindication of the right of the universities of Great Britain to a copy of every new publication*. As a result of the debate a bill was introduced in parliament in 1808 by John Charles Villiers, which sought to secure the libraries' rights. But there was huge resis-tance by the publishers to what they saw as an invasion of their private prop-erty, and the bill lapsed.[4]

Although the Trinity authorities, like the other beneficiaries, may not have shown much enthusiasm for the privilege in the early years of the century, they did make a speedy appointment in 1802 of Cadell and Davies as their agent in London to collect the books deposited at Stationers' Hall and other works.[5] These were anticipated to be so few that it was felt half-yearly deliv-eries to Dublin would suffice. The clerk at Stationers' Hall, George Greenhill, was to be allowed two guineas per year for gathering together TCD's books.

The first delivery from Stationers' Hall is recorded in the library minute book on 10 August 1802.[6] It took time to process these works, not surprising when it is remembered that the enormous Fagel Collection, recently pur-chased, had just arrived in the library. Some of the legal deposit books, received in sheets, were sent off to the binders on 16 August. It is also evi-dent that there was a screening process in operation. On 15 October the librar-ian sent a residue to the provost 'for his inspection', no doubt to get a final decision on whether the books were worthy to be catalogued and placed in the library.

The intake at the start was small, but was soon to change. Again Cam-bridge provided the motivating force. In 1811, at the instigation of Edward Christian, it instituted a case against the printer Henry Bryer for not send-ing legal deposit copies to Stationers' Hall; a verdict in its favour was handed

3   Partridge, p. 45 and table p. 315; John Feather, *Publishing, piracy and politics: an historical study of copyright in Britain*, London 1994, p. 100.
4   Partridge, pp 47-8; Feather, pp 101-2.
5   Letter, J. Barrett to Cadell and Davies, 2 May 1802, MUN/LIB/13/3.
6   Library Minute Book, 10 Aug. 1802, MUN/LIB/2/1; recorded as 'the first parcel' on 8 Oct.

down in 1812.[7] The publishers were incensed and succeeded in having a parliamentary select committee established in 1813 to examine the whole issue
of copyright and the attendant obligation of legal deposit. The publishers
made a submission to the committee in which they conceded the obligation
to make legal deposits, but they wanted the number of benefiting libraries
reduced to five, of which TCD was to be one. They were bitterly disappointed
when the committee reported in favour of the status quo.[8]

Lobbying on the publishers' behalf continued, however. After two abortive
bills the result was the Copyright Act of 1814 (54 Geo.III c.156). During the
consideration of the bill it is evident that Trinity had been in contact with
Edward Christian seeking his advice on how best to defend its position, and
it made a submission to parliament on 6 June.[9] Again the publishers were disappointed at the outcome. The act retained the eleven deposit libraries, and
insisted that all works be registered and copies deposited at Stationers' Hall.
One crumb thrown to the book trade was the extension of the period of copyright protection to 28 years.[10]

The publishers efforts to circumscribe the privileges of the legal deposit
libraries had backfired by making the libraries more aware of their entitlements. Soon the libraries were acting in concert. A meeting of representatives
was held in Sion College in London on 26 March 1816 at which Henry
Monck Mason represented the interests of the Dublin libraries. In a letter to
the provost he gave a report on the meeting, stating that an association of the
libraries was to be formed for mutual communication. Evasion by the publishers was so great that it was felt that prosecution was absolutely necessary.
All works, except novels and school-books, were to be claimed 'as the most
trivial pamphlets become very frequently important and valuable in the lapse
of time'.[11] (This is a very early recognition of the value of the so-called
ephemeral works, which was not universally appreciated by succeeding generations of librarians.)

This principle of inclusivity amazed the publishers. The act had stipulated that Stationers' Hall was to send quarterly lists of works registered to
the libraries, from which each would select what was wanted. Instead they
were being presented with printed forms in the names of all the libraries
(except the British Museum) demanding ten copies of every work registered.[12]
These demands were sent by George Greenhill, the warehouse-keeper at

7   Partridge, p. 49; Feather, pp 103-4.
8   Partridge, pp 53-4.
9   Letter, J. Palmer, London, to the Provost, 26 May 1814, MUN/LIB/22/19/1; Feather, pp
    110-11.
10 Partridge, pp 60-1.
11 Letter, H. Monck Mason to the Provost, 10 May 1816, MUN/LIB/13/15.
12 Partridge, p. 62; text of demand of 8 Apr. 1816 given on p. 313.

Stationers' Hall, who was acting as agent for the libraries. (This is the earliest version of the Copyright Agency which exists today, acting for all the legal deposit libraries under British law except the British Library.)

There was a dramatic rise in the number of works registered at Stationers' Hall following the 1814 act. In 1814 'literary works and books of prints' numbered 541; in 1815 this rose to 1244.[13] The first consignment since the passing of the act arrived in Trinity in July 1815, and the second in October.[14] The July consignment contained 163 works, and that of October 96 works, giving a total of 259 works in that half year. This was far short of what was being registered, so there must have been many rejects. Nonetheless the intake led rapidly to a storage problem, a recurrent headache for any legal deposit library, and on 15 March 1817 the Board had to agree that new books could be stored in the presses in the Reading Room.[15]

The earliest parcels of books had been shipped direct to Dublin from London port. One shipment in 1811 was captured by a French privateer and landed at Gravelines on the Normandy coast.[16] This may have been the reason why soon afterwards parcels were being sent overland for shipment from the ports nearest to Dublin – Liverpool, Preston, Holyhead.[17] Sea journeys presented problems other than privateering. A parcel was damaged in March 1817 when the vessel on which they were being shipped, the Sutton, was 'cast away', that is shipwrecked. Something however was salvaged – the bookbinder George Mullen was given volumes from the parcel to try and save; but others were beyond repair.[18]

The publishers were still straining against their obligations and succeeded in having yet another select committee established, this time solely to consider the question of legal deposit. Among the charges levelled by the trade was that the libraries, besides being indiscriminate in their demands, were even selling unwanted legal deposit books. TCD was at pains to point out in its submission that legal deposit books were always retained. Its instructions to its London agent was not to claim music, novels or school-books. Of what arrived at the library a selection was made of those that were to be catalogued and placed on the shelves, 'a considerable part' having to be bound (no mention being made in the acts of delivering bound volumes). What remained – imperfect works or 'such as there occurred some difficulty in determining

---

13 Partridge, pp 62-3 and table pp 315-16.
14 'First consignment from Stationers' Hall since passing 54 Geo. III', 15 July 1815, MUN/LIB/12/8; another list, 3-4 Oct. 1815, MUN/LIB/12/9.
15 Board Register, 15 Mar. 1817, MUN/V/5/6.
16 Library Minute Book, 23 Jan. 1811, MUN/LIB/2/1.
17 Board Register, 31 Jan. 1815, MUN/V/5/6; Library Minute Book, 14 Aug. 1818, MUN/LIB/2/2.
18 Library Minute Book, 5 Mar. 1817, MUN/LIB/2/2.

upon the propriety of placing them in the public library' – were in the custody of the librarian, 'none having ever been disposed of'.[19] Although the
committee reported in 1818 in favour of the publishers – suggesting that the
British Museum, or a reduced number of libraries (including TCD), retain
the legal deposit privilege – parliament ignored the report.

It soon became apparent that Greenhill was not carrying out his duties as
agent for the libraries as rigorously as was expected. When the bursar, James
Wilson, was in London early in 1821 he had remonstrated with him for losing
many valuable works for the college because he had not claimed them within
the statutory twelve months.[20] In 1821 some of the other libraries had chosen
another agent, Robert A. Durham. But Trinity kept faith with Greenhill until
December 1822 when it too opted for Durham.[21]

If Trinity was not getting all it should have under legal deposit at this
date, the appointment of James Henthorn Todd as a salaried assistant librarian in July 1834 led to a considerable tightening up in its claims over the following decades.[22] He brought a tenacious rigour to the task of legal deposit
claims that was later mirrored by Antonio Panizzi at the British Museum and
Edward B. Nicholson at the Bodleian. When Todd subsequently gave evidence before the Dublin University Commission, which reported in 1853, he
stated that as a result of the reforms he had introduced the number of legal
deposit books received was 'three times as great as it was in 1835', so that the
library received 'nearly all that we can legally claim'.[23]

Trinity changed its agent in 1834 when Hodges and Smith, the University
Bookseller in Dublin, was appointed in place of Durham.[24] (This was a strange
appointment as most of the work to be done was in London, and in fact the
firm had to appoint a sub-agent, Mawer Cowtan, to do the work there.)
Hodges and Smith was soon in trouble with Todd. On 8 April 1835 he sent
it a 23-page list, containing 560 works which should have been claimed.
Publishers' names are appended as well as references to the *Literary Gazette*
and various newspapers. Todd was obviously being very thorough, and
demanded such works as *Crowquill's comic keepsake*, *Mrs Copley's Housekeepers'
guide*, and *Selwyn in search of a daughter* and other novels, works that would

19 Library Minute Book, 7 July 1817, MUN/LIB/2/2.
20 Letter, J. Wilson to the provost, 8 Jan. 1821, MUN/LIB/13/23.
21 Library Minute Book, 22 Feb. 1819, MUN/LIB/2/2; Board Register, 10 Dec. 1822,
   MUN/V/5/6.
22 Board Register, 5 July 1834, MUN/V/5/7; he had been a supernumerary assistant librarian
   without salary since 23 Nov. 1831. For an assessment of him see George O. Simms, 'James
   Henthorn Todd', *Hermathena* 109 (1969) pp 5-23.
23 *Report of Her Majesty's Commissioners appointed to inquire into the state ... of the University
   of Dublin*, Dublin 1853, evidence p. 173.
24 Board Register, 1 Dec. 1834, MUN/V/5/7; Library Minute Book, 1 Dec. 1834, MUN/V/2/3.

surely have been rejected in earlier decades. (Hodges and Smith obviously did a poor job – none of these works is in the library). And there were several other demands in the same year.[25] It was obvious that Hodges and Smith's tenure would shortly end.

In the meantime the publishers, whose smoldering resentment was now rekindled, succeeded in having another bill introduced into parliament attacking legal deposit. It was sponsored by James Silk Buckingham who argued that legal deposit hampered rather than encouraged learning because it increased the price of books and prevented the publication of many expensive editions. He proposed the abolition of all legal deposit, but allowed for monetary compensation to the libraries affected. The 1836 Act (6 & 7 Will. IV c.110) when it was passed was a compromise: the British Museum, the Bodleian, Cambridge, Advocates in Edinburgh, and Trinity retained their privileges; the others were given an annual grant in lieu, King's Inns getting £433.[26]

Todd had not let up in his crusade. Early in 1837 he was in London visiting publishers. From a letter to the bursar it is evident that Trinity was contemplating bringing an action against a publisher named Macrone for not depositing books. But Todd was advised against it by some of the principal booksellers because Macrone was 'not respectable'; he was told it would be better to tackle one of the better law publishers, like Butterworth, because 'if we compel him to submit our victory will make a greater noise & strike a greater terror into the rest'.[27] No legal action appears to have been taken. On his visit Todd had also been scouting for a replacement agent. His letter goes on to state that Robert Cowtan, son of the British Museum's agent, had been recommended to him. Cowtan was employed in a minor capacity at the British Museum and would have access to that library's accessions' lists, as well as benefiting from his father's experience. Cowtan was duly appointed on 29 April.[28]

There is evidence that only about 70 per cent of accessions at this date were processed and placed on the library shelves. The library minute book records that the total value of all books and periodicals received in 1836 was £740 but that 'novels and others' to the value of £214 were not put in the library. The ledger from which these figures derive shows, despite the protestations of 1817, that not everything was retained. A small number of textbooks were sent to King's Hospital school; novels, which were stored in the 'Lumber Room', were sometimes recorded as 'borrowed'.[29]

25 Library Minute Book, 26 Feb., 3, 8, 24 Apr., 29 Jun., 10 Nov. 1835, MUN/LIB/2/3.

26 Partridge, pp 74-7, 141. This sum is still included in the Irish government accounts and paid annually to King's Inns.

27 Letter, J.H. Todd to R. MacDonnell, 3 Apr. 1837, MUN/LIB/22/20/2.

28 Board Register, 29 Apr. 1837, MUN/V/5/7.

29 Library Minute Book, Jan. 1837, MUN/LIB/2/3. 'Books received Feb. 23rd [18]35 to Decr. 1838', Dept. of Early Printed Books.

The growth in the intake was creating problems for the agent. At the beginning of the century books were assembled in a somewhat haphazard fashion for shipment to Dublin; the muniments record the arrival of 'cases', 'bundles', and 'parcels' of books at the library. By 1839 it is evident that tea chests had been in use for some time. On 12 December Cowtan wrote to say that because of the increased weight of the deliveries, sent on a monthly basis, he was now using packing cases.[30]

The publishers expressed their dissatisfaction with their obligations by making matters as awkward as possible for the libraries. When the publisher Pickering was asked to deposit copies of Henry Shaw's *Encylopaedia of ornament* he declined, stating that the work, issued in parts, was wholly made up of plates, and therefore did not come within the terms of the act.[31] He went on to state that the author intended 'to present' the descriptive letterpress to the purchasers with the last part, a ruse used by other publishers. (It appears that Pickering lost this battle as there is a copy in the college library.)

After the 1836 act, which dealt solely with legal deposit and reaffirmed the rights of selected libraries, there was no reason why legal deposit should not have been treated as a separate issue from copyright. But the traditional association of the two meant that whenever the copyright law was reconsidered, legal deposit too came under scrutiny.[32] And that was what happened in 1842 when the Imperial Copyright Act (5 & 6 Vict. c.45) was passed in an attempt to regulate copyright throughout the Empire. It provided a clean sweep; by it the acts of 1710, 1801 and 1814 were repealed. There were various adjustments to the deposit obligations, but all the privileged libraries retained their rights.

Hitherto the publishers had been extracting every penny they could from the legal deposit libraries, charging as much as they dared for colouring plates or boarding books, neither of which was required under former acts.[33] The 1842 act however required them to deliver copies in the form in which most were offered for sale, which at this date meant cased books, with coloured plates where applicable. The publishers were vexed at these new obligations and avoided them when they could. Todd had to send a stiff letter to John Gould threatening him with legal action for not supplying his sumptuous bird books with coloured plates.[34]

Robert Cowtan was not finding the job as agent easy. In March 1842 he wrote plaintively to Joseph Dobbs at the library: 'I assure you it is very tedious

30 Cowtan to TCD librarian, 12 Dec. 1839, MUN/LIB/22/20/18.
31 Letter, R. Cowtan to J. Dobbs, 27 May 1841, MUN/LIB/22/20/27.
32 Feather, p. 119.
33 Letter, Cowtan to Joseph Dobbs, 15 Sept. 1842, MUN/LIB/22/20/38. Strangely as late as 1912 some publishers were still seeking payment for hand-colouring plates (see letter, Bradford to Abbott, 30 Apr. 1912, MUN/LIB/22/20/330).
34 Library Minute Book, 24 Oct. 1842, MUN/LIB/2/3.

work to get decisive answers from the publishers – they will not give us a down right refusal or we should know what to do. A London collectorship is no sinecure.'35 There was a phenomenal amount of works issued in parts, reflecting no doubt the lack of wealth across broad swathes of an increasingly literate society, and these had to be kept track of. This also applied to issues of periodicals and the agent found it efficient to have lists of the regular journals printed up on which he entered in manuscript the issue numbers being forwarded.36 The library for its part prepared extensive lists of deficiencies in its holdings of these part issues and periodicals, which were returned to the agent to chase up.37

Cowtan had not long to worry about his onerous task. His relationship with the warehouse keeper at Stationers' Hall, now Joseph Greenhill, had deteriorated. It appears that Greenhill, no doubt afraid of losing the registration fees which were his to keep, was canvassing the publishers to deposit their books with him and not to send them direct to the agent, even stating that it was illegal to do so.38 It must have been evident to TCD that it would be more efficient to appoint the warehouse keeper as its agent, as it had done in the period 1816-22. Accordingly, although Cowtan had given 'the most entire satisfaction', Joseph Greenhill, who also acted for some of the other libraries, was appointed as agent to begin on 25 March 1845.39

The chronic lack of space in the library was drawn to the attention of the board at its annual visitation on 23 October 1843. Todd was authorized to seek legal opinion on the sale of duplicates and imperfect works, and also of those books received under legal deposit '[which] are useless for the purposes of the library, such as merely ephemeral novels, children's books, and other insignificant publications'.40 Mountifort Longfield counselled against disposal of legal deposit books, stating that the object of the act was 'to preserve copies of the works in the most important public institutions'. He added that publishers would be aggrieved to find these books appearing on the market in competition with their stocks. He saw no objection to the return of 'insignificant' works to the publishers.41

Shortly after this period, in September 1850, Antonio Panizzi was given power of attorney by the British Museum to enforce its entitlements under the act. He insisted that comprehensiveness was the only criterion for acqui-

35 Letter, Cowtan to Dobbs, 4 Mar. 1842, MUN/LIB/22/20/33.
36 Printed lists of periodicals sent to TCD, May 1843 – June 1849, MUN/LIB/22/4/1-41.
37 Annual lists prepared by TCD library of deficiencies in part works and periodicals, 1845 – 1847, MUN/LIB/22/6-8.
38 Letter, Cowtan to Dobbs, 17 Mar. 1843, MUN/LIB/22/20/45.
39 Library Minute Book, 16 Dec. 1844, MUN/LIB/2/4.
40 Library Minute Book, 23 October 1843, MUN/LIB/2/4.
41 Opinion of Mountifort Longfield, 25 October 1843, MUN/LIB/12/21 a-b.

sitions under legal deposit. (This was to mark the watershed in the shift of attitudes among the legal deposit libraries away from selectivity.) There followed a period of merciless pursuit of defaulting publishers, even in the provinces and across the sea in Ireland. The results were staggering. Between 1851 and 1854 the British Museum's annual intake nearly doubled.[42] All the legal deposit libraries benefitted by his rigour. At TCD the annual intake of printed volumes in 1850-1 was 1,560; the following year it was over double that. (Volumes could contain several works bound up together, so the actual number of works was considerably more.)

Todd was appointed as librarian in February 1852 and by March was reporting to the board on the cataloguing backlog.[43] With the present staff, he stated, it was only possible to process 250 works per month, that is 3,000 per year. There was a backlog of 5,000 works in the librarian's room and the annual intake was about 3,000. Even though the backlog continued to grow, it is clear that a library clerk was still assiduously scanning the major Irish newspapers looking for book advertisements and claiming those not deposited. One list compiled for the period 1850 to 1858 survives and runs to 40 folio pages.[44] And it is also evident that the library was now taking music, which it formerly had rejected.[45]

The increased intake added considerably to the storage problem, already critical. It was solved in an unforeseen and drastic manner. It was found that the roof of the Long Room was in danger of collapse, and during 1859-60 it had to be renewed. As a strengthening measure the bookcases at the floor level were continued up onto the gallery, thereby almost doubling the shelving space.

The Dublin University Commission report of 1853 had little to say about the legal deposit privilege, beyond mentioning that because of it admission to the library should be liberalized for the public, and recommending that publishers be obliged to deposit books without demand, placing the privileged libraries on the same footing as the British Museum.[46] Todd's evidence to the commission put some flesh on the bones. His policy as librarian was that everything known to be published in Great Britain and Ireland was claimed. As regards publications in the Dominions he stated that it was very difficult to discover what exactly had been published there; it was his opinion that

42 Partridge, p. 85 and table p. 327.
43 Board Register, 6 Mar. 1852, MUN/V/5/10.
44 'Advertisements of books from Saunders's Newsletter' and other newspapers, 1850-8, MUN/LIB/22/12.
45 Lists of music sent to TCD, Oct. 1859, Sept. 1860, MUN/LIB/22/16-17. The representation of music in the library at this period is very poor and much of this must not have been retained.
46 *Report of Commissioners* 1853, pp 76, 78.

there was a flaw in the act and the library would have difficulty enforcing its privilege. He mentioned too that not all the intake was put up on the shelves; the inferior class of publication was stored in 'large chests and boxes'.[47]

The difficulty of enforcing legal deposit obligations was highlighted in 1855 when Greenhill sent a list of recalcitrant London publishers, which included some of the best known houses, 'to whom it would be well to send threatening letters': Austin, Collins, Vizetelly, Griffin, Bagster, Skeat, Wildy, Berger, Gilbert and Cradock. Todd wrote to them all 'severely', threatening proceedings if they did not comply.[48]

Obstinate publishers were not the only problems the legal deposit libraries were having. A meeting of librarians was arranged in London for 30 May 1859 'for the purpose of considering the steps to be taken in order to secure a better delivery of the books ...'[49] Greenhill was being dilatory in his duties. Some of the libraries wanted to dismiss him but he was resisting, claiming that the wording of the act required all books to be received through him.[50] The Advocates Library led the way, and in 1860 appointed Gregory W. Eccles, who was employed in the British Museum, as its agent. But the other libraries reluctantly decided to stick with Greenhill although stringent conditions were imposed on his delivery times.[51] Matters, however, did not improve and by mid-1863 there was a general determination to opt for Eccles. Cambridge was first to join the Advocates, and the Bodleian followed shortly afterwards.[52] Eccles then wrote to Todd in an attempt to pursuade Trinity to join the other libraries, outlining the efficient service he could provide.[53] The board was not long in making a decision and on 4 July approved the appointment of Eccles, beginning from September.[54] (Thus was started the Copyright Agency which has survived continuously since then.) Not unnaturally Greenhill proved to be very uncooperative to the new agent, and when another copyright bill was being drafted in 1864 (which was later withdrawn) Eccles urged that provision be made for the delivery of books to the agent and not to Stationers' Hall.[55]

The Ordnance Survey was another area which received Todd's attentions. On 9 February 1863 Sir Henry James wrote to him to state that the acquisi-

47 Ibid. Evidence, pp 173–4.
48 Letter, Greenhill to the Revd B. Dickson, 5 Apr. 1855, MUN/LIB/22/20/65; Library Minute Book, 10 Apr. 1855, MUN/LIB/2/4.
49 Board Register, 21 May 1859, MUN/V/5/11/348.
50 Edmund Craster, *History of the Bodleian Library 1845–1945*, Oxford 1981, p. 63.
51 Library Minute Book, 31 Mar. 1860, MUN/LIB/2/4.
52 David McKitterick, *Cambridge University Library: a history*, Cambridge 1986, p. 578.
53 Library Minute Book, 1 July 1863, MUN/LIB/2/4.
54 Board Register, 4 July 1863, MUN/V/5/12/68.
55 Letter, Eccles to Todd, 2 Mar. 1864, MUN/LIB/22/20/90.

tion of parish and town maps 'would be of little practical utility' to an institution like TCD. The librarian wrote back in irate terms: 'I have always
regarded the Act ... as an expression on the part of the legislature of their
desire to make this Library keep every thing, & I do not allow the question
of the utility or merit of the publication to interfere with our right to it ...'[56]
Todd may well have rued his demand the following August when 14,000 maps
and a box of Admiralty charts were deposited.[57] (Successive generations of
librarians have been defeated by the intake of maps – for example, there was
a 50ft high stack of maps awaiting binding in 1900[58] – and it is only since
1987 that a map librarian was appointed and space allotted to store and catalogue the collections.)

Todd died in June 1869. It was not long before the new librarian, John
Adam Malet, made his dissatisfaction with Eccles felt. In fact it appears that
he summarily sacked the agent in March 1870, who appealed his dismissal to
the board. A sub-committee was appointed to consider the librarian's objections. It reported in May in favour of Malet's decision and the board, part-
ing company with the other legal deposit libraries, dismissed Eccles.[59] It
proved to be a bad decision. It is not clear what arrangements were made,
but in April 1872 the librarian had to be dispatched to London to try to find
a suitable agent.[60] The Reverend Dr T.S. Gray was the man chosen, but he
too proved to be unsatisfactory. By 1877 Trinity was again seeking a suitable
candidate. J.P. Mahaffy, on behalf of the library committee, wrote to the
Bodleian's librarian, Henry O. Coxe, asking for suggestions. Coxe replied that
he could think of no one more efficient than Eccles, and admonished: 'I always
thought that in rejecting Mr Eccles ... your authorities acted ... very injudi-
ciously'.[61] The college had to swallow its pride and ask Eccles to resume as
its agent. The answer was positive and from 22 June TCD again joined with
the Bodleian, Cambridge and Advocates in Edinburgh in having the same
agent.[62]

The whole question of legal deposit, having lain relatively dormant since
the 1842, burst on the scene again over thirty years later. In 1875 a Royal
Commission was established to consider what changes were needed in the
copyright laws, and of course legal deposit again came under scrutiny. The
Commissioners wrote to the various libraries asking for the annual figures for
the numbers of books received under the 1842 act and their value. Malet

56 Library Minute Book, 11 Feb. 1863, MUN/LIB/2/4.
57 Library Minute Book, 21 Aug. 1863, MUN/LIB/2/4/85.
58 Library Minute Book, Jan. 1900, MUN/LIB/2/5/77.
59 Board Register, 8 Mar., 28 May 1870, MUN/V/5/12.
60 Board Register, 6 Apr. 1872, MUN/V/5/13.
61 Letter, Coxe to Mahaffy, 8 Mar. 1877, MUN/LIB/22/20/94.
62 Board Register, 17, 22 Mar., 7 Apr., 30 June 1877, MUN/V/5/13.

wrote back giving estimated figures of 3,000–4,000 books to a value of per-haps £1,500, comparable to the figures supplied by Advocates, but much less than the Bodleian's £4,775.[63] None of the libraries was invited to make a fur-ther submission and all were astonished when the report, published in 1878, recommended that the British Museum be the sole library to retain the legal deposit privilege, the others to be compensated by an annual sum of £1,200.[64]

With a bill pending to implement the recommendations, the libraries were busy marshalling their forces. It is evident that part of Trinity's defence was to feed the story to the press. On 18 February 1879, before the board had even decided to send a deputation to London to make representations, the *Free-man's Journal* carried an extensive article, the first of several, on the Commiss-ion's report and the damage it would do to the TCD library.[65] The article in the issue of 7 March spoke of the 'grevious calamity to their noble national library'. The report in the *Irish Times* on 12 March also stressed the national element: 'Enlightened public opinion will not lean towards the recommenda-tion of so great a national loss as the entire abolition of the surety which at present exists in having a complete treasury of reference in at least one place in Ireland.' Also mentioned was the fact that the privilege did not cost the publishers much beyond the price of the paper in the books, and that the dis-play of the books in Trinity's library provided substantial advertisement value. All these points and more are to be found in Trinity's printed petition, car-ried to London by Malet and Mahaffy for presentation to Lord Manners who was sponsoring the bill.[66] The *Freeman's Journal* reported on 17 March that the delegation had been well received. It is stated that Manners had been under the impression that the libraries had refused to make submissions to the commission, and were not particularly interested in the privilege. In the event all the alarms and excursions were redundant – the bill was never dis-cussed in parliament due to pressure of business.

There were some further hints at changes in the legal deposit law in the 1890s, which were most sternly met by a barrage of letters to the other libraries from Edward Byron Nicholson, librarian at the Bodleian. But these projected changes too came to nothing. Trinity library's most pressing prob-lem at this date was again the lack of storage space. The east pavilion of the library building was remodelled twice in the 1880s to provide more shelving, and still the books poured in. Parliamentary papers and patents were especial problems.[67] A radical solution was called for, which is only hinted at in the

63 Partridge, pp 329-31.
64 Partridge, pp 89-90.
65 Library Minute book (cuttings of this and other reports pasted in), Feb., Mar. 1879, MUN/LIB/2/4, f. 142ff.
66 Board Register, 8 Mar. 1879, MUN/V/5/14.
67 Library Minute Book, 17 Dec. 1886, MUN/LIB/2/4.

muniments. Late in 1896 two workers were employed to sort out material, mostly Indian Papers and patents. One of their duties was to assemble waste-paper for dispatch to Drimnagh Paper Mills. Over a period of four months 170 sacks were sent off to be pulped and there can be no doubt that legal deposit material was silently included.[68] Another solution was to pass on novels and suchlike books to workhouses and hospitals. The first evidence we have of this at this period is on 8 July 1897 when 146 novels were sent to the North Dublin Union workhouse. Once the authorities had steeled themselves to take this course the floodgates seem to have opened. The seventeenth of February 1899 saw a van load of papers being sent to the National Library, and on 18 September Charles Soule, a Boston (Mass.) book dealer, purchased 807 volumes for £40. The fourteenth of March 1902 saw the dispatch of boxes of novels to the troops in South Africa. There proved to be a great demand for these and over the following years hundreds of novels were disposed of in this way. With the start of the Great War these numbers grew into thousands, even prisoners of war benefiting. This means of creating space continued at least down to 1920.[69] One of the most radical clearouts occurred in July 1918, no doubt sanctioned as part of the war effort. 778 volumes of patents for the period 1876-88, which had lain in the basement of the Engineering School since 1902, were sent to be pulped. Consciences must have been pricked, however, because a note is added to the reference in the library minute book: 'These vols. have never been asked for by readers and as a matter of fact were inaccessible.'[70]

Despite the fact that the library was discarding some of the lesser-used material, pursuit of recently-published works was still assiduously carried out. *The English Catalogue of Books*, *Willings Press Guide*, *The Bookseller*, the *Musical Times* and the *Publishers' Circular* were all scanned for information on publications at this time. And the library staff went even further. S.E. Brambell wrote to the agent in March 1919 informing him that 'We find the Dublin publishers as a rule very willing to recognize the obligations, but as there is no general list of books pubd. in Dublin we have to note them in the shop windows & local newspapers.'[71] The agent for his part was reluctant to press some claims if he thought it would upset good working relationships with various publishers. Thus in November 1896 Eccles advised against hounding Eyre and Spottiswoode for the second editon of Sharpe's *Students' handbook to the Psalms*; it was merely a stereotyped reprint with a memoir added. And as Eyre and Spottiswoode sent their books spontaneously,

68 Library Minute Book, 21 Sept. 1896 ff., MUN/LIB/2/7.
69 Library Minute Book, 8 July 1897 onwards, MUN/LIB/2/7.
70 Library Minute Book, 25 July 1918, MUN/LIB/2/7.
71 Letter, Brambell to Bradford, 7 Mar. 1919, MUN/LIB/22/20/556.

he was loath to start claiming from them in case 'that very laudable practice' ceased.[72]

Not all books were so assiduously sought. In September 1901 Eccles wrote to the librarian, T.K. Abbott, informing him that he had written to the University Press Ltd claiming books on sexual matters 'which profess to be scientific'. Among the books mentioned were Mortimer's *Chapters on human love*, Ellis's *Studies in the psychology of sex*, and Tarnowski's *Sexual instinct and its morbid manifestations*. Eccles had received a negative reply from the publisher and asked for instructions. The letter is annotated 'Dr A. doesn't want the books'.[73] (There remains to this day in the Special Collections' closed stacks a small cache of such 'tabooed' books, unrecorded in the public catalogues; they are mixed in with other works withdrawn by publishers for various legal reasons.)

The agency had become very streamlined under Eccles. By 1889 it was being called the 'Agency of the University Libraries', as its claim forms attest.[74] In February 1903 it had to move from Great James's Street to larger premises in Chapel Street off Bedford Row, a move made necessary by the growth in the number of deposits.[75] In a memorandum of June 1910 Eccles recorded the numbers of boxes dispatched to each library in previous years:[76]

1881	34
1890	42
1900	49
1905	63
1909	68
1910 (to end of May)	32

Eccles was preparing for his retirement. In July 1911 his assistant of 27 years standing, J.G. Bradford, took over the agency, assisted by Frederick G. Osborne; Osborne himself became head in January 1922.[77]

In 1910 a new bill was drafted to consolidate the law of copyright throughout the Empire. This became the Copyright Act of 1911 (1 & 2 Geo. V c.46). During the discussions on the bill it was again threatened that the legal deposit privilege might be withdrawn from all but the British Museum. Francis Jenkinson, librarian at Cambridge, was most vocal in defence of the right,

72 Letter, Eccles to Brambell, 17 Nov. 1896, MUN/LIB/22/20/116.
73 Letter, Eccles to Abbott, 27 Sept. 1901, MUN/LIB/22/20/163.
74 Printed claim form, 1889, MUN/LIB/22/20/97.
75 Correspondence, 11 Feb. 1903, MUN/LIB/22/20/144.
76 Memorandum, Eccles, 1 June 1910, MUN/LIB/22/20/286.
77 Board Register, 1 July, 10 Oct. 1911, MUN/V/5/20/157, 165; correspondence from Agency being signed by Osborne, Jan. 1922 onwards, MUN/LIB/22/20/639 ff.

stressing the importance of preserving the national literature; one copy in the British Museum, he argued, was too vulnerable to destruction (as the looming war was soon to prove).[78] Trinity too defended its rights, sending a detailed memorandum to selected peers. It is evident that Trinity feared that its privilege might even be transferred to the National Library. The memorandum stressed that the Trinity library was much richer in older books than was the national institution. There followed the enlightened statement quoted at the head of this article. In the event the status quo as regards the legal deposit libraries remained. The act also finally abolished the requirement that books had to be registered at Stationers' Hall.

The publishers were incensed that the legal deposit obligation had survived. Bradford reported in despair: 'The new act enraged the trade & though there are certain publishers who still send spontaneously there are a lot from whom I have to claim.'[79] Several of the larger firms had been ignoring demands from the agency, Heinemann, Hodder and Stoughton, Ward, Lock and Co. among them.[80] Trinity was having difficulty in getting G.T. Rivoira's *Lombardic architecture*, published by Heinemann, and W.B. Yeats's *Collected works* in eight volumes, printed at the Shakespeare Head Press.[81] In May 1912 Abbott wrote to Jenkinson asking what Cambridge was doing about defaulting publishers. While counselling caution, Jenkinson stated that Constable was one of the most blatant defaulters, and that it might be time to mount 'an attack on him'.[82] It is not clear if any legal action followed, but it is likely that it did not. The legal deposit libraries seldom brought publishers to court and there is no evidence in the muniments that Trinity ever did so. A letter from each library was usually sufficient. Such was the case with Martin Secker, whom Bradford found 'contumacious'. The Bodleian and Cambridge only got satisfaction from him after threats of legal action. J.G. Smyly, librarian since 1914, wrote to him in March 1921 enclosing a list of books claimed. They were delivered to the agency shortly afterwards.[83]

The spate of transport and general strikes in the first two decades of this century caused chaos at the agency. Books mounted up awaiting the return of empties to London, on occasions forcing the agent to rent more space for storage. After one prolonged crisis Bradford wrote in ecstatic relief: 'Mirabile dictu! 11 empties I found on coming back from grub to-day, I felt I ought to take a week's holiday to celebrate it, now that we shall get rid of the Dublin

---

78 Partridge, p. 107ff.
79 Letter, Bradford to TCD, 17 June 1914, MUN/LIB/22/20/415.
80 List of books claimed by the Agency, May 1911, MUN/LIB/22/20/309.
81 Letter, Brambell to Bradford, 17 May 1912, MUN/LIB/22/20/331.
82 Letter, Jenkinson to Abbott, 31 Oct. 1912, MUN/LIB/22/20/344.
83 Letter, Bradford to TCD, 1 Mar. 1920, MUN/LIB/22/20/553. Draft of letter, Smyly to Secker, 7 Mar. 1921, and outcome, MUN/LIB/22/20/608-9, 616.

stacking ...'[84] The circumstances of the Great War added to the woes. Pickfords organized the transport of the cases, using the London and North Western Railway and its associated steamers on the Irish Sea. This line was appropriated by the government during the war and transport had to be shifted to the Great Western Railway, connecting to Fishguard.[85] The war also introduced another cause for concern. In 1915 Bradford reported a recent air raid – 'damage within a minute's walk of here is shocking.' All the legal deposit libraries were alarmed and arranged for further insurance to cover losses through enemy action.[86]

The cost of the agency had been growing steadily in the first decades of the century, reflecting the increased workload and also the huge rises in inflation of this period. In 1900 the annual cost was £404, which was £101 for each of the four libraries. At the end of the war in 1918 it had increased to £600. Two years later it had almost doubled to £1,105.[87] The bursar, not unnaturally, was alarmed at the increases in the cost of the agency, but there was little that could be done. The college in general was in deep financial trouble and was appealing to the government for state funds. Meanwhile storage in the library was again in crisis and the stables attached to the Provost's House had to be used for the overflow.[88] And at the same time Independence loomed, adding uncertainty about its legal deposit status to the library's woes. Another chapter in the history of the library was about to begin.

APPENDIX – LIST OF AGENTS

Some dates are indicative of earliest evidence found, and therefore are not absolute dates of appointment or dismissal.

Date	*Agent*	*Stationers' Hall*
1802, May	Cadell & Davies	George Greenhill
1816, Apr.	George Greenhill	
1822, Dec.	Robert A. Durham	
1834, Dec.	Hodges & Smith (Dublin; Mawer Cowtan sub-agent in London)	
1837, Apr.	Robert Cowtan	

84 Letter, Bradford to TCD, 3 June 1921, MUN/LIB/22/20/623.
85 Letter, Bradford to TCD, 23 Dec. 1914, MUN/LIB/22/20/439.
86 Letter, Bradford to TCD, 15 Sept. 1915, MUN/LIB/22/20/465.
87 Library Minute Book, 18 Apr. 1922, MUN/LIB/2/7.
88 Library Minute Book, 10 Oct. 1921, 10 May 1922, MUN/LIB/2/7.

Date	Agent	Stationers' Hall
1845, Mar.	Joseph Greenhill	Joseph Greenhill
1863, Sept.	Gregory W. Eccles	
1870, May	Unknown	
1872?, Feb.	Revd Dr T.S. Gray	
1877, June	G.W. Eccles	
1911, July	J.G. Bradford	
1922, Jan.	Frederick G. Osborne	

GROWTH IN THE PRINTED BOOKSTOCK

N.B. the numbers represent volumes not individual works; a volume might contain many pamphlets. The figures include purchases and gifts and therefore can only indicate the general trend of legal deposit intake.

Year	Count	Increase	Year	Count	Increase
1836	78,686		1860	135,592	2,343
1837	81,721	3,035	1861	137,332	1,740
1838	83,814	2,093	1862	140,138	2,806
1839	86,452	2,638	1863	142,335	2,197
1840	88,036	1,584	1864	145,209	2,874
1841	90,677	2,641	1865	148,238	3,029
1842	92,643	1,966	1866	150,337	2,099
1843	94,831	2,188	1867	152,759	2,422
1844	96,002	1,171	1868	155,409	2,650
1845	97,227	1,225	1869	158,217	2,808
1846	98,918	1,691	1870	159,654	1,437
1847	100,634	1,716	1871	161,511	1,857
1848	101,962	1,328	1872	164,137	2,623
1849	103,898	1,936	1873	167,433	3,299
1850	104,578	680	1874	171,072	3,639
1851	106,138	1,560	1875	174,340	3,268
1852	109,485	3,347	1876	178,011	3,671
1853	113,159	3,674	1877	181,624	3,613
1854	115,908	2,749	1878	185,316	3,692
1855	119,400	3,492	1879	188,383	3,067
1856	126,095	6,695	1880	191,270	2,887
1857	128,780	2,685	1881	194,616	3,346
1858	130,954	2,174	1882	187,305	2,689
1859	133,249	2,295	1883	199,603	2,138

Year	Count	Increase	Year	Count	Increase
1884	202,037	2,434	1904	285,206	6,498
1885	204,519	2,482	1905	291,580	6,374
1886	207,312	2,793	1906	297,009	5,429
1887	210,114	2,802	1907	303,189	6,180
1888	213,291	3,177	1908	309,511	6,322
1889	216,303	3,012	1909	315,148	5,637
1890	219,398	3,095	1910	321,347	6,199
1891	222,648	3,250	1911	327,402	6,055
1892	226,091	3,443	1912	333,110	5,708
1893	229,531	3,440	1913	338,854	5,744
1894	233,084	3,553	1914	343,946	5,092
1895	236,597	3,513	1915	349,010	5,064
1896	239,806	3,227	1916	353,071	4,061
1897	242,865	3,059	1917	356,925	3,854
1898	249,853	6,988	1918	359,021	2,096
1899	255,296	5,443	1919	362,871	3,850
1900	262,048	6,752	1920	365,784	2,913
1901	267,909	4,861	1921	369,091	3,307
1902	273,080	5,171	1922	372,413	3,322
1903	278,708	5,628			

Sources: Library Minute Books, MUN/LIB/2/3-4, especially list near the beginning of the latter volume, and Library Annual Reports, MUN/LIB/17/Box 1.

The Library as Revealed in the Parliamentary Commission Report of 1853

ANNE WALSH

A revealing account of the library of Trinity College Dublin almost 150 years ago can be gleaned from the findings of the Dublin University Commission at work between 1851 and 1853.[1] The older universities of England and Ireland were under scrutiny at this period and the commission was established to enquire into the state, discipline, studies and revenues of the university. There was a widespread feeling that the universities were too limited, both in the subjects they taught and in the social classes from which they drew. In addition to sectarian exclusiveness, their critics also accused them of inefficiency, medievalism and sloth. Oxford and Cambridge were similarly under review with parallel commissions appointed in April 1850 to inquire into the finances and educational work of these institutions.[2] The nature of the examination was by means of 36 papers of written questions directed to the relevant officers of the college. At Trinity the co-operation received from the college authorities was greatly appreciated, and because of the completeness of the information supplied it was considered unnecessary to address enquiries to other members of the university. 'Our proceedings ... have been greatly facilitated by the spirit in which our communications have been received by the different officers of the College, and by the promptness and courtesy with which they have replied to our inquiries'.[3] The commission worked steadily for eighteen months and sent in its report early in 1853.

The librarian of the day was James Henthorn Todd, an eminent scholar who obtained a fellowship in 1831, was elected treasurer of St Patrick's

---

1 *Report of Her Majesty's commissioners appointed to inquire into the state, discipline, studies and revenues of the University of Dublin, and of Trinity College; together with appendices, containing evidence, suggestions, and correspondence*; report pp 74-9; evidence pp 171-80 [1637], H.C. 1852-53, xlv. (Hereafter cited as *Dublin University Commission*, 1853.)

2 *Royal Commission to inquire into state, discipline, studies and revenues of University and Colleges of Oxford: report, evidence*, appendix [1482], H.C.1852, xxii.i. (Hereafter cited as *Oxford University Commission*, 1852); *Royal Commission on state, discipline, studies and revenues of University and Colleges of Cambridge*, report, evidence, appendix [1559], H.C.1852-53, xliv.i (Hereafter cited as *Cambridge University Commission*, 1853.)

3 *Dublin University Commission*, 1853, p. 2.

Cathedral in 1837, became regius professor of Hebrew in the university in 1849 and held the position of president of the Royal Irish Academy for five years from 1856. He was appointed assistant librarian in 1834, a position he retained until 1850 when he resigned, and had no further official connection with the library until February 1852 when he was elected librarian on the resignation of Charles William Wall. Todd was the chief promoter of the Irish Archaeological Society, and for it he edited the Irish version of the *Historia Britonum of Nennius*, with a translation and notes, and the *Liber Hymnorum*. He was the author of introductions to the works of other contributors to the publications of the same society, and he edited the *Wars of the Gaedhill and the Gaill* for the Master of the Rolls' series. His other major publications include the *Life of St Patrick* (1864) and the *Catalogue of graduates who have proceeded to degrees in the University of Dublin* (1866).[4]

The report sets out in detail how the library operated. The provost and senior fellows were responsible for the appointment of library staff. They inspected the library on an annual basis and received an annual report from the librarian as head of department. William Lee was appointed assistant librarian in 1850 for a five year period, and shortly after his appointment as librarian, Todd was successful in obtaining permission from the board to nominate a second assistant to be paid out of his own salary on condition that he also be given the post of senior lecturer or bursar. The librarian's salary was £115 8s. and his assistant earned £60 per annum. The second assistant also received £60 a year, reducing Todd's salary to £55 8s. The other library personnel included five clerks and four attendants or porters. The library was financed by two sources namely grants made by the board from the general funds of the college, and from fees. Every student admitted to a degree contributed a portion of his fees to the library. For example, a *filius nobilis* for the bachelor's degree made a contribution of £1 17s., a doctor of law or of medicine £3 3s., and a doctor of divinity contributed £4 4s. In 1851, the library received £484 7s. 9d. from college fees, and in addition the board allocated £667 15s. 1d. to the library fund. The salaries of the librarian, wages of porters, repairs of furniture, painting and other incidental charges were paid out of the general funds of the college.

Todd was suitably qualified to answer the questions posed by the commissioners. A total of 71 questions was addressed to the librarian covering all aspects of library policy and administration. Based on the evidence received, the commissioners were in a position to make comments on the service, and recommendations for the future. The library of the mid-nineteenth century comprised over 100,000 books and 1,500 manuscripts. The number of books

4 For further information on Todd, see the *Dictionary of National Biography*, and G.O. Simms, 'James Henthorn Todd', *Hermathena* no. 109 (Autumn 1969), pp 11-16.

and pamphlets received annually under the Copyright Act amounted to between three and four thousand, and about 800 items were purchased. The purchase of English books to supply deficiencies and of foreign books was entrusted to a committee appointed by the board. Foreign books accounted for the majority of purchases consuming almost 70 per cent of the budget. The library stock was counted on 20 September at the end of the library vacation, and statistics were maintained on the annual growth to the stock, the number of volumes purchased and receipts by donation. Fifty-two books were donated to the library in 1853 including the *United States patent laws* and *Statistics of American railroads*. Material was also donated by the United States Government, the British Archaeological Society and the East India Company.[5] In the summer of 1852 some books were stolen from the library by a member of the cleaning staff. The theft was quickly discovered and all the books were ultimately recovered. This initiated changes in maintenance procedures, and in 1853 the library was cleaned before the books were counted and not afterwards as had previously been the practice. The work was now carried out by the porters and some assistants for whom they were responsible.[6]

Books were generally accessible to readers in the library within a month of receipt except when binding was required and delayed availability for at least three or four weeks. The library did encounter problems with commercial binding. In October 1852 Todd wrote a letter of complaint to Frederick Pilkington, a bookbinder with premises in Middle Abbey Street, Dublin. The nature of his complaint was twofold. He was not satisfied with the quality of the work or with the unreasonable length of time it took to complete the task. At this period Pilkington was paid almost £200 for his annual services to the library. Todd insisted that all library books in his possession were to be returned within a month, and in future he intended pursuing a new arrangement regarding binding.[7] However, three years later Todd was again in communication with Pilkington to complain about the inconvenience experienced in the library due to the length of time the books were detained at binding. On this occasion Todd provides information on the extent of the problem which was now intolerable. Books dispatched eight months previously were still not returned, and books 'sent for classing' were detained for at least six months.[8]

Considering the extent and value of the collections, the commissioners expressed surprise at the low level of usage. Plans to convert the Divinity

5 TCD Library, Library Minute Book, Report on the library for the year ending 1853, MUN/LIB/2/4. (Hereafter all MSS refs. are to TCD Library).
6 Ibid.
7 Ibid., 23 October 1852.
8 Ibid., 15 June 1855.

School on the ground floor of the library building at the east end into a reading room were approved in July 1846. The reading room was opened two years later and for the first three years of its existence the average number of daily readers was 47 and the greatest number in any one day during that period was 90. The opening hours – except during a vacation of six weeks and a few special holidays – were from 9 a.m. to 4 p.m. in summer, and from 10 a.m. to 3 p.m. in winter. The library statutes at this period limited the use of the library to graduates resident in the college, but this restriction had not generally been insisted on. During the period 1848-1853 the number of non-graduate admissions averaged nine per annum, and never rose above twenty. In 1852 only three non-graduates were allowed access to the library, and two were admitted in 1853.[9] All graduates were apparently admitted but this privilege was not extended to the undergraduate community. The clause in the statutes which prohibited the admission of undergraduates was considered objectionable, and in 1851 a committee was appointed to consider this and other obsolete clauses with a view to dispense with them. The outstanding objections to admitting undergraduates to the library centred on the 'danger of injudicious reading', and the expense of providing attendants. The commissioners however, strongly recommended that the privilege of admission be extended to undergraduates and asserted that the system of dockets had a great tendency to check 'desultory' reading, and could also be employed as a means of testing by observation the use which undergraduates would make of the library.

> We do not think, therefore, that any class of them should now be excluded, from a *priori* considerations of the extent to which they might abuse the privilege, but only on its being clearly ascertained that a considerable number of them had abused it.[10]

However, the undergraduates continued to be denied access to the library until 1856 when the librarian was empowered to issue admission tickets for six months to undergraduates who had passed their final senior freshman examination. These tickets were renewable provided the student remained on the college books.[11] At the Bodleian in Oxford there was little difficulty in undergraduates gaining admission to the library, and it was recommended that they should have every facility and every encouragement to make use of the collections.[12] Similarly at Cambridge undergraduates frequently obtained

9   Ibid., Report on the library for the year ending 1853.
10 *Dublin University Commission*, 1853, p. 76.
11 Library Minute Book, Decree of the Board of Visitors, 13 February 1856, MUN/LIB/2/4.
12 *Oxford University Commission*, 1852, p. 119.

the use of library facilities, although they were not entitled to the privileges enjoyed by graduates of consulting the catalogues and taking down the books from the shelves.

The provost, fellows and college professors were allowed to remove the books from the shelves and replace them without submitting a docket for their use. All other readers were denied access to the shelves and forbidden to read in the recesses, windows or on the short bookcases. In order to obtain a book they were obliged to submit a docket to the library attendant who fetched it on the reader's behalf. The average daily number of dockets recorded was 41 and the greatest number in any one day was 63. The docket system was introduced in 1843 to prevent books being lost and misplaced and appears to have worked satisfactorily. In almost a decade only two volumes were reported as missing: Lucianus, *Excerpta quaedam ex Luciani operibus*, Dublin 1819, and Taylor, *Notes of a tour in the manufacturing districts of Lancashire*, London 1842. Both of these books were recovered by the library and are currently in place at their original locations.[13] The British Museum, the Bodleian and other large libraries had adopted a similar docket system to control their stock. Borrowing privileges were restricted to the senior members of the college (the provost, fellows and professors) who were permitted to borrow a maximum of six books from the uncatalogued stock in the librarian's room. The borrower was obliged to return the books by 21 March and 21 November without any notice or demand being sent to the reader. All books not returned on these designated days were ordered by the librarian, and the account sent to the bursar who forwarded the charge to the borrower.[14]

Prior to 1838 undergraduates at Trinity were also excluded from the Lending Library. This library had been in existence in the eighteenth century, but was re-organized in some unspecified way in 1800 and occupied the ground floor room at the west end of the library. The collection consisted mainly of books bequeathed to the college by Claudius Gilbert and Provost Richard Murray. The Lending Library served as a venue for law lectures and was often referred to as the Law School. Some divinity lectures and examinations were also held in this room. Students on the college books who had taken the library oath were allowed to borrow, with the exception of the divinity and mathematical books which were made available for loan only to students who attended these lectures. In the early decade of the century the books were issued 'on a certificate from the professor or lecturer whom they attended, that they were deserving of such an extraordinary indulgence'. In order to borrow a student was required to deposit with the librarian a sum equal to the value of the book which was then sealed and deposited in an iron box and retained until the book

13 Shelfmarks TT.gg.28 and E.t.48.
14 Board Register, 17 November 1849, MUN/V/5/9.

was returned in good order. The library was open during term from 1 p.m. to 3 p.m. on Tuesdays and Fridays, and out of term for the same two hour period on Fridays only. Heavy fines were imposed on those whose books were overdue. In consequence of the elaborate rules and the fact that there were rarely any additions of new books on the shelves, students did not utilize the Lending Library and very few were in fact aware of its existence.

In 1838, at the instigation of Todd, reforms were introduced extending the use of the Lending Library to all students on the college books. The library oath was not imposed and no deposit was required in order to borrow books. The opening hours however were still restrictive with borrowing facilities available from 3 p.m. to 4 p.m. on Tuesdays and Thursdays only. On admission a catalogue of the collection was given to each reader for which he paid one shilling. A student was entitled to borrow a maximum of two books at any one time on a two-week or monthly loan, and the fine for late returns was two shillings and six pence. Returns were accepted on Saturdays from 3 p.m. to 4 p.m. only. In 1838-9 £200 was granted by the board for the purchase of books, and subsequently £50 per annum was granted for that purpose. The selection of books to purchase for the Lending Library was entrusted to the junior dean who was invariably elected librarian. Foreign books were selected and purchased by Todd from 1834 to 1845, when the duty of purchasing all books was transferred to a committee nominated by the board. There was also a 'Want Book' kept in the reading room in which readers were invited to enter the details of books recommended for the library to purchase. The librarian and junior dean would subsequently submit to the board which of these books they would recommend to be purchased. In 1855 the duty of superintending the Lending Library was transferred from the junior dean to the librarian, and it was from this date considered a department of the library. A fixed sum of £560 was now allocated annually to defray the expenses of book purchases and binding both for the main library and the Lending Library.[15] By the mid-century the library held a stock of about 3,000 volumes, and Todd was confident that it now contained all the books necessary for undergraduate academic studies. The number of books borrowed annually from this collection represented a quarter of the number of dockets used in the main library.[16] The 'Borrowers' book'[17] records an average of 226 issues a month from the Lending Library during the period May 1849 to April 1850 when the undergraduate population was 1,096.

At Cambridge lending books were borrowed from the library on a ticket signed by a member of the senate. Graduates were entitled to borrow a max-

15 Board Register, 19 December 1855, MUN/V/5/10.
16 *Dublin University Commission*, 1853, pp 78, 176.
17 Lending Library Books, 1849-54, MUN/LIB/8/6.

imum of ten books and an undergraduate was entitled to five, provided his
ticket was counter-signed by his tutor. The borrowing period extended for
three months. Despite the generous lending arrangements, it was apparently
very rare for a student to fail to return a book, and when this did occur he
was compelled to replace it. Cambridge University Library was in fact further prepared to consider admitting 'strangers' to its reading-room 'in accor-
dance with the liberal principle which has been so generally acted upon by
the University of late years of throwing open their collections of every kind
as widely as was deemed consistent with their safety.'[18] This liberal approach
is in stark contrast to the policy adopted at the Bodleian where it was forbidden to remove any book from the library. There were objections raised to
such a restriction and examples of the library of Göttingen, and of many
others on the continent, of the university library at Cambridge, and of the
Advocate's Library at Edinburgh, were cited as proof of the advantages in
relaxing such a stringent rule.[19]

During the summer vacations arrangements were made at Trinity to allow
visitors view the library at certain hours and a book was kept in which one
of each party was required to sign and include his address and the number
of his party. Tourists from around the world signed the register, and during
the six-month period from May to October 1853, 18,675 people visited the
library. The busiest day was 30 August, the day after the Queen's arrival in
Dublin, when 519 people paid the library a visit.[20]

Connected with the use of the library was the question of providing a catalogue of the stock. Sometime after the publication of the Bodleian Catalogue
in 1843, an interleaved copy of it was annotated with TCD shelfmarks and
additions, and this served as a reading room catalogue. A catalogue of the
Lending Library was printed every three or four years,[21] and the printing of
a catalogue of the main library was begun in December 1848. The progress
of this catalogue was very slow as Todd was the 'sole superintendent of so
difficult and laborious a work'. He had undertaken the task without any remu-
neration or salary and up to July 1852, only 26 sheets, not extending beyond
letter A of the catalogue, were printed off.[22] There were also at least 5,000
volumes remaining uncatalogued in the librarian's room. As a result an additional clerk was recruited specifically to deal with the cataloguing arrears, and

18 *Cambridge University Commission*, 1853, p. 132.
19 *Oxford University Commission*, 1852, p. 117.
20 Library Minute Book, Report on the library for the year ending 1853, MUN/LIB/2/4.
21 Lending Library Books, MUN/LIB/8. Catalogues covering the period *c.*1830-1894.
22 For a detailed consideration of the Catalogue see V. Kinane and A. O'Brien, ' "The vast
    difficulty of cataloguing": the Printed Catalogue of TCD (1864-1887)', *Libraries & Culture*
    vol. 23 no. 4 (Fall 1988) pp 427-49.

a year later the backlog had decreased to between 1,500 and 2,000 volumes.[23] The purpose of the catalogue was to provide a complete description of the books 'perfectly arranged'. The analytical approach adopted by the librarian was somewhat criticized by the commissioners who recognized that such a catalogue possessed great value from a bibliographical point of view; but they considered a list of books arranged alphabetically, or according to subjects to be sufficient. Increasing the use of the library was paramount, and such a catalogue could be completed within a reasonable time, and at a moderate expense. To help make this a reality, it was recommended that a parliamentary grant might defray at least half the cost. The liberal-minded commissioners recommended that admission should also be granted to the public for a limited period on any respectable recommendation. They viewed the library as a national as well as a collegiate institution because of its privilege of receiving a copy of every book published in the 'British dominions' under the Copyright Acts:[24]

> The publication of the catalogue, with the more liberal concession of admission to the reading-room, would give to the reading public in Dublin all the advantages which the Library of the British Museum secures to the same class in London.[25]

The commissioners questioned the librarian on the practical applications of Legal Deposit, and specifically on whether the privilege extended to all books published in the colonies. Todd's understanding was that the terms of the Act applied to books published in the United Kingdom only. As no means existed of ascertaining what books were published in the colonies, it would have been impossible to enforce a claim to them.

The board drew the attention of the commissioners to what it regarded as a defect in the Copyright Act, and proposed a modification so as to place every privileged library on the same footing as the British Museum. In the case of the British Museum the onus was on the publisher to deliver his book, whereas the other libraries were obliged to demand it within a year from the date of publication. This procedure entailed not only considerable expense and delay but also enabled publishers to evade the intention of the Act, as it was extremely difficult to prove demand within the time required.[26] It was the duty of one of the library clerks to examine the advertisements and booksellers' lists, and to

23 Board Register, 28 January 1854, MUN/V/5/10.
24 1836 Act (6 & 7 Will. IV c.110); 1842 Imperial Copyright Act (5 & 6 Vict. c.45).
25 *Dublin University Commission*, 1853, p. 77.
26 The libraries at Cambridge and Oxford similarly objected to this defect in the Copyright Act.

communicate with Joseph Greenhill, the warehouse keeper of the Company of Stationers in London, who was the accredited agent of the college for demanding books in London. Parcels were received from Stationers' Hall on a monthly basis, and usually contained books published within the preceding six months. Books not received via this route were demanded by letter addressed to the publishers. Todd felt confident that since the appointment of permanent clerks to examine the publishers' catalogues, the library received nearly all that could legally be claimed. Occasionally, difficulties did arise with regard to ascertaining the exact time of a book's publication or who the real publisher was. A bookseller in an advertisement may have represented himself as acting merely as the publisher's agent, and tracking down the actual publisher often proved difficult. On the representation of Greenhill, the librarian wrote 'severally' to eleven London booksellers in 1855 stating that if they did not comply with the Act, legal proceedings would be instituted immediately.[27] The librarian admitted that children's books, school books, the 'inferior class of novels, and insignificant publications of various kinds' were not placed in the library, but were stored in large chests and boxes. Lists of these items were maintained, but due to shortage of space they were not very easily accessible.

The college officers not only utilized the library for academic purposes but also borrowed material for their leisure reading. The 'Light reading borrowers' book 1857-1869'[28] reveals some interesting insights on the reading habits of the college lecturers and on the works of fiction they chose purely for enjoyment. The register is scant in detail and merely records the date and title of the book under the borrower's name. No information is provided on the lending period or whether the book was ever returned. The most enthusiastic readers of the period were Todd and his successor John Adam Malet; William Lee, John Anster and Edward Perceval Wright. During 1865 for example, Todd borrowed 70 books from this category; 16 in June presumably to entertain him over the summer and 14 in November to help shorten the winter. Malet was also an avid reader of fiction and on 1st April 1868 succeeded in borrowing 27 books. Todd's housekeeper was very privileged and allowed to borrow works of fiction in 1862 and 1863. These items were recorded under Todd's name. At the back of the register the books borrowed by a Mrs Hitchcock are itemized. Her reading list extending throughout the period 1857 to 1869 is very impressive and occupies several pages. No information is given on the status of this woman or what connections she had with TCD. However, we can assume that she was married to Richard Hitchcock, a library clerk, whose salary receipts for the period 1849-56 survive.[29] He

27 Library Minute Book, 10 April 1855, MUN/LIB/2/4.
28 Records of the use of printed books, MUN/LIB/6/17.
29 Library Accounts, MUN/LIB/11/23; MUN/LIB/11/32; MUN/LIB/11/34.

would have been in an ideal position to keep his wife updated on the latest works of fiction as his duties included claiming publications under the Copyright Act, and dealing with new material before it was catalogued.[30]

At Cambridge the librarian, Joseph Power,[31] shared Todd's objections to the great number of children's books received under the Copyright Act:

> I have taken upon myself to deprecate the sending of infantile publications ... which served only to swell out the lists inconveniently and to embarrass us at the library.[32]

The commissioners at Cambridge cast further aspersion on the Act, regarding the majority of legal deposit material as being of little worth or better suited for a popular circulating library. They recommended that the legal deposit requirements of the Act be commuted for a money payment to be expended in purchasing and binding worthwhile material, and favoured the exclusion of works of a 'frivolous' nature. They maintained that with these adjustments the use of the library would be confined to those who required it and not as a substitute for an ordinary book-club.[33]

Power made a visit to TCD library and was highly impressed by the accurate and systematic records maintained by Todd and his clerks. He paid special tribute to the registers describing them as extremely beautiful 'harmonizing as it does in the most complete and convenient manner with the binding, placing and cataloguing of the books'. His admiration for the library extended to his desire to model its procedures and establish 'as far as possible the exact system of Trinity College Dublin'.[34] The visiting librarian also commented on the spacious and lofty working conditions. In particular, he paid tribute to the facilities provided for the clerks, suitably supplied with desks, tables and shelves for receiving, collecting and distributing the incoming material. Todd however, was concerned about improving conditions in the library and in particular making easier access to the books on the gallery. When for example, the reading room attendant was requested to fetch books at the east end of the gallery, the route he was obliged to take involved walking the whole length of the library four times and repeating the journey four times when replacing the books. Todd considered two possible courses of action to remedy this inconvenience. A spiral staircase connected the reading room on the ground floor of the east pavilion with the Fagel library above.

30 Library Minute Book, 29 September 1848, MUN/LIB/2/4.
31 Joseph Power (1798-1868) remained librarian at Cambridge for 19 years, until he retired in 1864.
32 *Cambridge University Commission*, 1853, p. 56.
33 Ibid., p. 129.
34 Ibid., p. 59.

A proposed solution was to extend it into the manuscript room on the level above that again, thus gaining access to the north gallery. This plan would not however have been ideal because it would cause draughts in the reading room. Todd's preferred solution was to construct a light spiral staircase of iron at the opposite end of the Fagel library which could also be conveniently used in place of a ladder to gain access to the books in the three sides of the recess in which it would stand.[35] (In the event the spiral staircase was constructed at the east end of the Long Room.)

The board had sanctioned Todd's proposal to cater for four years' growth by erecting low bookcases in the windows of the gallery capable of holding a total of 35,200 volumes. The bookcases were cleverly designed revolving on hinges with shelves on both sides. Two of these were planned for the central part of the building where the walls are thicker, so that with the fixed shelves at the back, there were five shelves in depth and four in height. Progress had been slow and in 1852 only a small proportion of this work had been completed making room for 4,500 volumes. He similarly suggested making additional space in the Fagel library by bringing the shelves closer together and placing short bookcases in the stalls. By carrying out these minor adjustments and removing the seats and desks from the area, Todd calculated that an additional 6,500 volumes could be accommodated in the Fagel library. The manuscript room could be modelled on a similar design and a spiral staircase constructed to facilitate access to the upper room. The librarian also saw potential in converting the Law School which occupied the ground floor room at the west end of the library into a manuscript library. By this arrangement room would be created for about 17,000 volumes.[36]

With regard to the manuscript collection of 1,512 items, there was an incomplete catalogue in circulation at this time and no steps had been taken towards the printing of a catalogue. A single-volume catalogue[37] organized as a shelflist was compiled by Canon John Lyon who was appointed assistant in the library in charge of the manuscripts until he had completed his catalogue of them in 1747.[38] When the Irish Board of the Commissioners of Public Records was established in 1810 one of the sub-commissioners, Henry Joseph Monck Mason was instructed to compile a new catalogue of the college manuscripts as part of their survey of historical sources. This five-volume work

35 *The book of Trinity College Dublin 1591-1891*, Belfast 1892, pp 177-9.
36 The Law School was converted into a manuscripts room when law lectures were transferred to the Museum Building completed in 1855.
37 Catalogues and book lists, MUN/LIB/1/53.
38 In 1747 he was paid £40 for the catalogue of manuscripts and pamphlets (MUN/V/57/3), and he received further payment in 1755 for the charters he included in the same volume (MUN/V/5/3). Todd, in his evidence to the commissioners dates Lyon's catalogue to about 1780 (*Dublin University Commission*, 1853, p. 175).

was organized on a shelf basis covering cases A-M and is more detailed than Lyon's catalogue.[39] It was purchased by the college in 1837 for £120 and attempts made by Todd to have it published were unsuccessful. In 1836 John O'Donovan was employed by the board to catalogue the Irish manuscripts and according to Todd he completed 'a very minute and accurate catalogue'.[40] When Todd was appointed assistant librarian he devoted much attention to the manuscripts. His efforts included 'a tolerably complete Catalogue of the Wickliffe and Waldensian Manuscripts' and work on a catalogue of the biblical manuscripts which he abandoned due to time constraints. The commissioners recommended that the completion of a comprehensive catalogue of manuscripts was indispensable, and suggested that half the expenses should be defrayed by a parliamentary grant and the other half from the funds of the college. From 1840 the board granted £50 per annum for the purpose of transcribing Irish manuscripts and made an enormous outlay of £6,000 in the publication of the works of Archbishop Ussher under the superintendence of Charles Richard Elrington. The scholarly approach adopted by the librarian to catalogues and transcriptions was again at variance with the more practical and short-term approach preferred by the authors of the university report:

> The publication of well-selected manuscripts, at a moderate cost, is likely to excite interest in the subjects of them, and promote similar publications in future; whilst the publication of a voluminous collection, at a great expense, is likely to discourage any further efforts in the same direction.[41]

Some of the treasures in the manuscript collection had been recent purchases, and included the *Book of Dimma*: 'An Irish *Textus*, or copy of the Four Gospels, in an ante-Hieronymian Latin version, written in the seventh century, with its ancient silver shrine or *cumhdach*.'[42] The board had purchased this manuscript in 1836 for the sum of £150. For four guineas the manuscript of Keating's History of Ireland was acquired. In 1840 a collection of the manuscripts of Archbishop William King was purchased and supplemented later by a large number of autographed letters by the prelate. Joseph D'Arcy Sirr sold manuscripts collected by his father Major Sirr to the college, and in 1842 at the sale of Lord Kingsborough a collection of State Papers relating to Ireland was purchased for £89. Todd was commissioned by the

---

39 Catalogues and book lists, Monck Mason Catalogue, MUN/LIB/1/55 (MS 1708).

40 *Dublin University Commission*, 1853, p. 175; John O'Donovan's catalogue of Irish manuscripts made between 1836 and 1851, MUN/LIB/1/61.

41 *Dublin University Commission*, 1853, p. 77.

42 Ibid., p. 174.

board to attend an auction in 1849 where the Stowe manuscripts were offered for sale. He was allocated a budget of £400 but the entire collection was bought by a private collector without going to public auction. During the decade 1842-52, 89 manuscripts were acquired by the library, 78 of which were purchased and the remainder represented donations.[43]

The library at this period also had in its possession a collection of 1,881 coins bequeathed to the college by Claudius Gilbert. The majority of these were Roman silver coins; 300 remained uncatalogued, and about 300 were Roman and Greek brass coins. The collection occupied two large iron presses in the manuscript room at the east end of the library. The catalogue of Roman silver coins was compiled by the numismatist, John Adam Malet, and published at the expense of the college.[44] Malet admitted that very little interest had been expressed in the collection, and applications were seldom, if ever, made for permission to see it. The commissioners, however, blamed the low level of interest on a lack of awareness, and listed several practical suggestions to assist in promoting the collection. For example, increased interest may have been achieved by advertising the collection in the college calendar, maintaining a register of the places in which the ancient coins had been found, and extending the collection to include modern coins. They also recommended exhibiting a selection of the most interesting pieces in a glass case either in the library or museum.

The report on the university provides a fascinating overview to the workings of its departments at an interesting stage of development. The library was not harshly criticised and emerged relatively unscathed from the scrutiny. The contribution made by Todd to the library was significant in terms of his commitment to improving access to the collections by reassessing the stringent rules and regulations in force, and by his scholarly approach to cataloguing the stock and transcribing Irish manuscripts. His dedication and commitment to the job was constantly tested and he was even prepared to execute tasks at his own expense for the benefit of the library. He also adopted a strategic approach to managing the library and the policies and plans he alluded to in his evidence were progressive and student-oriented. The proposals he outlined for the interior design of the library would ultimately have resulted in the accommodation of an additional 50,000 volumes. Except on issues of cost-effectiveness with regard to catalogues, the commissioners are generally supportive of the endeavours of the librarian. The conclusions of the report reiterate and reinforce the observations of Todd as presented in his evidence, and point the way to a more inclusive and outward-looking organization.

43 Ibid.
44 John Adam Malet, *A catalogue of roman silver coins in the library of Trinity College Dublin*, Dublin 1839.

The Study of German in TCD and the Acquisition of German Language Works by the Library in the Nineteenth Century

VERONIKA KOEPER-SAUL

OVERVIEW OF NINETEENTH-CENTURY ACQUISITIONS

An inspection of the library acquisition books at Trinity College Dublin quickly reveals the great changes that took place in the nineteenth century. The needs of new subjects like civil engineering (1841), geology (1844), and modern languages (introduced in 1775) were catered for;[1] other subjects, like Irish, enjoyed renewed and systematic attention; and the foreign publications received were so numerous that they had to be registered in separate volumes.[2] Thanks to the extension of the legal deposit privileges to TCD library after the union of Great Britain and Ireland in 1800 and the acquisition of major collections, like that of the Fagel library in 1802, the general influx to the library became many times larger than that of the previous centuries.[3]

The new open-mindedness and widening of interest evident in the acquisition books reflects the shift from a theologically centered towards a scientific world-view, in which German philosophers, writers and scientists played a leading role.[4] In consequence a considerable increase in German language material can be observed in the course of the century. Under letter *A* in the foreign publication books for example numerous German journals, called *Annalen*, *Anzeiger* or *Abhandlungen* on subjects like physics, chemistry, archaeology, and Eastern studies, are listed along with German books in these sub-

---

1 See TCD Library, Registers of Publications Received, MUN/LIB/20 (all subsequent MS references are to TCD Library unless otherwise stated); Foreign Publications Books, MUN/LIB/9/3-4; J.V. Luce, *Trinity College Dublin: the first 400 years*, Dublin 1992, pp 58-9, 87-8 and 103. All TCD manuscripts quoted in this article are reproduced by kind permission of the Board of Trinity College Dublin.
2 Foreign publications were listed separately from 1843 onwards; on Irish books, see below.
3 See Peter Fox, *Trinity College Library Dublin* (1982), new ed., Dublin 1993, pp [6] and [9-10].
4 An overview of the German role in nineteenth century science is given in David Knight, *The age of science: the scientific world-view in the nineteenth century*, Oxford 1988, pp 52-69.

151

ject areas.[5] Likewise German journals named *Zeitschrift* with nineteenth-century issues on subjects such as theology, philology, archaeology, Eastern studies, geology, geography, linguistics and sciences take up a long section in the Printed Catalogue of the library, which lists acquisitions up to 1872.[6] Other German language material listed in the nineteenth-century foreign publications books treats philosophy, theology, literature, linguistics, history, astronomy, classics, geography, mathematics and medicine. In addition, there were numerous donations of German language items on these and other subjects, including geology and engineering. Separate lists of acquisitions, such as booksellers' accounts, also suggest an interest to catch up on German material during these years.[7] Exchanges with foreign societies, institutions and libraries also contributed to the accumulation of German language material at this time. Since some of the items are listed several times, e.g. in the library minute book and in the presentation book, and others only once, it is hard to give an exact account of the frequency with which German language acquisitions occurred in the different subjects. It can be said with certainty, however, that Germanic studies did not account for the largest influx of German material; items of and on German literature and language studies seem to form a background to the general picture only. Instead, the amount of German material acquired seems to be more in line with the importance given to the individual subjects at the time, with theology still taking first place overall, followed by classics, archaeology and history, with the science subjects catching up during the course of the century, evident for example in a specific order of a number of German medical works in 1872.[8]

The 20,000-volume library of the Dutch politician Greffier Fagel, incorporated into TCD library in 1802, accounted for the greatest share of the

5 The Foreign Publications Books, MUN/LIB/9/3, list for example *Anzeiger für Kunde der Deutschen Vorzeit, Annalen der Physik und Chemie* ('von Poggendorf'), and *Abhandlungen für Kunde des Morgenlandes* from 1863 onwards; books on related matters include Schumacher, *Die Krystallisation des Eises*, 1844, listed March 1853, Schaaf, *Chinesische Literatur*, Berlin 1854, listed 1854, Wachsmuth, *Hellenische Alterthumskunde*, pt. 1-9 listed 1845, and Spiegel, *Die Altpersischen Keilinschriften*, listed 1864.

6 *Catalogus librorum impressorum qui in Bibliotheca Collegii Sacrosanctae et Individuae Trinitatis ... juxta Dublin, adservantur*, Dublin 1864-87, 9 vols.

7 See e.g. Accounts of Messrs Bossange Barthes & Lowell, foreign booksellers, London, for foreign books, MUN/LIB/11/4, especially the account of 14 June 1844. Other German material was supplied by Hodges & Smith, MUN/LIB/11/5, C.J. Steward, London, MUN/LIB/13/44F, and Milliken (according to the Foreign Publications Books, e.g. Franz Bopp, *Vergleichende Grammatik*, received December 1843, from Milliken; 2nd ed. of the same received November 1852 from Lowell).

8 See A. Malet, TCD Library, letter to Hodges & Figgis concerning a proposed purchase, with a list of German medical works, MUN/LIB/13/50 a & b; A. Malet succeeded J.H. Todd as librarian in 1869; Hodges & Figgis was one of the library's regular suppliers of foreign books.

older German language material during the century. Subject areas include fine arts, geography, politics, history, social science, and theology, and the copies are particularly noteworthy for their high quality engravings in mint condition,[9] as for example in the complete run of the M. Zeiler/M. Merian *Topographia* of the German-speaking area or the *Theatrum Europaeum* volumes. Most of the German works acquired thereafter were contemporary publications, but there were also numerous donations of older German language imprints, mostly in the area of theology,[10] and even some retrospective buying of German books can be observed. In 1859, for example, the librarian James Henthorn Todd acquired a seventeenth-century work on the Apocalypse, Johannes Andreas Lucius, *Die Offenbahrung des heiligen Apostels und Evangelistens Johannis, in der Churfürstlichen Sächsischen Schloßkirche zu Dresden*, Dresden 1670.[11]

READING GERMAN AT TCD IN THE NINETEENTH CENTURY

It has been alleged that the knowledge of German was not very widespread in nineteenth-century Britain, except that, since around 1840, 'ignorance in German thought was no longer a feature in chemists. Outside their ranks, however, there were many like Darwin who struggled rather hopelessly with the language'.[12] The nineteenth-century loan books of the TCD library clearly reveal, however, that German material was read by scholars from all subject areas. The professor of German, Ignaz Abeltshauser, not surprisingly borrowed the largest quantity. Staff of German origin, like the professors for Sanskrit and assistant librarians, Rudolf Thomas Siegfried and his follower Carl Friedrich Löttner, are naturally to be expected to have read German. However, English and Irish colleagues, most of whom were clergymen, also repeatedly consulted German books, so that one may assume their language studies to have been sufficiently successful. They included the Archbishop King's lecturer in divinity, the Reverend Dr Thomas McNeece, and his assistant in this department, James William Barlow; the mathematician, theologian and later provost of the college, the Reverend George Salmon; the archae-

---

9 See Vincent Kinane, 'The Fagel collection', in Peter Fox ed., *Treasures of the library, Trinity College Dublin*, Dublin 1986, pp 158–69.

10 See for example Presentations Book, 7 December 1840, MUN/LIB/1/32, a large donation of older German imprints by Thomas Parnell.

11 Lucius's work and Matthias Hoe, *Commentariorum in beat apostoli ...*, Leipzig and Frankfurt 1671, bound in one volume, were acquired from Stewarts, London, in 1859 (see Letters, MUN/LIB/13/44-45, and Foreign Publications Book, MUN/LIB/9/3, 31 October 1859, under Hoe).

12 David Knight (cited note 4), p. 67.

ologist and mathematician the Reverend Dr Charles Graves; the classical scholar and theologian Dr William Lee; the professors for Greek, Thomas Stack and his successor John Kells Ingram, as well as the lecturers in this department, Thomas Kingsmill Abbott and Charles Ferrar; the professor of modern history, John Toleken; the professor for civil law, John Anster; the professor for Arabic, William Wright; the professor in physic, William Stokes; and last but not least, theologian, professor of Hebrew and librarian James Henthorn Todd. Apart from theology they read in German on their own subjects as well as on antiquities and historical matters. William Wright for example studied German works on linguistics, history and geography, and regularly read the *Göttinger Gelehrter Anzeiger* between 1857 and 1860; Dr Ingram studied German books on classical mythology; and the professor for medical physic and archaeological researcher Dr William Stokes, amongst other items, also consulted a German work on traditional costume.[13] German language material on philosophy, physics, music, classics, and literature were also borrowed from the library.

THE ROLE OF JAMES HENTHORN TODD

Among these and other scholars who would have had an influence on the increase of German language acquisitions in this century, the Reverend James Henthorn Todd, who served as a librarian from 1852 to his death in 1869,[14] stands out as a person with a particular long-standing interest, to whom the acquisition of several German language items can be traced back. He is known to have been a hard-working man in all the areas he dealt with: as an Irish high-churchman, TCD professor of Hebrew, supporter of the Church Educational Society, precentor of St Patrick's Cathedral, founder of St Columba's College, but most notably as a librarian and scholar of Irish studies, who founded the Irish Archaeological Society and later became president of the Royal Irish Academy.[15]

It was in the course of his pursuit of Irish studies that Todd developed his profound interest in German language, culture and antiquities. Throughout the nineteenth century questions about the Indo-Germanic origin of the Celtic languages and the precise relationship between Celtic and Germanic languages and nations caused heated debates among European scholars, especially in

---

13 In 1863.

14 An overview of his activities as a librarian is given in G.O. Simms, 'James Henthorn Todd', *Hermathena* no. 109 (Autumn 1969), pp 11–16.

15 See R.B. McDowell and D.A. Webb, *Trinity College Dublin 1592–1952: an academic history*, Cambridge 1982, pp 276–7.

Ireland and Germany. In both countries scholars were anxious to raise the level of Celtic studies from 'guess-work-etymology' to scientific standards.[16] In Ireland Todd was one of the key figures, together with George Petrie, John O'Donovan and Eugene O'Curry, who argued against the far-fetched etymological views of the then leading Irish archaeological researcher, Sir William Betham, seeking to replace his 'a priori method' with the detailed study of the ancient Irish monuments.[17] Todd in particular was untiring in uncovering, collecting, editing, translating and evaluating Irish manuscripts himself, and in recruiting and supporting collaborators for this great cause. One of the functions of the Irish Archaeological Society was to promote the translation and editing of Irish texts.[18]

As Germany was a major centre of Celtic studies in the nineteenth century,[19] Todd soon learnt about its leading scholars, such as Franz Bopp, who is thought to have been the first to prove the Indo-Germanic origin of the Celtic language in a scientifically acceptable fashion in 1839,[20] and Johann Kaspar Zeuss. Zeuss 'wrote vehemently against those who attempted to discuss historical questions without the necessary linguistic qualifications'[21] and, like Petrie and Todd, he did not hesitate to include even influential contemporaries in such a category, notably in his book *Die Herkunft der Bayern von*

---

16 Patrick M. MacSweeney, *A group of nation-builders, O'Donovan – O'Curry – Petrie*, Dublin 1913, pp 89-90, likewise pp 128-9 (on Ireland); on German-Celtic studies in the nineteenth century see Helmut Bauersfeld, *Die Entwicklung der keltischen Studien in Deutschland*, Berlin 1937 (=Schriftenreihe der 'Deutschen Gesellschaft für keltische Studien', Heft 1). Though both of these booklets have to be read with a certain scepticism, due to strong nationalist tendencies (MacSweeney rides attacks against 'foreigners' and 'faddists' (e.g. p. 10); Bauersfeld plays down non-German research, e.g. p. 20), the overall development of the discipline seems to be described adequately, and is well backed-up by the writings of the described researchers themselves.

17 For a general discussion see MacSweeney, op. cit., p. 89; on Todd in particular see his letter to O'Donovan of 25 February 1842, where he blames Betham and Vallancey (also then a member of this section of the RIA) for mistakes by the Oxford Professor James Ingram (National Library of Ireland, Letters from Todd to O'Donovan, MS 5373 no. 16). All NLI manuscripts quoted in this article are reproduced by courtesy of the National Library of Ireland.

18 See MacSweeney, op. cit., pp 18-20.

19 For information on the role of Celtic studies in Germany in the nineteenth century see Helmut Bauersfeld (cited note 16). I am most obliged to Diarmaid Ó Catháin, Cork, for sending on this article and other information on Celtic studies in Germany and Ireland to me.

20 Bauersfeld (cited note 16), p. 4. Francis Shaw, 'The Background to Grammatica Celtica', *Celtica* vol. 3 (1956) pp 1-16, argues however that this had already been proven by the Dane Rusk in 1817, whilst Bopp was still in doubt as late as 1838 (p. 3).

21 Francis Shaw, 'Johann Kaspar Zeuss', *Studies* vol. 43 (Summer 1954) pp 194-206; quote from pp 196-7.

den Markomannen (1839), where he proved the then fashionable idea of a German Celt to be entirely unfounded.[22] In 1853 he published the first comparative grammar of Celtic languages, *Grammatica Celtica*.[23] The work, written in Latin for an international readership, was greeted with enthusiasm by Celtic scholars everywhere.[24] Various letters to Todd give evidence that Zeuss's *Grammatica* was also seen as the fundamental tool for Celtic studies among the Irish Celtic scholars of Todd's acquaintance. For example, William Reeves, bishop of Down and Connor, in a letter to Todd of 18 May 1855, complained about the typical lack of understanding by the English critics of Irish publications, such as Todd's edition of an 'Antiphonary' (hymn book):[25]

> But this I know that Irish productions run two risks with the English public, namely that the Reviewer has not the *ability* or the *soul* to do them justice. Why does not the Quarterly, or Athenaeum or any of the Literary Dictators take Zeuss in hands?[26]

Similarly William Stokes, in a letter to Todd of 11 November 1858 concerning translations from the Irish, recommended reliance on what 'Zeuss correctly states'.[27] Stokes followed Todd as president of the Royal Irish Academy in 1874,[28] and in 1876 received the Prussian order *Pour le Mérite* for his medical writings. John O'Donovan, who among other things assisted Todd in the cataloguing of manuscripts in the college, had his own Irish Grammar published with Todd's support in 1845, and won the praise of leading German scholars like Bopp and Grimm; but he praised Zeuss as 'Jupiter Tonans'.[29]

Thanks to such tremendous interest, German language works on Celtic philology and antiquities acquired in the nineteenth century are plentiful in Trinity College library. In the library's Printed Catalogue of items acquired up to 1872, which is in itself another of Todd's superior legacies,[30] Zeuss fea-

---

22 Ibid., p. 197; see also pp 199 and 203 on Zeuss's fight against the 'Celtomaniacs'.

23 Johann Kaspar Zeuss, *Grammatica Celtica*, Leipzig 1853.

24 See Francis Shaw, 'Zeuss', p. 202. Francis Shaw, '*Grammatica Celtica*', p. 13, also describes the relationship between Zeuss's work and O'Donovan's *Grammar of the Irish language*, Dublin 1845.

25 *The book of hymns of the ancient Church of Ireland, edited from the original manuscript in the library of Trinity College, Dublin, with translation and notes by J.H. Todd*, pt. 1, Dublin 1855.

26 NLI, Letters to James Henthorn Todd, MS 2252, no. 34.

27 Ibid. no. 40.

28 For information on Stokes see his entry in the *Dictionary of National Biography*.

29 Patrick M. MacSweeney (cited note 16), p. 26. On O'Donovan's grammar see p. 29.

30 On the catalogue see Vincent Kinane and Ann O'Brien, '"The vast difficulty of cataloguing": the printed catalogue of Trinity College Dublin (1864-1887)', *Libraries & Culture* vol. 23 no. 4 (Fall 1988) pp 427-53.

tures not only with several editions of his *Grammatica Celtica*, but also with his earlier works *Die Deutschen und die Nachbarstämme* (Munich 1837) and *Die Herkunft der Bayern von den Markomannen gegen die bisherigen Muthmassungen bewiesen*, the latter in the second, enlarged edition (Munich 1857). Works by Franz Bopp, mostly grammars and glossaries on Sanscrit, take up an even more impressive long section in the catalogue. Another example of an acclaimed German book on the relationship between Germans and Celts, contained in the 1872 catalogue, is Adolf Holtzmann, *Kelten und Germanen: eine historische Untersuchung* (Stuttgart 1855). One could continue this list. Todd and his assistant librarian Rudolf Thomas Siegfried, and probably Stokes, whom we have quoted above, were most likely to have been the driving forces behind these acquisitions.

Siegfried, born in Dessau, Germany, in 1830, had entered the college in 1854 to study Irish[31] and was formally appointed assistant librarian in 1855,[32] a position in which he remained until his death in 1863. After the introduction of the courses in Sanskrit in 1856, Siegfried became the first lecturer of this language ever appointed in Ireland in 1858,[33] and from 1862 until his death, he served as professor in Sanskrit and comparative philology.[34] Bopp's books on the Sanskrit language would have served him and Carl Friedrich Löttner, his successor as professor and as assistant librarian, in their teaching and researches. The fact that Siegfried came to study Irish also indicates his interest in German books on Celtic languages. Indeed he even contributed a memoir of Johann Kaspar Zeuss to the *Ulster Journal of Archaeology*.[35] He seems to have gotten on particularly well with Todd.[36] Thus in a letter to

---

31 Information according to his entry in F. Boase, *Modern English biography*, 6 vols., Truro 1892-1921.

32 Information on the precise date of his appointment varies in the different sources; Boase, op. cit., give 1854 as year of appointment; the Library Minute Book 1843-1887, MUN/LIB/2/4, mentions an appointment of two assistant librarians, 'neither of whom shall be fellows' in the report for 1854, without giving any names, and under 'May 1. 1855' states 'Dr. Rudolph Thos. Siegfried Dr. Phil of Tubingen was elected by the Board Junior Assistant Librarian'. This refers to an entry in the Board Register, MUN/V/5/10, under 30 April 1855, 'Rudolf Thomas Siegfried (Doctor in Philosophy of the University of Tubingen) was elected Junior assistant Librarian, upon the recommendation of the Librarian', i.e. Todd. I suppose Siegfried in fact started his library work in 1854 and was approved in this position by the board in 1855.

33 See *Trinity College Dublin Record volume 1991*, comp. D.A. Webb, ed. J.R. Bartlett, Dublin 1992, p. 127 and Alfred W. Bennett, 'Obituary' for Rudolph Thomas Siegfried, *The Athenaeum* no. 1838 (17 January 1863), p. 88.

34 According to Boase (cited note 31).

35 See Alfred W. Bennett (cited note 33), p. 88, and S.A. Allibone, *A critical dictionary of English literature*, 3 vols, Philadelphia and London 1859-71, under Siegfried.

36 McDowell and Webb (cited note 15), p. 278, count it as Todd's achievement that he

Todd, dated 11 November 1858, William Stokes gave the following advice regarding Todd's planned edition of the manuscript Book of Leinster: 'I hope you will collate *with your own eyes* every bit you take from the bk of Leinster, & that you will print the text exactly as it stands', but then inserts, over 'with your own eyes', 'or Siegfried's'.[37] There even seems to be some evidence that Todd and Siegfried co-operated in an attempt to persuade the great master of Celtic studies in Germany, Johann Kaspar Zeuss, to come to Trinity himself. As Francis Shaw reported in his commemorative article on Zeuss, it is likely that Zeuss was about to travel to Dublin, just before he died. Zeuss had written a letter to Siegfried in July 1856:

> It is clear from Zeuss's letter that in the summer of 1856 he had received an invitation from Dr Todd, regius professor of Hebrew in Trinity College and President of the Royal Irish Academy, to come to settle in Dublin, and it is evident that some work or post was to be offered to him. In this letter Zeuss expresses his intention of accepting and discusses his plan to travel to Dublin with Siegfried who was visiting Germany at the time. ... Siegfried visited Zeuss at Kronach in the summer and found there, to use his own words, 'a dying man'.[38]

Zeuss died on 10 November 1856, and sadly Siegfried himself was soon to follow, on 10 January 1863, aged only 33. The Royal Irish Academy attended his funeral as a body, 'as a mark of respect'.[39] Siegfried is now commemorated by a bust in the Long Room of the library.

The 'tradition' that Zeuss was to become a professor at Trinity College on Todd's suggestion,[40] has been disputed by some, but there is clear evidence of Todd attempting to influence the teaching of Irish in the college, and of preparing the library in this view. On 18 June 1838 for example, he wrote to the archbishop of Tuam to win support for the establishment of 'a school of Irish in connexion with the University', which he thought 'would be more useful than any separate establishment in the country, remote from such helps as our Library supplies.'[41] Stressing that the 'Professor should be elected by public Examination', Todd asked the bishop to write to the provost

---

'attracted foreign scholars like Siegfried and C.F. Lottner to double the teaching of Sanscrit with doing both skilled and semi-skilled work in the library, and succeeded in making them happy.'

37 National Library of Ireland, Letters to Todd, MS 2252, no. 40.
38 Francis Shaw (cited note 21), p. 204.
39 Alfred W. Bennett (cited note 33), p. 88.
40 See Francis Shaw (cited note 21), p. 204, where he refers to an article in *Die frankische Presse* of 22 July 1946.
41 Letters to and by the Revd J.H. Todd, MS 2214, no. 75.

about this matter and, after apologizing for the length of his letter, concluded, the 'establishment of an Irish Professorship' had been one of his 'favourite project[s] ... for years'. The bishop correctly pointed out that Irish had already been taught at the college before, but still reassured Todd of his support.[42] According to the *Trinity College Record volume 1991* the professorship in Irish was then indeed 'founded' in 1838 and the first professor appointed in 1840.[43] Thus the idea that Todd may have tried to install the admired scholar Zeuss as a professor in Trinity College is at least a tradition that illustrates Todd's character and intentions in this field very well.

Todd's connections with the elected professors of Irish seem not to have been very strong, and the most notable Celtic scholars in the college for this period remain Todd himself and his friends and correspondents Stokes and Reeves, besides poet and Trinity graduate Sir Samuel Ferguson.[44]

As an untiring collector, editor and translator of Irish manuscripts,[45] Todd himself can clearly be shown to have added not only to the field of Irish studies, but also to have been a keen supporter of language studies including German, and a specialist in networking with European libraries. Todd's first visit to German speaking countries seems to have taken place in 1843.[46] Writing to the Reverend Dr Charles Richard Elrington, who himself had visited Germany before, knew the language and was well acquainted with Todd's archaeological interests, Todd summed up how he had criss-crossed the country West to East, North to South and back, staying 'scarcely ... more than a day or two in any one place'. Paderborn in Westphalia, however, kept him a bit longer and he gave an exceptionally detailed account of this visit. Not only had he searched for manuscripts and admired the rich antiquities, which he described, but he also had taken some very independent steps to brush up his German. Paderborn, he explained, is in 'a region not often visited by the English, where we found German manners + the German language in their purity, + where we were forced to scrape up what little we could muster of the latter in noble defiance of all number, gender, + declension', and went on:

42 See Letters to and by the Revd J.H. Todd, MS 2214. no. 76, where the bishop points out that he himself had been taught Irish at TCD. On earlier teaching of Irish in the college see J.V. Luce, *Trinity College Dublin, the first 400 years*, Dublin 1992, pp 29-30, a description of Irish classes introduced under Provost Narcissus Marsh (Provost 1679-1683) and the re-establishment of the Irish 'professorship' in 1708.

43 See *TCD Record volume 1991* (cited note 33), p. 119. The endowment was at first secured through a special fund raised by public subscription. From 1840 onwards Irish was continuously taught at the college as opposed to the earlier arrangement (see note 42).

44 See Luce (cited note 42), p. 112, where he summarizes Lecky's tercentenary speech.

45 See e.g. Simms (cited note 14), pp 11-13.

46 A very short account of this visit is also given in Simms (cited note 14), p. 13. Simms does not consider the language and cultural aspect of this journey however.

> Here also we got into the interior of the Franciscan monastery + were
> most kindly received by the monks – but what a place it was for dirt
> + abominations – the monks all grossly ignorant – there was but one
> of them that could speak a little Latin, all the rest had no tongue but
> German + seemed utterly at a loss to comprehend why we felt a dif-
> ficulty in understanding it ...47

He concluded with a promise to give Elrington a full account of what he
had seen after his return. Whatever he said about the dirt and the difficulty,
Todd must have been pleased enough with this method of self-exposure to a
genuine mother-tongue environment, as we find him applying the same
method to improve his oral Irish on Achill and Clare islands, from where he
sent similar letters.48 On 6 August 1844 he wrote to Dean R. Butler:

> by the latter end of Septr. ... I hope to be able to carry on a conver-
> sation in my native tongue – This is an excessively dull place, + affords
> but few temptations to idleness – everyone speaks Irish, + many speak
> no-thing else – I have therefore every facility for the prosecution of
> my purpose ...49

He enthusiastically encouraged others to follow his example. In a letter of
25 November 1863 he advised a nephew, who was staying in Dresden, to
work hard on the languages:

> I entreat you to make the best use you can of your present opportu-
> nity of learning modern languages, especially French + German – in
> the age of the world which is now come they are most important, +
> without them no man can expect to get any advancement of impor-
> tance, especially in the line of life you have selected. If India is to be
> your destination you ought also to learn Sanscrit.50

He went on to urge his nephew to take advantage of the facilities at TCD,
where there was 'a regular department to prepare men in all the subjects',
pointing out that 'we have also Sanscrit'. At this date it was taught by C.F.

---

47 Letters to and by the Revd J.H. Todd, MS 2214, no. 140, of 28 August 1843, addressed
  to 'Revd Dr Elrington, Deanery House, Armagh, Irlande'.
48 See Letters to and by the Revd J.H. Todd, MS 2214, no. 148, a letter by Todd to Elrington
  from Achill Island, written 11 August 1844, where he describes cultural aspects, the services and activities of the protestant church there with special attention to the use of the
  Irish language.
49 NLI, Letters by J.H. Todd, MS 2253, no. 36.
50 Letters to and by the Revd J.H. Todd, MS 2214, no. 166.

Löttner, who was to become Todd's new assistant librarian in February 1864.[51] The recommendations match the requirements of the British Civil Service,[52] but would also have offered a good foundation to follow the lines of Todd's chosen line of archaeological and language studies.

Todd's practical language exercise in Paderborn apparently did not quite have the desired result though. Subsequent correspondence between Todd and librarians and scholars of the German mother-tongue, such as Ferdinand Keller from Zürich, Hermann Ebel from Schneidemühl, or the theologian Konstantin von Tischendorf from Leipzig, were all written in English or French. Despite some unease with the German language, Todd however did not give up visiting the country. The contact with the monastic library in St Gall, Switzerland, proved to be a quite fruitful one. Todd went there several times, e.g. in 1845, 1846 and 1852, taking notes of Irish manuscripts for a paper to be given at the Royal Irish Academy, and with the librarian Ferdinand Keller he organized an exchange of publications between the RIA and the Society of Antiquaries in Zürich. Keller evidently also took Todd to see other libraries and antiquities in the area, and in discussions with him also drew Todd's attention to Germanic marginals in the manuscripts which they examined.[53] An institution found among listed donors in the library minute book at TCD was the K.K. Geologische Reichsanstalt, who presented their yearbook in 1862.[54] Furthermore a letter is retained in Trinity College, sent by the librarian of Göttingen university library on 25 February 1899, complaining of failure to send publications in return for those dispatched from Göttingen.[55]

A previously regular purchase of the *Göttingen Transactions*, as well as that of the *Berichte der Sächsischen Gesellschaft zu Leipzig* in place in Todd's time as librarian, had to be discontinued in 1856 though, due to lack of funds.[56] Todd tried to make up for such shortages not only by claiming every single British publication due to the library under the Copyright Act,[57] among which were many translations from the German,[58] but also through encouraging per-

---

51 Library Minute Book, MUN/LIB/2/4, under 14 February 1864.
52 See Luce (cited note 42), p. 103 (Sanscrit and Arabic required for British imperial administration) and Gilbert Carr, 'Literary historical trends and the history of the German syllabus in TCD, 1873-1972', *Hermathena* no. 121 (1976) p. 38ff.
53 On the exchange of publications see NLI, Letters, MS 5941, no. 26, by Ferdinand Keller to Todd from Zürich, written 24 May 1845; on this as well as on the manuscripts and Todd's library visits see also NLI, Letters to Todd, MS 2252, no. 9, by Ferdinand Keller to Todd, dated 17 January 1846.
54 Library Minute Book, MUN/LIB/2/4, Donations 1862.
55 Library Muniments, MUN/LIB/13/110.
56 Library Minute Book, Library report for 1856, MUN/LIB/2/4.
57 On these activities see for example Simms (cited note 14), pp 11ff.
58 For example J.G. Fichte, *The nature of the scholar* [*Über das Wesen des Gelehrten*, Engl.],

sonal donations of foreign publications, including German language material.
He himself contributed to this section: '*Munchhausen*. Von K. Zimmermann
(4 vols in 2) Düsseldorf 1841' and '*Ijob* with German translation, edited by
A. Wolfssohn' in 1867, along with numerous older donations mostly in Latin.
His assistant librarian C.F. Löttner followed his example, leaving German
items such as '*Gedichte* von L. Uhland, 50th ed. Stuttgart 1866', '*Nibelungen
im Frack – Ein Capriccio* von Anastasius Grün, 2nd ed Leipzig 1853' and '*Die
Verfassungs-Urkunde für den Preußischen Staat 31 Jan 1850* Köln 1863'.[59] The
Reverend Thomas McNeece, professor of divinity, had contributed a folio
volume of *Cipriani Hilaria evangelica oder theologisch historischer Bericht vom
andern evangelischen Jubelfeste*, Gotha 1719, in 1860 already.

Various illustrious visitors as well as graduates of the college made further donations of German books, most notably the king of Prussia, who presented a complete run of Lepsius's *Denkmäler aus Aegypten und Aethiopien* in
1860,[60] and Thomas Parnell, who presented 25 German titles published
between 1524 and 1795 in 1840.[61]

One particularly amusing nineteenth-century addition to the library, a seventeenth-century German language imprint, presented to Todd in 1850, may
have originated from the mathematician, theologian and future provost, George
Salmon, who is known to have had some interest in German New Testament
criticism,[62] and travelled in Germany and Switzerland himself.[63] The *Catalogus
etzlicher sehr alten Bücher, welche neulich in Irrland auff einem alten eroberten
Schlosse in einer Bibliothec gefunden worden* (no imprint), 1649 (Catalogue of
some very old books, which have been found recently in Ireland, in the library
of an old conquered castle), bears the manuscript annotation 'From G S to
Revd Dr Todd'. Most features of the handwriting, including the initials,
resemble Salmon's.[64] The item is bound in a volume of 'Tractatus Varii',
comprising an assortment of tracts from 1523 to 1649 in Dutch, French, Latin
and German, with a binding date of 'Feby 1853'.[65] The German catalogue is
a satirical classified listing of titles for sale at the upcoming fair in Frankfurt,
supposedly from ancient and biblical times, such as 'Judae Ischarioths

translated by Wm. Smith, London 1845, was received Nov. 1845 (see Publications Received
1844-1847, MUN/LIB/20/2); Todd was assistant librarian at this time.

59 Library Minute Book, MUN/LIB/2/4, Donations 1867 and Donations 1869.

60 Library Minute Book, MUN/LIB/2/4, Library report 1860, list of donations.

61 Presentations Book, 7 December 1840, MUN/LIB/1/32.

62 See Luce (cited note 42), p. 102.

63 Letters of George Salmon to J.H. Bernard 1891-1903, MS 2384; includes postcards and
letters from German-speaking Switzerland.

64 Admittedly Salmon seldom wrote the 't' with an upstroke, although there are other examples of this, such as Salmon's letter to Todd of 22 March 1859, MUN/P/1/1843.

65 Shelfmark Gall. C. 11. 22, no. 17.

Leichenpredigt, gehalten vom Apostel Simon Petro ...' (Judas Ischariot's funeral sermon, delivered by the apostle Simon Peter); 'Der Königin Cleopatrae Eheordnunge, in 4. Revis. Gabriele de Plurimis' (Queen Cleopatra's marriage regulations, in its 4th revision by Gabriel of the Many); mixed with some similarly satirical titles of political and theological relevance, like 'Des Ablaß=Krämers Tezels Paßbrieffe wieder den Teuffel ... in 4o. [*sic*] Autore ipso Tezelio' (The indulgence-grocer Tezel's passports against the devil, in a small miniature edition, written by Tezel himself); or 'Funfftzig Ursachen ... warumb Franckreich nicht in Deutschland, und Deutschland nicht in Franckreich liege ...' (Fifty reasons why France is not situated in Germany, and Germany not in France). As opposed to his other numerous and valuable donations, Todd made no mention in any of the relevant library muniments of giving this original seventeenth-century imprint to the library. Possibly in this instance, Todd was not overjoyed by Salmon's present, which in fact seems to mock his own antiquarian activities.

Todd continued his acquisition of old imprints, affording a special treatment for an item on Irish and German history. Thomas Carve, *Reyßbüchlein, deß ehrwürdigen Herrn Thomae Carve Irrländers, ..., Auß dem Latein. ins Teutsch ubersetzt durch P. K.*, Mainz 1640 (Itinerary of the Reverend Thomas Carve from Ireland ..., translated from the Latin into German by P. K.), was received through the Dublin bookseller Milliken in November 1843.[66] It was bound in red morocco by John Mackenzie in London, with gold tooling and gauffered edges. The binding could have been carried out to the order of Todd, as booksellers Hodges & Smith's account for 6 July 1849 states: 'Paid McKenzi's (Dr Todd's order) nett 11.4.0'.[67] The book describes the journey from Ireland of Irish mercenaries through Britain to Germany and interprets their conduct in the Thirty Years War in a favourable way. The special binding could have been intended to encourage interest in the book, as Todd is known to have left new acquisitions on the tables for inspection by readers.[68]

OTHER GERMAN LANGUAGE ACQUISITIONS

A more modern interest in collecting German language items can be observed in relation to the German department. The nineteenth-century professors of German were originally concerned with grammar and basic language skills,

---

66 Foreign Publications 1843-1864, MUN/LIB/9/3.
67 Accounts of Hodges & Smith, MUN/LIB/11/5.
68 For further information see Veronika Koeper-Saul, '17th-century German language imprints at Trinity College Dublin, acquired up to 1872', unpublished minor thesis for MLIS, University College Dublin 1995.

especially for public service examinations, but increasingly added literature studies to the course.[69] A list of German books ordered by the library through Barthes & Lowell in 1844 gives a good insight into such strands of interest. The books were probably requested by Ignatius Gerorge Abeltshauser (professor of German, 1842-66), and show a focus on classical and the then 'modern' German literature (from the eighteenth century onwards), rather than on older German language documents.[70] The invoice includes a series of biographies on such classic authors as Goethe, Klopstock, Wieland, Schiller, and others. Also included were Klopstock's works in nine volumes; collections of works by several romantic writers, for example Hauff (10 volumes), Jean Paul Richter (33 volumes (!) plus biography), and Tieck (three volumes); works of nationalist character, such as poems by Körner and Freiligrath;[71] and recent publications like Grillparzer's 'Des Meeres Wellen' (i.e. *Des Meeres und der Liebe Wellen*, 1840) or 'Weh dem, der Lught' (i.e. *Weh dem, der lügt*, 1840). Ancient times and the middle ages provided the thematic sources for this 'modern' literature, both in the works by Grillparzer, and in secondary literature, such as 'Hagen. Anmerkungen zu den Nibelungen'. 'Raumer Geschichte der Hohenstaufen' (History of the Stauffer), was also acquired in 1844,[72] an interest reflected in exam questions at the time.[73] While it is typical of the period's methodology that several German multi-volume works on general literary history were acquired, the purchase of a specialized work 'Über Moderne Litteratur'[74] (About modern literature, by 'Marbach', 4 volumes), is evidence of the growing interest in modern works, whilst medieval literature was only seen as a part of history in general.

Abeltshauser's successor, Albert Maximilian Selss (professor of German, 1866-1907), went even further in a 'modern' direction. His *Critical outline of the literature of Germany*, London 1865, clearly argued against 'the exaggerated importance hitherto given to the Middle Ages'.[75] In his first chapter, an introduction to the German language, Selss sought to demonstrate

69 See M.M. Raraty, 'The chair of German at TCD 1775-1866', *Hermathena* no. 102 (1966) pp 53-72 and Carr (cited note 52), pp 36-53.
70 On Abeltshauser's teaching goals see M.M. Raraty, op. cit., pp 66-9. The booklist is incorporated in an invoice dated 14 June 1844, in Accounts of Messrs. Bossange, Barthes & Lowell, foreign booksellers, London, for foreign books, 1836-1857, MUN/LIB/11/4.
71 'Korner' and 'Freilegarth' in the accounts are obviously misspellings; there are many others.
72 Both titles are quoted from Bossange, Barthes & Lowell's invoice of 14 June 1844, MUN/LIB/11/4.
73 Raraty (cited note 69), p. 69, quotes exam questions from 1843, including '2.a. What were the *Minnesänger*? ... c. Under which imperial family did they principally flourish?'
74 MUN/LIB/11/4, 14 June 1844.
75 Carr (cited note 52), p. 42.

the superior importance of high German over low German dialects and older forms of German, and shed doubt even on the research by the brothers Grimm, who he reported, recently 'thought fit to publish some specimens of Low German tales'.[76] In the second chapter Selss went on to explain how the 'Zenith of Literary Excellence' in German literature was reached as late as 'about 1800 A.D.' only,[77] and attempted to isolate the particular nationalist characteristics in German literature, as opposed to the English and French ones. The chapters following illustrated his argument with details mostly on recent writers, including not only poets, playwrights and novelists, but also philosophers and historiographers. In Selss's view 'the literary fame of Germany is in a high degree due to her philosophical productions'.[78] It is evident from this what kind of material he and Abeltshauser would have ordered for the library, beyond German literature and language works. Schleiermacher's collected works, received in 1863, and critical works by Schlegel, received in 1844,[79] would certainly have served them well.

Thus whilst Todd and his friends researched the historic origins of the Celtic and Germanic languages and nations, Selss's starting point, and similarly Abeltshauser's, was of contemporary literary output. However, closer examination of the context of their primary field reveals an overlap between the interests of both groups. We see Todd and Löttner contributing recent German language publications, and Selss and Abeltshauser studying the past through the newly systematized methods of literary history and through the content of the literary canon. Both pairs resemble each other also in their interdisciplinary approach: Todd learned German to study Irish linguistics and archaeology, Selss was drawn to philosophical and historical studies through German literature. In consequence both groups significantly encouraged the study of the German language, and from different directions, added to the German language material in the library, complementing each others' contributions. Many scientists, as for example Stokes, had a side interest in the above disciplines too, especially in archaeology, and applied their language knowledge further to the study of their own disciplines. Part of the influx of scientific German language items into Trinity College library in the nineteenth century may be explained this way. But we also notice a lot of other independent minds, like Salmon, making their own contributions, which finally led to the acquisition of German language items in all subject areas. In this truly international orientation, Trinity College stands out amongst universi-

76 Albert M. Selss, *A critical outline of the literature of Germany*, 2nd, rev. and enl. ed., London 1880, p. 5.

77 Ibid., p. 14.

78 Ibid., p. 224.

79 Foreign Publications Books, MUN/LIB/9/3.

ties in nineteenth-century Great Britain and Ireland. As James Henthorn Todd proudly explained to his nephew:

> We [i.e. TCD] are particularly great in the Languages, whether it be from the excellence of our teachers, or because Paddy has in a remarkable way a gift for every species of gab, I cannot tell ...[80]

---

80 Letters to and by the Revd J.H. Todd, MS 2214, no. 166, dated 25 November 1863.

A Select Bibliography of the Library

CIARAN NICHOLSON AND ANN O'BRIEN

P.K. Fox ed., *Treasures of the library, Trinity College Dublin*, Dublin 1986, includes Ann O'Brien's 'A select bibliography of the library'. Ciaran Nicholson has prepared for the present volume a continuation, with some additions, of the O'Brien bibliography. For the convenience of readers the editors have decided to republish the O'Brien list, rearranging it in one alphabetical sequence, and to integrate it into the Nicholson list. Nicholson entries are distinguished by asterisks.

Annual Bulletin is used as an abbreviation for the entry included in full below.

Abbott, T.K., *Catalogue of fifteenth-century books in the Library of Trinity College Dublin, in Marsh's Library Dublin, with a few from other collections*, Dublin 1905.
—, *Catalogue of the manuscripts in the Library of Trinity College Dublin; to which is added a list of the Fagel Collection of maps in the same library*, Dublin 1900.
—, 'The Library', in *The book of Trinity College Dublin 1591-1891*, Dublin 1892.
— & Gwynn, E.J., *A catalogue of the Irish manuscripts in the Library of Trinity College Dublin*, Dublin 1921.
Alexander, J.J.G., *A survey of manuscripts illuminated in the British Isles. Vol 1.: Insular manuscripts from the sixth to the ninth century*, London 1978.
'Alterations of library building, Trinity College Dublin', *Dublin Builder* (1860) p. 196.
Alton, E.H., 'Some notes on the Library and cost of its building', *Annual Bulletin* (1948) pp 10-12.
Anderson, Glynn & Deegan, Mark, 'Computerizing the Printed Catalogue using optical character recognition', *Alumnus* (1991) pp 65-71.*
Andrews, J.H., 'Maps and atlases', in P.K. Fox ed., *Treasures of the library, Trinity College Dublin*, Dublin 1986, pp 170-83.*
Annual Bulletin of the Friends of the Library of Trinity College Dublin, 1946–57.
Annual Report: Library, 1972/3–.
Barnard, T.C., 'The purchase of Archbishop Ussher's library in 1657', *Long Room* 4 (1971) pp 9-14.*
Bell, R., 'Legal deposit in Britain', *Law Librarian* 8 (1977) pp 5-8, 22-6.
Bennet, M.B., *Trinity College Library Dublin*, Palm Springs, Calif. 1959.
Benson, Charles, 'Anatomizing early printed books in Trinity College Dublin', *Eighteenth-century Ireland*, 1 (1986) pp 195-99.*

—, *A checklist of plays in the English language printed before 1700, held in Trinity College Library, Dublin*, Dublin 1993; 27 leaves.*

—, 'The drama collection at Trinity College, Dublin', *Antiquarian Book Monthly Review* xiv, 6 (June 1987), pp 216-19.*

—, 'A friend of the Library', *Long Room* 9 (1974) p. 40.

—, '"Here's fine work! Here's fine suicide, paracide and simulation"', in P.K. Fox ed., *Treasures of the library, Trinity College Dublin*, Dublin 1986, pp 143-7; about the library's collection of play texts in English before 1820.*

—, 'Trinity College: a bibliographical essay', in C.H. Holland, *Trinity College Dublin and the idea of a university*, Dublin 1991, pp 357-71.*

Benyon, W.H., *Portfolio of Trinity College Dublin: a series of illustrations, photogravure, etc. from original negatives*, Cheltenham 1901.

Bloomfield, Barry C. ed., *A directory of rare book and special collections in the United Kingdom and the Republic of Ireland* 2nd ed., London 1997, pp 610-14.*

Boran, Elizabethanne, 'The libraries of Luke Challoner and James Ussher, 1595-1608', in Helga Robinson-Hammerstein ed., *European universities in the age of reformation and counter reformation*, Dublin 1998, pp 75-115.*

—, 'Luke Challoner's library: 1595-1608', *Long Room* 37 (1992) pp 17-26.*

Braches, Ernst, 'The first years of the Fagel Collection in Trinity College, Dublin', in Sue Roach ed., *Across the narrow seas: studies in the history and bibliography of Britain and the Low Countries*, London 1991, pp 189-96.*

Brawne, M., *Libraries: architecture and equipment*, London 1970, pp 108-11, 148, 173.

Brown, P., 'Trinity College Library', *Protean* (Winter 1972) pp 24-7.

Building for books. Documentary film, colour. 1958.

Buschkühl, M., 'Die Bibiothek des Trinity College in Dublin' Unpublished thesis. Bibliothekar-Lehrinstitut des Landes Nordrhein-Westfalen, Cologne 1980.

Cains, A., 'Book conservation workshop manual, pt 1-', *New Bookbinder* 1- (1981-) pp 11-25.

—, 'In-situ treatment of MSS and printed books in Trinity College Dublin', in N. Hadgraft and K. Swift eds., *Conservation and preservation in small libraries*, Cambridge 1994, pp 127-31.*

—, 'A recently discovered Apollo & Pegasus medallion binding', *Long Room* 41 (1996) pp 19-24; in the Claudius Gilbert collection.*

—, 'Repair treatments for vellum manuscripts', in Guy Petherbridge ed., *Conservation of library and archive materials and the graphic arts*, London 1987, pp 183-94.*

—, 'Roger Powell and his early Irish MSS in Dublin', in N. Hadgraft and K. Swift eds., *Conservation and preservation in small libraries*, Cambridge 1994, pp 151-6.*

—, 'Roger Powell's innovation in book conservation: the early Irish manuscripts repaired and bound, 1953-1981', in John L. Sharpe ed., *Roger Powell: the compleat binder*, Turnhout 1996, pp 68-87; includes the Book of Kells and other TCD library MSS.*

—, 'The work of the Conservation Laboratory', *Trinity College Gazette* (10 March 1983) pp 5-6, 11.

— and Sheehan, Paul, 'Preservation and conservation in the library of Trinity College Dublin, *International Library Review* 18 (1986) pp 173-8.*

— and Swift, Katherine, *Preserving our printed heritage: the Long Room Project at TCD*, Dublin 1988; 24p. Revised ed. 1999.*

Caldicott, C.E.J., 'The drawings of Nicholas Robert in Trinity College: a seventeenth-century view of nature', *Long Room* 20 & 21 (1980) pp 7-15; on a collection of the French botanist's drawings in the library.*

Catalogi librorum manuscriptorum Angliae et Hiberniae, Oxford 1697.

A catalogue of the books in the Lending Library of Trinity College Dublin, Dublin 1861.

Catalogus librorum impressorum qui in Bibliotheca Collegii Sacrosanctae et Individuae Trinitatis Reginae Elizabethae juxta Dublin adservantur ... Dublin 1864-87. 8 vols. *Supplementum addenda et corrigenda*, 1887.

Catalogus librorum in Bibliotheca Collegii Sanctae et Individuae Trinitatis Reginae Elizabethae juxta Dublin, Dublin (*c.*1720?).

Catalogus librorum quibus aucta est Bibliotheca collegii SS. Trinitatis reginae Elizabethae juxta Dublin anno exeunte Kal. November MDCCCLIII, Dublin 1854.

Ceadel, E.B., *Adaptation of computer programs for catalogues for use in another library*, Cambridge 1977. (British Library research & development report 5352.)

Chepesiuk, R.J., 'Great libraries of Dublin: a scholar's delight', *Wilson Library Bulletin* 57 (1983) pp 657-61.

Clarke, Aidan, 'The 1641 depositions', in P.K. Fox ed., *Treasures of the library*, *Trinity College Dublin*, Dublin 1986, pp 111-22.*

Clarté: art et decoratif, n. 9 (Septembre 1935) (includes an illustrated account of the Library).

Colker, Marvin L., 'The recataloguing of the mediaeval Latin manuscripts', *Long Room* 1 (1970) pp 13-16.*

—, *Trinity College Library Dublin: descriptive catalogue of the mediaeval and renaissance Latin manuscripts*, Aldershot 1991; 2v.*

Colquhon, A., 'Library, Trinity College Dublin', *Architectural Review* (October 1967) pp 265-77.

'The Crofton pamphlets', *Annual Bulletin* (1956) pp 15-18.*

Crookshank, A., *The Long Room*, Dublin 1976.

—, 'The Long Room', in P.K. Fox ed., *Treasures of the library, Trinity College Dublin*, Dublin 1986, pp 16-28.*

— and Webb, David, *Paintings and sculptures in Trinity College Dublin*, Dublin 1990; 205p., illus. (some col.).*

Cruickshank, Dan, 'Berkeley Library: Trinity College, Dublin 1967-1997', *RIBA Journal* v. 104 no. 10 (Oct. 1997) pp 69-75.*

Cuala Press archive 1902-1986: a general descriptive listing rev. ed., Dublin 1998; 27p.*

D., X., 'Trinity College Library', *Irish Penny Journal* (1841) pp 340-2.

DeArce, Miguel, 'The Berkeley Library', in Miguel DeArce, *Campus poems*, Dundalk 1998, p. 32.*

Delaney, P., 'Trinity College Library Dublin', *Architectural Design* 37 (1967) pp 459-68

Dixon, W.M., *Trinity College Dublin*, London 1902. (College histories.)

Donat, J., 'Magic box: Trinity College Library in Dublin', *Architectural Forum* (October 1967) pp 78-85.

Dougan, R.O., *A descriptive guide to twenty Irish manuscripts in the Library of Trinity College Dublin, with an appendix of five early Irish manuscripts in the Royal Irish Academy*, 2nd ed, Dublin 1955.

—, 'The rebinding of the Book of Kells', *Annual Bulletin* (1953) pp 11-12.*

Dublin University Commission, Dublin 1853.

Duffin, E.A.R., 'Conservation, we can afford it! The good news from TCD', *Rare Books Newsletter* 34 (November 1989), pp 24-8.*

Edwards, Edward, *Memoirs of libraries: including a handbook of library economy*, London 1859, v. 2 pp 45-63.*

Edwards, George, ed., *The Grolier Club iter Hibernicum*, New York 1998; pp 30-46 provides an account of a visit to the library.*

Esposito, M., *Inventaire des anciens manuscrits français des bibliothèques de Dublin*, Paris 1914-21.

Farr, Carol, *The Book of Kells: its function and audience*, London 1997, 196p. (The British Library studies in medieval culture).*

Ferguson, Lydia, 'The implementation of the UKMARC rare books fields at Trinity College Library, Dublin', *Rare Books Newsletter* 47 (July 1994) pp 29-32.*

Ferguson, Paul, and Cains, M. 'Map conservation project at Trinity College Library Dublin', in *Cartographic Journal*, 27 (1990) pp 3-6.*

—, *News from the Map Library: new look for Map Library*, Dublin 1991; [4]p., illus.*

Fitzgerald, John Andrew, and Ní Mhoitleigh, Colette, *System manual: Trinity College Library Dublin, card catalogue conversion project*, Dublin 1987; 1 v. (unpaged).*

Fox, Peter K., 'The Book of Kells facsimile', in *Antiquarian Book Monthly Review*, xvii no. 3 (March 1990) pp 98-108.*

— (ed.), *The Book of Kells: MS 58 Trinity College Library Dublin: commentary*, Lucerne 1990, 383p.; includes Gerard Marmion, 'Select bibliography [on the Book of Kells]', pp 357-73.*

—, 'A library well deserving the notice of the traveller', in C.H. Holland ed., *Trinity College Dublin and the idea of a university*, Dublin 1991, pp 135-52.*

—, 'Peter Brown, in memoriam', *IFLA Journal* v. 10 no. 2 (1984) p. 121.*

—, 'They glory much in their library', in P.K. Fox ed., *Treasures of the library, Trinity College Dublin*, Dublin 1986, pp 1-15.*

— (ed.), *Treasures of the library, Trinity College Dublin*, Dublin 1986; 258p., illus. (some col.).*

—, *Trinity College Library Dublin*, Dublin 1982. (Irish heritage series.)

'French texts in the library of TCD: 1. Medieval French manuscripts, Lisa Shields. 2. Holdings and acquisitions of French, 1750-1850, F. M. Higman. 3. The Fagel collection, J.-P. Pittion. 4. The Bonaparte-Wyse collection, Mina Kelly', *Hermathena* v. 121 (Winter 1976) pp 90-120.*

French, R.B.D., 'Great Library of Trinity College Dublin', *Library Journal* (1959) pp 3533-5.

—, *The Library of Trinity College Dublin: a great library and its needs*, Dublin 1954.

Gabel, Gernot U., 'Dublin. 400 Jahre Trinity College Dublin Library', *Bibliotheksdienst* 26 (1992) p. 1903.*

Garau Aunós, M., 'Manuscripts españoles de la biblioteca del Trinity College de Dublin', *Il Biblioteconomia* (1965) pp 52-8.

Gilbert, J.T., *Facsimiles of the national manuscripts of Ireland*, Dublin 1874–84.

Gleeson, E., *Union list of current legal periodicals held in Dublin law libraries*, Dublin 1978.

Gougad, Don L., 'Répertoire des façsimiles des manuscrits irlandais', *Revue celtique* (1913) pp 14-37.

'Great British libraries – VI: the library of Trinity College, Dublin', *Times Literary Supplement* 2820 (16 Mar. 1956) p. 172.*

Grene, Nicholas, 'Modern Irish literary manuscripts', in P.K. Fox ed., *Treasures of the library, Trinity College Dublin*, Dublin 1986, pp 230-8.*

Griffith, Margaret C., 'The College muniments', *Long Room* 12 & 13 (1976) pp 6-12.*

—, 'From the College muniments, 1: Depredations in the library, 1715', *Long Room* 4 (1971) pp 15-18; about book thefts.*

Harris, N., 'Pilot projects using variable length library records', *Program* (1968) pp 13-16.

Hayes, R.T., *Manuscript sources for the history of Irish civilisation*. Boston, Mass. 1965. *First supplement* (1965–75), 1979.

Heron, D.C., *The constitutional history of the University of Dublin*, Dublin 1848.

Hincks, E., *Catalogue of the Egyptian manuscripts in the Library of Trinity College Dublin*, Dublin 1843.

Hobson, A.R.A., *Great libraries*. London 1970. (Trinity: pp 174-85.)

Hurst, F.J.E., 'The College Library', *Kosmos* (1967) pp 20-1.

—, 'Dr Herbert William Parke [obituary]', *Library Association Record* v. 88 no. 3 (March 1986) p. 117.*

—, 'Trinity College Dublin proposed new library', *Library Association Record* (February 1961) pp 45-8.

Hutton, H.D., *Impressions of twelve years cataloguing in a great library*, London 1886.

'In the Library', *TCD: a College Miscellany* (9 March 1904) p. 44. (Dramatic vignette.)

International architectural competition for a new library building, Dublin 1960.

[International architectural competition] *Decisions and report of the jury of award*, Dublin 1961.

Jeffares, A.N., *Trinity College Dublin founded 1591: 34 drawings and descriptions*. Dublin 1944.

Jessop, N.R., & Nudds, C., *Guide to collections in Dublin libraries: printed books to 1850 and special collections*, Dublin 1982.

Kells Ingram, J., *The Library of Trinity College Dublin: being an address delivered at the seventh annual meeting of the Library Association of the United Kingdom, September 30, 1884*, London 1886.

Kinane, Vincent, 'The Fagel Collection', in P.K. Fox ed., *Treasures of the library, Trinity College Dublin*, Dublin 1986, pp 158-69.*

—, 'A fine set of the Irish Common's Journals: a study of its production history', *Long Room* 30 (1985) pp 11-28; the set was presented to the library by Dr Maurice Craig.*

—, 'Some aspects of the Cuala Press', *The Private Library* v. 2 no. 3 (Autumn 1989) pp 118-29; based on the archive and printing equipment of the press, donated by the Yeats family to the library.*

—, 'Trinity Closet Press 1973-1994: a chronology and a bibliography', *Long Room* 39 (1994) pp 60-3; the press is part of the library.*

— and O'Brien, Ann, '"The vast difficulty of cataloguing": the Printed Catalogue of Trinity College Dublin (1864-1887)', *Libraries and Culture* 23 (1988) pp 427-53.*

Koralek, Paul, *The New Library, University of Dublin, Trinity College, opened by Eamon de Valera, President of Ireland, July 12th 1967*, Dublin 1967; [16]p.*

Lancashire, Ian, 'The provenance of *The worlde and the chylde*', *Papers of the Bibliographical Society of America* v. 67 (1973) pp 377-88; about the thefts from the library by Edward Barwick in 1813-5, including the unique copy of *The worlde and the chylde*, London 1522.*

'Lending libraries and copyright', *Hibernia* (1882) pp 179-80.

'The Library' (by Pip), *TCD: a College Miscellany* (15 December 1921) p. 65. (Sonnet.)

'The Library Association at Dublin', *Library Chronicle* (1884) pp 161-4.

'The Library, Trinity College Dublin', *Architect and Building News* (11 October 1967) pp 611-18.

Libri in publica Collegii Bibliotheca 29 Febr. anno 1600: entry no. 49 in the Particular Book, Trinity College Dublin. Facsimile with introduction and appendices by J.P. Mahaffy, London 1904.

List of the collections of modern papers, 18th-20th century in the Library of Trinity College Dublin, London 1975.

List of current and recent foreign periodicals, Dublin 1906.

Long Room (Friends of the Library of Trinity College Dublin), 1972–.

Luce, A.A., 'A list of editions of the works of George Berkeley in the College Library', *Annual Bulletin* (1946) pp 11.

Luce, John V., 'A report on the progress of the Library extension appeal', *Annual Bulletin* (1958) pp 14-15.*

—, *Trinity College Dublin: the first 400 years*, Dublin 1992; x, 246p.*

McCormack, William J., 'William Elliot Mackey (1924-1996): an appreciation', *Long Room* 41 (1996) pp 15-17; Mackey was editor of *Long Room* (1970-1991) and Research Librarian.*

McDonnell, Joseph, and Healy, Patrick, *Gold-tooled bookbindings commissioned by Trinity College Dublin in the eighteenth century*, Leixlip 1987; ch. 1, pp 1-13.*

McDowell, Robert B., 'The acquisition of the Fagel Library', *Annual Bulletin* (1947) pp 5-6.*

—, 'Henry Dix Hutton – positivist and cataloguer', *Friends of the Library of Trinity College Dublin Annual Bulletin* (1956) pp 6-7.*

—, and Webb, D.A., *Trinity College Dublin 1592–1952*. Cambridge 1982.

McGing, Brian C., and Parke, Herbert W., 'Papyri', in P.K. Fox ed., *Treasures of the library, Trinity College Dublin*, Dublin 1986, pp 29-37.*

MacManaway, Norma, and Benson, Charles, '"A sceliton with taffety hangings": the early college library', in David Scott ed., *Treasures of the mind: a TCD quatercentenary exhibition*, London 1992, pp 143-50.*

MacNiocaill, Gearoid, 'The Irish-language manuscripts', in P.K. Fox ed., *Treasures of the library, Trinity College Dublin*, Dublin 1986, pp 57-66.*

Maconchy, E., *Ina Boyle: an appreciation with a select list of her music*, Dublin 1974.

McParland, Edward, 'The buildings of Trinity College Dublin', *Country Life* (1976) p. 203; the library is included in a series of articles published in the issues for 6, 13, and 20 May 1976.*

—, 'The College buildings', in C.H. Holland ed., *Trinity College Dublin and the idea of a university*, Dublin 1991, pp 153-84.*

McPhail, I., 'A short list of Elizabethan books in the Library', *Annual Bulletin* (1958) pp 3-7.

Mahaffy, J.P., *An epoch in Irish history: Trinity College Dublin, its foundation and early fortunes, 1591-1660*, London 1903 (reprinted 1970).

—, 'The Library of Trinity College Dublin: the growth of a legend', *Hermathena* 27 (1902) pp 68-78

Malet, John A., *A catalogue of silver coins in the library of TCD*, Dublin 1839; 96p.*

Matteson, Robert S., 'Archbishop William King's library: some discoveries and queries', *Long Room* 9 (1974) pp 7-16; TCD MS 1490 lists 649 volumes from his library.*

Maxwell, C.E., *A history of Trinity College Dublin 1591-1892*, Dublin 1946.

Meehan, Bernard, *The Book of Durrow: a medieval masterpiece at Trinity College Dublin*, Dublin 1996; 94p., illus. (some col.).*

—, *The Book of Kells: an illustrated introduction to the manuscript in Trinity College Dublin*, London 1994; 95p., illus. (some col.).*

—, 'The manuscript collection of James Ussher', in P.K. Fox ed., *Treasures of the library, Trinity College Dublin*, Dublin 1986, pp 97-110.*

—, '"A melody of curves across the page": art and calligraphy in the Book of Armagh', *Irish Arts Review Yearbook* 14 (1997) pp 90-101.*

Morrow, Veronica, 'Bibliotheca Quiniana', in P.K. Fox ed., *Treasures of the library, Trinity College Dublin*, Dublin 1986, pp 184-96.*

—, 'Bibliotheca Quiniana: a description of the books and buildings in the Quin collection in the Library at Trinity College Dublin'. Unpublished thesis. University of London, 1970.

—, 'An unrecorded Grolier binding', *Long Room* 39 (1994) pp 30-1; in TCD library, shelfmark QQ. n. 39.*

—, 'What do we mean by "copyright"?', *TCD Library News: User Newsletter* 12 (1998) pp [2-3].*

Murphy, H.L., *A history of Trinity College Dublin from its foundation to 1702*, Dublin 1951.

Murray, R.H., *A short guide to some manuscripts in the Library of Trinity College Dublin*, London 1920.

Newsletter (Friends of the Library of Trinity College Dublin), 1984–.

Ní Mhoitleigh, Colette, Fitzgerald, John, Hogan, Gail and Peare, Trevor, 'Retrospective conversion at Trinity College Dublin', *Vine* 69 (1987) pp 13-24.*

Nineteenth-century short title catalogue ... extracted from the catalogues of the Bodleian Library, the British Library, the Library of Trinity College Dublin, the National Library of Scotland and the university libraries of Cambridge and Newcastle, Newcastle-upon-Tyne 1984–.

Nixon, Howard M., *Roger Powell & Peter Waters*, Froxfield 1965; includes an account and illustrations of the rebinding of some of the TCD library MSS.*

Novae bibliothecae SS Trin. Coll. Dub. descriptio, poema. In duabus partibus. Ad calcem accesserunt nonnulla varii argumenti epigrammata ..., Dublin 1735.

Nudds, Christine, 'The Dolmen Press Collection', in P.K. Fox ed., *Treasures of the library, Trinity College Dublin,* Dublin 1986, pp 239-48.*

'Obiit tranquillitas', *TCD: a College Miscellany* (27 October 1927) p. 8. (Poem on the pleasure of silence in the library.)

O'Brien, Ann, 'A select bibliography of the library', in P.K. Fox ed., *Treasures of the library, Trinity College Dublin,* Dublin 1986, pp 249-51.*

O'Callaghan, Julie, *The Long Room Gallery,* Dublin 1994; [4]p.; a poem.*

O'Dwyer, Frederick, *The architecture of Deane and Woodward,* Cork 1997; includes an account of the mid-nineteenth century alterations to the library, pp 349-55.*

Oldham, C.H., *Trinity College pictorial account of the foundation of the College: a tercentenary souvenir,* Dublin 1892.

Olley, John, 'Berkeley Library, Trinity College Dublin, 1961-7: Ahrends Burton Koralek', in Becker, Annette, Olley, John and Wang, Wilfried eds., *Ireland: 20th-century architecture,* Munich 1997, pp 124-5.*

O'Mahony, Felicity ed., *The Book of Kells: proceedings of a conference at Trinity College Dublin, 6-9 September, 1992,* Aldershot 1994; xi, 603p.*

Ó Seanóir, Stuart, 'The Dillon papers', in P.K. Fox ed., *Treasures of the library, Trinity College Dublin,* Dublin 1986, pp 215-21.*

O'Shaughnessy, Ron, 'Memoirs of a dust boy', *Trinity Trust News* v. 11 no. 1 (Nov. 1986) pp 16-17; anecdotal description of the library 1943-86.*

O'Sullivan, William, 'Binding memories of Trinity Library', in Agnes Bernelle ed., *Decantations: a tribute to Maurice Craig,* Dublin 1992, pp 168-76.*

—, 'The eighteenth-century rebinding of the manuscripts', *Long Room* 1 (1970) pp 19-28.

—, 'George Carew's Irish maps', *Long Room* 26 & 27 (1983) pp 15-25.*

—, 'The Library before Kinsale', *Annual Bulletin* (1952) pp 10-14.

—, 'The new Manuscripts Room', *Annual Bulletin* (1958) pp 12-13.

—, 'The new Manuscripts Room', *Long Room* 5 (1972) pp 23-5.

—, 'Notes on the Trinity Liber Hymnorum', in John L. Sharpe ed., *Roger Powell: the compleat binder,* Turnhout 1996, pp 130-5.*

—, 'The rebinding of the Book of Durrow', *Annual Bulletin* (1954) pp 4-5.*

—, 'Ussher as a collector of manuscripts', *Hermathena* 88 (1956) pp 34-58.*
(Further articles by William O'Sullivan on the history of the library and its collections will be found in the select bibliography appended to Toby C. Barnard et al. eds, *'A miracle of learning': studies in manuscripts and Irish learning: essays in honour of William O'Sullivan,* Aldershot 1997, pp 284-5).*

Parke, H.W., *The Library of Trinity College Dublin,* Dublin 1961.

—, 'Mr Timothy Casey's robberies: an episode from the Library Minutes', *Annual Bulletin* (1949) pp 7-9.

Pollard, Mary, *The architects' and builders' new song; addressed to the New Library from the ruins of the Old,* Dublin 1967. (Broadsheet ballad.)

—, 'The "College Binder" – Thomas Whitehouse?', *Long Room* 38 (1993) p. 17.*

—, 'The Sáirséal agus Dill collection', *Long Room* 1 (1970) p. 43.*

Pressley, Stuart, 'The archives of the *Dublin Magazine*, 1923-58', *Long Room* 7 (1973) pp 27-32.*

Roberts, C.B., 'The Slavonic Calvinist reading primer in Trinity College Library', *Long Room* 28 & 29 (1984) pp 7-14; TCD MS 1684/16.*

Roberts, E.F.D., 'Trinity College Library, University of Dublin', in *Encyclopaedia of the library and information science*, vol. 7, pp 308-14.

Saddlemyer, Ann, '"Infinite riches in a little room": the manuscripts of John Millington Synge', *Long Room* 3 (1971) pp 23-31.*

Santamaría, José, 'Apéndice al catálogo de manuscritos españoles en la Biblioteca del Trinity College de Dublin (Fagel Collection)', *Revista Alicantina de Estudios Ingleses* no. 1 (Nov. 1988) pp 171-80.*

Shackleton, Lydia K., *Trinity College Library Dublin: a checklist of recent accessions in the French language in the Department of Early Printed Books*, Dublin 1990; 17p.*

Sheehan, Paul E., 'A condition survey of books in Trinity College Library Dublin', *Libri* v. 40 no. 4 (December 1990) pp 306-17.*

Shields, Hugh, 'Nineteenth-century Irish song chapbooks and ballad sheets', in P.K. Fox ed., *Treasures of the library, Trinity College Dublin*, Dublin 1986, pp 197-206.*

Shields, L., 'Medieval manuscripts in French and Provençal', *Hermathena* 121 (1976) pp 90-100.

Simms, George Otto, 'Early Christian manuscripts', in P.K. Fox ed., *Treasures of the library, Trinity College Dublin*, Dublin 1986, pp 38-56.*

—, 'James Henthorn Todd', *Hermathena* 109 (1969) pp 5-23.*

Simpson, Edward, 'Anthony Cains: Director of Conservation at Trinity College Dublin interviewed by Edward Simpson', *Paper Conservation* 74 (June 1995) pp 1-4.*

Smyly, J.G., 'Notes on Greek manuscripts in the Library of Trinity College', *Hermathena* (1933) pp 163-95.

—, 'The Old Library: extracts from the Particular Book', *Hermathena* 49 (1935) pp 166-83.*

'Songs of the College 4: the library', *TCD: a College Miscellany* (31 May 1928), p. 183. (Poem.)

Stanley, Roy, 'Trinity College Library, Dublin', in D. Paisley ed., *German studies: British resources. Papers presented at a colloquium at the British Library 25-27 September 1985* (British Library Occasional Papers 8), London 1986, pp 205-9.*

Stanwood, P.G., 'The Richard Hooker manuscripts', *Long Room* 11 (1975) pp 7-10.*

Sullivan, E.,'The Library of Trinity College Dublin', *Book Lover's Magazine* 7 (1908) pp 1-12.

Swift, Katherine, 'The Worth Library', *Friends of the Library Newsletter* 10 (1988) pp 2-3.*

The Synge manuscripts in the Library of Trinity College Dublin: a catalogue prepared on the occasion of the Synge centenary exhibition 1971, Dublin 1971.

Taylor, W.B.S., *History of the University of Dublin from its foundation to the end of the eighteenth century*. London, Dublin 1845.

Tedeschi, John, 'A "queer story": the Inquisitorial manuscripts', in P.K. Fox ed., *Treasures of the library, Trinity College Dublin*, Dublin 1986, pp 67-74.*

'To the gent who snored in the Library the other day: an ode' (by K.H.B.), *TCD: a*

College Miscellany (25 November 1908) pp 167.

Todd, J.H., *Books of the Vaudois: the Waldensian manuscripts preserved in the Library of Trinity College Dublin*, Dublin 1865.

Trinity College Dublin: Arts and Social Sciences buildings, Dublin 1978; pp 24-7; deals with the Lecky Library.*

Tucker, A.M., 'Experiences with MARC based systems at Trinity College Dublin', in *International Seminar on the MARC Format and the Exchange of Bibliographical Data in Machine Reliable Form, Berlin 1971: proceedings*, München-Pullach 1972, pp 157-71.

—, 'Library automation in Trinity College Dublin: a progress report', *Long Room 2* (1970) pp 36-7.*

'The university library', in *Dublin University Calendar* (1833) pp 187-96.*

Webb, D.A., 'Broadsides relating to Swift', *Annual Bulletin* (1946) pp 8-11.

A Selection of Published Illustrations Relating to the Library: Buildings, People, and Some Artifacts

arranged chronologically by date of first publication

CIARAN NICHOLSON

Charles Brooking, 'The colledge library' in *A map of the city and suburbs of Dublin*, London 1728; the full map and ancillary views were reproduced by the Irish Architectural Archive and the Friends of the Library, TCD, Dublin 1983.

Joseph Tudor, 'A prospect of the library of Trinity College Dublin', in *Six views of Dublin*, London 1753, plate 6; often reproduced in later publications.

Bernard Scalé, *A plan of Trinity College Dublin park, gardens, etc.*, London 1761; engraving, showing library attached at north-east and north-west pavilions to other buildings in Library Square.

Samuel Byron, 'Isometric drawing of the college', 1780; reproduced in colour in a limited edition print, published by the Trinity Trust and the Irish Architectural Archive, 1986; often reproduced in later publications.

James Malton, 'The college library, Dublin [i.e. the Long Room]' in *A picturesque and descriptive view of the city of Dublin*, London 1799; often reproduced in later publications; the original watercolour is reproduced in colour on the cover of Fox (1986) and in Holland (1991), p. 214.

W.B.S. Taylor, *History of the University of Dublin*, London 1819-20:
> View of the Dining Hall &c. from the provost [*sic*] garden (coloured aquatint showing the west end of the library).
>
> S.W. view of the library (coloured aquatint, showing the west and south faces of the library).

Dublin Penny Journal, 10 October 1835: The library viewed from the north.

W.B.S. Taylor, *The history of the University of Dublin*, London 1845:
> The Fagel Library, plate inserted between pp 308-20.
>
> The principal library [i.e. the Long Room], plate inserted between pp 308-20.
>
> S.W. view of the library, plate inserted between pp 308-20.

John W. Stubbs, *The history of the University of Dublin*, Dublin 1889: Trinity College as it was in 1750, from Rocque's map of Dublin (shows library forming one side of a quadrangle, joined at the north-east and north-west ends to other buildings; often reproduced in later publications), p. 191.

The book of Trinity College Dublin, 1591-1891, Belfast 1892:
> Interior of library 1858 (readers in gowns and mortar boards; no bookshelves on gallery, and the ceiling is flat), p. 154.

Satchel of Book of Armagh (from b/w photographs, front and back views), p. 164.

Shrine of Book of Dimma (from b/w photographs, front and back views), p. 165.

Book recesses in library (wood-engraving), p. 176.

Inner staircase in library (wood-engraving, one of the pair of staircases at the west end of the Long Room), p. 177.

Interior of library 1860 (from b/w photograph; bookshelves on gallery, and ceiling is barrel-vaulted), p. 178.

The library, 1891 (from a b/w photograph showing the low granite wall, with its high iron railings, which ran from the north-east corner of the library buildings to the side of the Examination Hall, before it was moved back some fifty feet in the spring of 1892), p. 179.

Library staircase and entrance to reading room (wood-engraving, staircase at west end), p. 180.

Royal arms now placed in library (Elizabethan arms believed to have come from the original college chapel), p. 181.

Parliament and Library Squares (looking towards the Rubrics with library on viewer's right), p. 201.

View in the College Park – Library, Engineering School (now the Museum Building), plate opp. p. 228.

Map of college 1892 (by J.E. Croasdaile; entrance to library at the west end is marked on the map), fold-out plate opp. p. 296.

Charles Hubert Oldham, *Trinity College pictorial*, Dublin 1892:

A view in the Great Quadrangle (from a b/w photograph, showing part of north side of library), p. 16.

West staircase to Long Room (wood-engraving), p. 25.

The Campanile and the library building (from a b/w photograph), p. 26.

The Great Room of the library (from a b/w photograph, looking east), p. 27.

The library reading room (from a b/w photograph; now part of the colonnades bookstacks), p. 46.

The Long Room in the library (from a b/w photograph, looking west, showing display cases and curtained display stands), p. 48.

W.H. Benyon & Co., *The portfolio of Trinity College, Dublin*, Cheltenham 1901: Library (Long Room, looking east from gallery).

W. MacNeile Dixon, *Trinity College Dublin*, London 1902:

The library – exterior (from a b/w photograph; Old Library from west in Fellows' Garden), plate opp. p. 108.

The library – interior (from a b/w photograph; taken from west end of gallery), plate opp. p. 224.

Dublin Corporation, *A book of Dublin: official handbook*, Dublin 1929: The Library, Trinity College, from a drawing by Hilda Roberts, plate opp. p. 51.

Trinity College Dublin, *A handbook of TCD*, Dublin 1929:

The Old Library from Fellows' Garden showing tennis courts (from a b/w photograph), facing p. 23.

The library interior (with no display cases), facing p. 26.

A.N. Jeffares, *Trinity College Dublin, founded 1591: thirty-four drawings and descriptions*, Dublin 1944:

The Campanile and the library.

The Rubrics and the library from the G.M.B.

The schools [Museum Building], the library and the back of the Rubrics.

One of the oak staircases which lead to the gallery in the Long Room.

K.C. Bailey, *A history of Trinity College, Dublin, 1892-1945*, Dublin 1947:

Interior of library reading room prepared for opening ceremony, 1937 (from a b/w photograph), plate opp. p. 65.

The Lecky statue in its original position in front of the library [west] door; plate opp. p. 70.

Long Room (b/w photograph taken from gallery looking east), plate opp. p. 165.

Illustrated London News, 19 November 1949, p. 783: Long Room (from a drawing by Bryan de Grineau; the original is now (1998) in the librarian's office).

R.B.D. French, *The library of Trinity College Dublin*, Dublin 1954:

West doorway (after a drawing by Seán MacManus), p. 1.

Long Room from the gallery (after a drawing by Bryan de Grineau by permission of the *Illustrated London News*), p. 4.

In the [1937] Reading Room (from a b/w photograph), p. 6.

Old Library from the south (after a drawing by Seán MacManus), p. 7.

The Old Library – and the New as it might take shape (after Seán MacManus; 'Impression of the proposed library extension is based upon a design by A.I.N. Robert', see p. 23), p. 9.

Staircase in Long Room (after a drawing by Seán MacManus), p. 11.

Readers in Long Room (after a drawing by Seán MacManus, eighteenth-century scene imagined by the artist), p. 14.

The [1937] Reading Room from the Dining Hall steps (after a drawing by Seán MacManus), p. 15.

Almost every sightseer in Dublin starts his tour with a visit to the library (from 2 b/w photographs showing tourists in the Long Room and leaving the west door), p. 16.

Newly arrived students wait to take the Oath of Admission to the library (from a b/w photograph, showing queue on west staircase), p. 22.

The classing room, too is overcrowded (from a b/w photograph, showing cataloguers at work in what is now the Manuscripts Reading Room), p. 22.

The old colonnades (after a drawing by Seán MacManus, who imagined what they looked like before being closed off to be used as bookstacks), p. 24.

Trinity College Dublin (from a b/w aerial photograph, showing the Magnetic Observatory which housed the Manuscripts Room, the Old Library, the 1937 Reading Room, and a roughly drawn outline of the proposed New Library), front endpapers.

Herbert W. Parke, *The library of Trinity College Dublin: an historical description by the librarian*, Dublin 1961: A corner of the [1937] Reading Room (from a b/w photograph), p. 11.

Paul Koralek, *The New Library, University of Dublin, Trinity College*, Dublin 1967:

The New Library from New Square (from a b/w photograph), p. 3.

The New Library from College Park (from a b/w photograph), p. 3.

A carrel on the second floor; view from the Iveagh Hall; the west side (from b/w
   photographs), p. 7.
Seven line drawings: block plan; west elevation; lower basement; upper basement;
   first floor plan; second floor plan; ground floor plan.
Anne Crookshank, *The Long Room*, Dublin 1976:
   General view of Long Room (from a b/w photograph, taken from the gallery at
      west end), cover.
   A staircase to the gallery of the Long Room (from a b/w photograph), p. 4.
   A bay of the Long Room (from a b/w photograph; bay SS-TT), p. 14.
Edward McParland, 'The buildings of Trinity College Dublin', *Country Life* (May
   1976):
   Thomas Burgh's library begun in 1712 (from a b/w photograph), illus. 3.
   Western entrance to the library (from a b/w photograph), illus. 4.
   The Long Room as it is today (from a b/w photograph), illus. 8.
   One of the staircases [in the Long Room] (from a b/w photograph), illus. 9.
Trinity College Dublin: Arts and Social Sciences buildings, Dublin 1978:
   Plan of levels 1 & 2 of Arts Building showing Lecky Library (line drawing), p. 8.
   The Old Library from the building (from a b/w photograph), p. 18.
   The Lecky Library (from a b/w photograph), p. 27.
Peter K. Fox, *Trinity College Library, Dublin*, Dublin 1982:
   The Long Room (from a colour photograph viewed from the main floor at the
      west end), front cover.
   The 1937 Reading Room (from a b/w photograph), fig. 19.
   The Berkeley Library (southern aspect, from a colour photograph), fig. 20.
   The Berkeley Library (the Morrison Room, from a b/w photograph), fig. 21.
   Conservation Laboratory – repairing damaged manuscripts, fig. 28.
   Conservation Laboratory – repair work on *The worlde and the chylde* (1522), fig.
      29.
   Fellows' Square, showing the 1937 Reading Room, the Old Library, the Berkeley
      Library (from a colour photograph), fig. 30.
   The Lecky Library (an interior shot showing the two levels, from a b/w photo-
      graph), fig. 31.
   (This work contains many other illustrations of artifacts, MSS and printed books
      in the library.)
Adrian Le Harivel, *National Gallery of Ireland: illustrated summary catalogue of draw-
   ings, watercolours and miniatures*, Dublin 1983: The Long Room in the Old Library,
   by Flora Mitchell, pencil on paper, no. 18,520.
Peter K. Fox, *Treasures of the library, Trinity College Dublin*, Dublin 1986:
   Peter Brown (from a b/w photograph), p. viii.
   Margaret Gertrude Chubb (from a b/w photograph), p. ix.
   The 'Brian Boru' harp (from a colour photograph), fig. 4.
   The Old Library today (b/w illustration, view from the north-west), fig. 5.
   Conservation Laboratory: cleaning the old binding adhesive from a leaf of the
      Winchcombe Psalter (b/w illustration), fig. 9.
   The Long Room (colour illustration, viewed from the main floor at the west end),
      fig. 11.

Staircase by Richard Castle in the west pavilion of the Old Library (1750) (b/w illustration), fig. 13.

(This work contains many other illustrations of artifacts, MSS and printed books in the library.)

'Dublin through the pages exhibition', *Cló* v. 5 no. 3 (Dec. 1988) p. 17: (shows wooden common press in the Long Room, on loan from the Boethius Press, set up for printing demonstrations during the exhibition).

Anne Crookshank and David Webb, *Paintings and sculptures in Trinity College Dublin*, Dublin 1990:

Barrett, John (1754?-1821), portrait by G.F. Joseph, oil on canvas, p. 18.

Berkeley, George (1685-1753), portrait by James Latham, oil on canvas; portrait, attributed to Francis Bindon, oil on canvas; portrait, by Robert Home, oil on canvas, pp 20-1.

Clement, William (1707-82), portrait attributed to James Latham, oil on canvas; marble bust, by Edward Smyth; portrait by an unknown artist, oil on canvas, pp 37-8.

Deane, Sir Thomas (1792-1871), oval plaster relief by Thomas Manly Deane, p. 45.

Gilbert, Claudius (1670-1742), marble bust by Simon Vierpyl, p. 59.

Ingram, John Kells (1823-1907), portrait by Sarah Purser, oil on canvas, p. 73.

Jones, Henry (1605-1682), portrait by an unknown artist, oil on panel, p. 76.

Malet, John Adam (1810-79), plaster bust by J.E. Jones, p. 97.

Palliser, William (1646-1727), portrait by Mrs Fairholme, oil on canvas, p. 107.

Sadleir, Franc (1774-1851), portrait by John Henry Nelson, oil on canvas, p. 117.

Siegfried, Rudolf Thomas (1830-63), marble bust by Joseph Robinson Kirk, p. 120.

Ussher, James (1581-1656), portrait by Robert Home, oil on canvas; portrait after an engraving after a portrait by Sir Peter Lely, oil on canvas; marble bust, signed 'P. S. fe'(i.e. Peter Sheemakers), pp 136, 152.

Wall, Charles William (1780-1862), portrait by S. Catterson Smith, the elder, oil on canvas; marble bust by Thomas Kirk, p. 137.

Woodward, Benjamin (1816-61), portrait by S. Catterson Smith, the elder, on brown prepared paper in black chalk, highlighted with white, p. 143.

Gilbert bequest: busts of 'men eminent for learning' adorning the Long Room, paid for by money bequeathed by Claudius Gilbert for the purpose, pp 149-52.

View of the Old Library by J.A. O'Connor, oil on canvas (c.1818-20), p. 168.

View of the Old Library by an unknown artist, oil on canvas (undated), p. 168.

View of the Long Room by Seán McManus, as it looked before the alterations of 1858, watercolour on paper. View of the Long Room by Seán McManus, as it looked after the alterations of 1858, watercolour on paper, p. 177. The attribution to McManus is disputed by Frederick O'Dwyer in his *The architecture of Deane and Woodward*, Cork 1997, who suggests T.N. Deane as the artist (n. 170, p. 589).

View of the interior of the Long Room by James Malton, watercolour on paper, p. 178.

David Evans, *The Long Room*, Dublin 1990: Colour print, no. 9 in the series of limited edition prints of TCD published by the Trinity Trust and the Irish Architectural Archive (reproduced in colour on the cover of Holland, 1991).

C.H. Holland, *Trinity College Dublin and the idea of a university*, Dublin 1991:

Provost McConnell being seen off at Dublin airport in the autumn of 1958 by Mr J.V. Luce as Executive Officer of the Library Extension Appeal (from a b/w photograph), p. 85.

Dr John (Jacky) Barrett from McCleary's *Public characters*, *c*.1810 (caricature), p. 139.

The Long Room in the late nineteenth century, showing exhibition cases (from a b/w photograph), p. 149.

College Park, *c*.1840, with view of proposed viaduct; ... the Old Library and New Square ... on the right ... (from an undated lithograph after George du Noyer), p. 154.

Plan of library reading room, proposed in 1873 by McCurdy & Mitchell, for the site between the west pavilion of the Old Library ... and the Examination Hall ..., where the 1937 Reading Room was eventually built, p. 164.

Elevation of library reading room, proposed in 1873 by McCurdy & Mitchell, p. 164.

Doorway, now leading into the nave of Christchurch Cathedral, Waterford, removed from Thomas Burgh's Old Library in 1891 (in the original spine wall, connecting Library Square with Fellows' Garden), p. 176.

Plan of the neighbourhood of the Old Library by Thomas Manly Deane, 1913, showing alternative sites for a new reading room for the library, p. 177.

Elevation of design B, for a proposed new reading room, by Sir Thomas Manly Deane, March 1912, p. 177.

John V. Luce, *Trinity College Dublin: the first 400 years*, Dublin 1992:

The Long Room of the Old Library, col. plate 1.

A view of the northern façade of the Arts and Social Sciences Building from Fellows' Square. In the background, the Berkeley Library, col. plate 8.

The Berkeley Library from the New Square, by Paul Koralek (1967), col. plate 9.

A plan of the campus 1990 (showing the locations of the various library buildings), b/w plate 6.

The memorial tablet to the Reverend Dr Michael Moore in the 1937 Reading Room, b/w plate 9.

Dan Cruickshank, 'Berkeley Library: Trinity College, Dublin 1967-1997', *RIBA Journal* v. 104 no. 10 (Oct. 1997) pp 69-75:

Berkeley Library and Lecky Library from Fellows' Square.

Section of Berkeley Library looking towards the east end of Old Library.

Floor plans of first floor, ground-floor and upper basement.

Section of Research Floor.

Two illustrations of Iveagh Hall.

View of Morrison Room looking down from the Research Floor.

Elevation drawing of Berkeley Library ('reveals how a series of rooflights allows light to fall deep into the interior').

John Donat's original pictures from 1967.
ABK's inspiration: four top-heavy compositions:
    Le Corbusier's Sainte-Marie-de-la-Tourette, Evaux (1959).
    Denys Lasdun's Royal College of Physicians, London (1960).
    Gerhard Kallmann McKinnell's Boston City Hall (1962).
    Marcel Breuer's Whitney Museum, New York City (1966).
Frederick O'Dwyer, *The architecture of Deane and Woodward*, Cork 1997:
    Trinity College, Dublin, library, perspective showing the Long Room, with the ceiling as existing in 1858, p. 351.
    TCD library, transverse section through the roof showing the proposed iron truss design, April 1858, by Robert Mallet, p. 352.
    Trinity College, Dublin, library, perspective showing the Long Room, with Deane and Woodward's timber barrel-vaulted roof, p. 353.
John Olley, 'Berkeley Library, Trinity College Dublin, 1961-7: Ahrends Burton Koralek', in A. Becker, J. Olley, and W. Wang eds., *Ireland: 20th-century architecture*, Munich 1997, pp 124-5: Three b/w views of the exterior, 1 b/w view of the interior, 2 elevation drawings, 1 plan, 1 section drawing and 1 conceptual sketch.
Miguel DeArce, *Campus poems*, Dundalk 1998: Philip Castle's painting, 'Town and gown', which is an elevated view of the west end of the TCD campus and shows several of the library buildings, is reproduced in colour on the cover; the original is at present (1999) in the front hall of the Berkeley Library.

A Select Chronology

ISOLDE HARPUR

1592		The 'College of the Holy and Undivided Trinity near Dublin' is founded by Queen Elizabeth I.
1590s		First college library.
1595		Catalogue of Luke Challoner's library – 473 titles. Some of Challoner's books have ended up in the college library.
1596	14 December	'Catalogus librorum Lucae Challeneri' – catalogue of Challoner's library containing 853 titles.
1601		Money is contributed by various people, including soldiers and officers in H.M. service, amounting to about £700 and used for purchasing books for the library.
		Ambrose Ussher is appointed the first library keeper.
	24 February	Earliest catalogue of the library is to be found in a volume called 'the Particular Book'; lists 39 printed books and a handful of manuscripts.
	June	Luke Challoner sent to London on a book-buying expedition; purchases about 350 books.
1603		Luke Challoner and James Ussher are sent to England to make extensive purchases for the library.
1604		Catalogue of library compiled by Ambrose Ussher.
1606		Luke Challoner and James Ussher are sent to England again to procure books for the college library.
1608		Catalogue of Challoner's library listing 885 titles.
1609		Challoner and Ussher are sent one more time to England for book-buying.
1610		Library catalogue lists almost 4,000 works.
1611	March	Randal Holland, library keeper, is paid six shillings 'for makinge an index of library bookes.'
1637		An order is made by the provost and senior fellows which introduces fines for not returning library books on time.

1650s		Samuel Winter (Provost) gives large sum for the purchase of books for the library.
1651		Henry Jones, then vice-chancellor of the university, adorns the library with a staircase and is responsible for other furniture additions to the value of about £400.
1661-82		The Book of Kells and the Book of Durrow are presented to the college by Henry Jones, during his tenure as bishop of Meath (1661-82).
1661	31 May	Order is passed by the House of Commons that Archbishop Ussher's books are to be removed from Dublin Castle to Trinity College Dublin. As a result the library acquires more than 10,000 books and manuscripts.
1670		Sir Jerome Alexander, one of the Justices of the Common Pleas, bequeathes to the college his collection of books and manuscripts and some money towards building a library for his collection. The books were received in 1674.
1671		Alexander donation augmented by the bishop of Kilmore.
		Rachel, countess dowager of Bath, gives £200 for purchase of books for the library in memory of her husband, Henry Bouchier, former fellow of the college.
1672	4 May	Agreement between TCD and Richard Mills, bricklayer, for the erection of Sir Jerome Alexander's Library.
1674		The college receives the books bequeathed by Sir Jerome Alexander.
	20 November	George Mercer is appointed library keeper of Sir Jerome Alexander's Library.
1675	20 November	Richard Acton is appointed library keeper. He is paid £10 for creating a catalogue of Spanish books.
1680s		Provost Robert Huntington donates some of his valuable collection of manuscripts.
1689		Manuscripts moved to England for safe keeping.
1689-90		Library preserved from the depredations of Jacobite troops through the efforts of Fr T. McCarthy and Fr M. Moore, although the shrine of the Book of Durrow was lost.
1691		Provost Robert Huntington divides his collection of Oriental manuscripts between Trinity College and the Bodleian, Oxford.
1693	20 November	Claudius Gilbert is appointed library keeper.

1697		Catalogue of the MSS is published in *Catalogi librorum manuscriptorum Angliae et Hiberniae*, Oxford 1697.
1707	20 November	Richard Helsham appointed library keeper; prepares catalogue of the library.
1709	1 June	The House of Commons successfully petitions the Queen for a grant of £5,000 to erect a new library building in the college.
	November	George Berkeley, the philosopher, is apppointed librarian.
1712	12 May	Foundation stone of the new library designed by Thomas Burgh, chief engineer and surveyor-general of her majesty's fortification in Ireland, is laid.
	16 May	In the college register of this date, it is ordered that £50 be paid to the person who solicited the payment of the £5,000 in England.
c.1715–20		The first printed catalogue of the library is published.
1717		Subscription of £1,000 towards the new library building is paid by outgoing Provost Benjamin Pratt.
	21 September	An application to Parliament is made for another £5,000. Request is granted.
	24 September	Entry in college register of this date reads that 'the degree of LL.D. is to be offered to all Members of the House of Commons who desire it, in consequence of an Address to the King for £5,000 to complete the Library.'
1720	January	Joseph Keddy [Caddy] is appointed librarian; prepares a new catalogue of the library (perhaps the version printed about this date).
	July?	A fire occurs in the library.
1721	6 October	A further application to Parliament is made for another £5,000. This again is granted.
1724		Main structure of library building is completed.
1726		Library bequeathed 4,000 volumes from the personal collection of William Palliser, archbishop of Cashel.
1732		New library building, started in 1712, is opened.
1733	20 November	The librarian, Edward Hudson, receives £60 to organize removal of the books from the old library to the Long Room; supervises the preparation of a new catalogue.
1735		Claudius Gilbert declares he will leave his library to Trinity.
	25 March	The bursar is ordered to pay Edward Hudson an advance of £112 for his present and future efforts in organizing the new library.

1741		Gift from John Stearne, bishop of Clogher, of the manuscript portion of his library. The collection included the 1641 Depositions.
1742		Edward Worth of Rathfarnham bequeaths 1,000 volumes to the library.
	21 July	The librarian, William Clement, is to go to Clogher to choose printed books from Bishop Stearne's library for the college.
1743		Claudius Gilbert, vice-provost and professor of divinity, leaves £500 'for the purchase of busts of men eminent for learning to adorn the library'.
		Trinity receives Claudius Gilbert's library of some 13,000 volumes.
1744	28 April	Henry Mercier is appointed to arrange and catalogue Gilbert's books.
1747		Canon John Lyon completes his catalogue of the college manuscript collection.
1749	21 March	The senior sophisters present Roubilliac's bust of Swift to the library.
1786	31 October	Sir John Sebright's Irish manuscripts, collected by Edward Lhuyd, received by library. These include the Book of Leinster.
1800	20 November	Thomas Prior is appointed keeper of the new Lending Library.
1801		Following the union of Great Britain and Ireland, the Copyright Act extended to Ireland, under which TCD becomes a legal deposit library.
1802	11-14 May	Arrival of the Fagel Library, consisting of 20,000 volumes which belonged to Hendrik Fagel, Greffier (Chief Minister) of Holland.
1805		Henry George Quin, a Trinity graduate and book collector, bequeaths his collection of 127 choice editions in fine bindings to the library.
1806		Purchase of first folio Shakespeare.
1807	24 October	The librarian, John 'Jacky' Barrett is given £100 'for his extra trouble in arranging and making a catalogue of the Fagel Library'.
1809	March	Richard Graves is paid £200 for arranging the Fagel Library.
	1 March	Board orders Fagel Library to be opened.
c.1811-14		Henry J. Monck Mason recatalogues the library manuscripts for the Irish Record Commission.
1813-15		Thefts by Edward Barwick of books from the library.
1817	27 September	Musgrave depositions on 1798 Rebellion are received.

1831	23 November	James Henthorn Todd is appointed as supernumerary assistant librarian without salary.
1834	14 July	'First College accounts book' and other muniments put in MSS Room.
1836		John O'Donovan is employed by the board to catalogue the Irish manuscripts.
	29 March	The Book of Dimma is purchased from Sir W. Betham for £150.
1837		College purchases catalogue of college manuscripts compiled by Henry J. Monck Mason.
	February	Board orders that £200 per annum be allocated to prepare a copy of the library catalogue for the press, under the supervision of Todd.
1838		Todd introduces reforms. Use of Lending Library is extended to all students.
		A collection of Egyptian papyri is presented by Lord Kingsborough.
1840		A collection of the manuscripts of William King (1650-1729), archbishop of Dublin, is purchased.
1841		Mr Dobbs is paid £10 for compiling a catalogue of the Lending Library.
1842		A collection of State Papers relating to Ireland is purchased at the sale of Lord Kingsborough's library.
1844	October	Sample swinging bookcases installed in the gallery window openings. Over the next ten years many more were put in place, to provide much needed storage space.
1846	July	Plans are approved to convert the Divinity School on the ground floor of the library building at the east end into a reading room.
1848	20 March	New reading room opened.
	December	Work starts on the printing of a catalogue of the main library.
1851	12 April	Undergraduate scholars ask to use the library – Lloyd and Todd to consider changes to statutes.
1852	7 February	Todd is elected librarian.
	13 March	Board agrees to appoint additional library clerk and assistant librarian.
1853		Report of the Dublin University Commission.
		First fascicle of new catalogue is printed.
1854		Purchase by Charles W. Wall, former librarian, of records of the Inquisition, which he presents to the library.
		Acquisition of the Book of Armagh from Lord George Beresford, archbishop of Armagh.

1855		Lending Library becomes a department of the main library, under the librarian, instead of being in the care of the junior dean.
1856		Sophister students are granted readers' tickets.
	November	Board asks John McCurdy, and Deane and Woodward to report separately on the dangerous condition of the roof of the library.
1858		The architectural firm of Deane and Woodward are employed to secure the roof of the library, and thereby remodelling the Long Room.
1859		Acquisition of Book of Mulling.
1861	May	Reconstruction of library is completed.
1864		Volume 1 of the Printed Catalogue is published.
1869	28 June	Librarian, J.H. Todd, dies.
1872	9 April	Library committee reactivated – to meet monthly.
1880	20 October	Remodelling of east pavilion completed.
1881		The Aiken Irvine collection of theology is acquired.
1884		John Kells Ingram, the librarian, is elected president of the British Library Association.
1887		Printed Catalogue of the library finally completed.
1892	April	Colonnades glazed in to provide a new reading room and space for book storage.
1896		The attic of the west pavilion is shelved for book storage.
1900		T.K. Abbott's *Catalogue of the manuscripts in the library of TCD* is published.
	8 December	Board approves evening opening of reading room.
1901	10 January	Library opens in the evenings.
	17 March	St Patrick's Day – library is closed for the first time on this day.
1911	20 May	Board first discusses need for a new reading room (eventually completed in 1937).
1912	24 February	Sir Thomas Deane is to be consulted about new reading room.
	19-22 March	W.E.H. Lecky's collection of books arrives – presented by Mrs Lecky.
1913-15		Steel shelving is erected in the colonnades by W. Lucy & Co., Oxford.
1915	29 November	Woman first employed on regular staff duties.
1916	25 April	Easter Rising. Library is closed.
	8 May	Library is re-opened. Books at binders are destroyed in the Rising.
1918	23 March	Miss A.R. Jackson is appointed superintendent of reading room.
1920	15 April	Appeal for state funds for library and new reading room.
1921		T.K. Abbott and E.J. Gwynn, *Catalogue of the Irish manuscripts in the library of TCD*, is published.

	21 June	Board endorses plan for a memorial to the 450 College members who died in the Great War. It is decided that a Hall of Honour be erected which will serve as an entrance hall to a new reading room for the library.
1922		Legal deposit books are withheld by two British publishers because of the establishment of the Irish Free State.
		Three rooms over the provost's stables are fitted out with shelving for newspapers.
1923	7 January	Legal deposit books are withheld by publisher because of establishment of Irish Free State.
	25 October	Further refusal of legal deposit books.
1924	21 March	Letter to copyright agent confirming TCD library's right to claim legal deposit books.
1925		Two old army huts are acquired for book storage, and space is also afforded in the east wing of Campus House.
	26 February	Provost is to visit USA and Canada seeking funds for reading room. He is to depart on 29 April.
1926	23 January	Board decides to start putting money aside towards the new reading room.
	May	Committee is set up on new reading room. Sir Thomas Deane is asked to invite tenders for the building work from P.J. Good and from G. & T. Crampton.
1927		The War Memorial Committee hands over the sum of £7,280 towards the erection of the Hall of Honour. The Industrial and Commercial Property (Protection) Act is passed by Dáil Éireann. This provides that Irish publishers must supply legal deposit copies of their publications to specified libraries including that of Trinity College.
	11 April	Start of building of Hall of Honour.
	May	The Lecky statue is moved to its present position between the Old Library and the campanile, to make way for the building of the Hall of Honour.
1928	10 November	The Hall of Honour is opened by the provost, Dr E.J. Gwynn.
1932		Albert M. Bender begins donation of mainly Californian private press printings; he continues to make additions to the collection up to the early 1950s.
1935	18 July	Excavations for new reading room are started.
1936	23 May	Board gives approval to the National Library to make 'photostatic' copies of all the manuscripts in the library.

1937	2 July	President Eamon de Valera opens new reading room.
1938	1 January	First use of mechanical book conveyor to the 1937 Reading Room.
1939		The space occupied by the old reading room in the colonnades is fitted with steel shelving.
1940	July	Because of the war the Books of Kells and Durrow, and other important manuscripts, are placed in a strong room cellar, specially constructed in 1939 at the north side of the west pavilion.
1942		American graduates donate money to mark the college's 350th anniversary. Board decides that the money should be used to buy books of American interest for the library.
	25 February	Board allows women students access to reading room between 6 p.m. and 8.45 p.m.
1943		Library committee is re-established.
1945	10 May	Board decides all manuscripts are to be brought back to library and that the Book of Kells is to be put back on daily display.
	June	'Friends of the Library' established at a meeting in the Graduates Memorial Building.
1946	2 October	Board allows teaching staff who are not fellows or professors access to library shelves.
1950		Full facsimile of the Book of Kells (mostly b/w illustrations) is published by Urs Graf Verlag, Berne.
1951		The British Copyright Committee recommends that the privileges of Trinity College under the Copyright Act be continued.
1952	21 November	Library committee minute book records first mention of the need for a new library extension.
1953		Approval of library extension.
		The Book of Kells is rebound by Roger Powell. He also rebound the Book of Durrow in the following year.
1954		Plans are approved to convert the Magnetic Observatory in the Fellows' Garden into a Manuscripts Room.
		Robert Butler Digby French's *The Library of TCD* is published as part of the appeal for funds for the new library.
1955		Bibliotheca Earberiana, a collection of *c.*2,000 mainly eighteenth-century Irish and English pamphlets, is presented by Miss A. Crofton.
1957	3 June	Opening of the new Manuscripts Room by the Taoiseach, Eamon de Valera.
		Appeal to graduates for library extension.

1958	15 July	Official launch of library extension appeal.
	September	'Building for books', a film directed by Vincent Corcoran as part of the library extension appeal, is first shown at Cork Film Festival.
1960	15 June	An international architectural competition is launched for the new library building.
1961		To further promote the extension appeal, an exhibition of TCD Library treasures is mounted in the Royal Academy, London, and includes the St Matthew volume of the Book of Kells.
		H.W. Parke's *The library of TCD: an historical description* is published.
	21 March	Closing date for entries for architectural competition.
	3 May	Paul Koralek selected as architect for the new library (later named the Berkeley Library).
	October	State grant is sanctioned for new library building.
1963	October	Government gives a further grant for the new library.
1965		H.W. Parke, the last of the fellow-librarians, resigns and is replaced by Francis J.E. Hurst, the first professional librarian to hold the post.
1966		New British act confirms Trinity College Library's legal deposit privileges.
1967		East pavilion of the Old Library is remodelled to provide a library shop, a new staircase, and a special Early Printed Books department.
	12 July	New Library opened by President Eamon de Valera.
1968		Manuscripts of John Millington Synge are purchased.
1969		Bonaparte-Wyse collection of Provençal literature deposited in the library.
		Samuel Beckett presents four of his notebooks.
		Introduction of the computerized Trinity College MARC-based acquisitions and cataloguing system.
		Many College archives, although still held in the Muniment Room in the Provost's House, are transferred to the responsibility of the library. Shortly afterwards the muniments were physically transferred to the library.
	December	Donation of Sáirséal agus Dill collection.
1971		The papers of the Incorporated Society for Promoting Protestant Schools in Ireland are presented, the largest outside collection since that of Archbishop Ussher.
	1 June	New Manuscripts Room in the west pavilion of the Old Library opens to readers.

	October	A new science reading room is established in the Biochemistry Building. A lending library for science, engineering and medical undergraduates is established in the Science Library Hut, which occupies part of Fellows' Garden.
1972-3		Work starts on the book repository at Santry and the conservation laboratory in the west pavilion of the Old Library.
		Full introduction of the new form of computer produced catalogue on microfilm; later it appeared on microfiche.
1973		Trinity Closet Press founded, run by members of the department of Early Printed Books as a museum of hand-printing and as a teaching tool for students of historical bibliography.
1974	May	Conservation Laboratory is officially opened.
1974-5		A medical library is established in the Trinity unit at St James's Hospital.
		First stage of the book repository at Santry (sufficient to hold 600,000 books) is completed.
		A special historical research collection of almost 25,000 volumes is established and organized on the research floor of the New Library with a specialist staff.
		The collections of official publications are brought together and administered by specialist staff.
		The music library is established under a specialist music librarian.
		'Near-binding' unit, under the supervision of the Conservation Laboratory, is set up to cope with binding of paperbacks and periodicals.
1977-8		The undergraduate science library moves to St Mark's Church, Pearse Street.
1977-1979		The Book of Kells and other Irish manuscripts are sent to the USA as part of a touring exhibition 'Treasures of early Irish art'.
1978	31 July	Lecky Library opens in the new Arts and Social Sciences building.
1979		Michael Freyer Dolmen Press Collection purchased.
1979-80		Major extension of online processing is introduced with the new library programmes developed by the Computer Laboratory. In the Cataloguing Department the introduction of VDUs mark the transition to online work.
1981		Science collections moved from St Mark's Church and the Biomedical Library, into space in the Sports Hall and the 1937 Reading Room.

1982		Peter K. Fox's pamphlet *Trinity College Library, Dublin* is published.
		William O'Sullivan retires. He joined the staff in 1949, became Assistant in charge of Manuscripts in 1953, and was appointed Keeper of Manuscripts in 1961.
1982-4		The Book of Kells and other Irish manuscripts are sent to to four European countries as part of a touring exhibition 'Treasures of Ireland'.
1984		Pollard School Book Collection is acquired. Consists of approximately 550 textbooks used in Irish schools up to 1910.
	7 January	The librarian Peter Brown dies.
	16 June	Margot Chubb, Keeper of Readers' Services, dies.
1985	March	The first woman to hold the post of deputy librarian, Elizabeth Duffin, is appointed.
1986		Cuala Press archive and printing equipment are presented by the Yeats family.
		The second phase of the library's book repository at Santry is opened.
	27 May	Publication of Peter K. Fox ed., *Treasures of the library, Trinity College Dublin.*
	1 October	Appointment of first map librarian.
1987		An edition of the Printed Catalogue, with MS additions and corrections, is published on microfiche.
1988		The Map Library opens in the old gymnasium.
		Installation of the Dynix Library Computer System.
	February	Dr Worth's collection of *c.*4,500 antiquarian books is transferred from Dr Steevens' Hospital to the library.
1989	November	Online Public Access Catalogues (OPACs) appear in the reading rooms; hitherto the current catalogue was on microfiche.
	27 November	Dr Patrick Hillery, president of Ireland, is presented with the first copy of the fine-art facsimile edition of the Book of Kells.
1990		Full colour facsimile of the Book of Kells is published by Faksimile Verlag Luzern; it is accompanied by a commentary volume edited by Peter K. Fox.
	November	The deputy librarian, Elizabeth Duffin, dies.
1991		Start of the Colonnades Project, which would provide a new display area for Irish manuscripts, a new library shop, and bookstacks for early printed books and manuscripts. The displaced books to be stored in the Santry repository.
		Marvin L. Colker's *Trinity College Library Dublin: descriptive catalogue of the mediaeval and renaissance Latin manuscripts* is published.

1992	13 March	Official opening of the Colonnades; on display is 'Treasures of the mind: a TCD quatercentenary exhibition'.
	13 July	Hamilton Science Library opens.
	July/August	Music library moves from the 1937 Reading Room to the Berkeley Library.
	6–9 September	An international conference on the Book of Kells takes place in TCD. This conference celebrates the college's quatercentenary through discussion of the college's greatest treasure.
1993		Medical library at St James's Hospital moves to the new Trinity Centre there. The library is to be known as the John Stearne Medical Library.
		Library joins CURL, the Consortium of University Research Libraries. At this time the other members are the university libraries of Cambridge, Edinburgh, Glasgow, Leeds, London, Manchester, Oxford and University College London.
	1 December	Retrospective catalogue conversion project, called the Stella Project, is launched, financed by a private donation.
1994	October	Publication of *The Book of Kells: proceedings of a conference at Trinity College Dublin, 6–9 September 1992*, edited by Felicity O'Mahony.
1995		Purchase of the *Aibidil gaoigheilge agus caiticiosma*, published in 1571 and one of only four surviving copies of the first book printed in Irish in Ireland.
	December	The Worth Library, which had been housed in Trinity since 1988, is returned to Dr Steevens' Hospital, after its destiny was decided by the courts.
1996	6 February	Opening of a major exhibition in the Colonnades entitled 'The Book of Kells. Picturing the word'.
1997	November	McCullough Mulvin and Keane Murphy Duff are selected as architects for a new library building to be built between the existing Berkeley and Lecky libraries.
1999	22 February	Opening of a new Colonnades exhibition entitled 'The Book of Kells: turning darkness into light'.

List of Contributors

DR ELIZABETHANNE BORAN is a part-time lecturer in Trinity College Dublin where she teaches on the history of ideas in the early modern period. Her doctoral thesis investigated the early history of the library of TCD and her recent publications concentrate on sixteenth- and seventeenth-century university history.

ANTHONY CAINS is a book and manuscript conservator and since 1972 director of the TCD Library Conservation Laboratory, which he established. He has contributed to the commentatory volume of the Book of Kells facsimile (1990), as well as several journals and publications on conservation techniques. He has taught and lectured in Europe, North America and Australia.

DR LYDIA FERGUSON is an Assistant Librarian in the Department of Early Printed Books in TCD Library. After being awarded a PhD for her thesis on Juan Goytisolo, a contemporary Spanish writer, she turned her attention to earlier centuries and older books. She now has a particular interest in the publication of early editions of French literature.

PETER KENDREW FOX has been University Librarian at the University of Cambridge since 1994. Prior to that he was Deputy Librarian at TCD Library from 1979 to 1984, and Librarian from 1984 to 1994. He has been chairman of the Consortium of University Research Libraries since 1997. Among his publications and works he has edited are *Treasures of the library, Trinity College Dublin*, Dublin 1986, *The Book of Kells; commentary volume*, Lucerne 1990, and *Cambridge University Library: the great collections*, Cambridge 1998.

BRENDAN GRIMES trained as an architect at the Dublin Institute of Technology (where he currently lectures in the School of Architecture) and at the Politecnico di Milano. His book *Irish Carnegie libraries: a catalogue and architecural history* was published by Irish Academic Press in 1998.

ISOLDE HARPUR graduated in Russian and German from TCD and holds a Diploma in Library and Information Science from the National University of Ireland. She joined the staff of Trinity College Library in 1990, and works as subject librarian for English, Irish, Russian and Linguistics. She is also Treasurer of the Friends of the Library.

VINCENT KINANE is an Assistant Librarian in the Department of Early Printed Books in TCD Library. Since 1996 he has been seconded on a part-time basis to catalogue the Worth Library in Dr Steevens' Hospital, Dublin. He has published widely in the field of Irish historical bibliography. His book *A history of the Dublin University Press, 1734-1976* was published in 1994. He is also editor of *Long Room: Ireland's Journal for the History of the Book*.

VERONIKA KOEPER-SAUL was born in Germany and came to Ireland in 1986, where she took a Master's degree in Library and Information Studies with a thesis on '17th-century German language imprints at Trinity College, Dublin, acquired up to 1872' (1996). She now lives in Liverpool, working as a translator and web editor.

JANE MAXWELL graduated from TCD in 1985. The following year she took the diploma course in Archival Studies in University College Dublin. She has been in the Manuscripts Department of the library in Trinity College since then, working with the college archives.

BERNARD MEEHAN is Keeper of Manuscripts at Trinity College Library.

CIARAN NICHOLSON is an Assistant Librarian, Collection Management Division, TCD Library. Since 1989 he has been a compiler of *Writings on Irish history*.

DR ANN O'BRIEN is a lecturer in the Department of Information Science, Loughborough University. Formerly she worked in the Cataloguing Department in Trinity College Library.

WILLIAM O'SULLIVAN worked for the Irish Manuscripts Commission after graduation from TCD with a moderatorship in history in 1942. He was appointed to TCD Library as superintendant of the reading room in 1949. In 1953 he was given charge of the manuscripts, becoming Keeper of Manuscripts in 1961, and retired in 1982. His abiding interest is the provenance of manuscripts.

ANNE WALSH is history librarian at TCD Library, with a special interest in local studies. She has published articles in local history journals and in the *Irish Arts Review*. She lectures part-time in the Department of Library and Information Studies at University College Dublin.

Index